Outlook® 2013

ABSOLUTE BEGINNER'S GUIDE

Diane Poremsky and
Sherry Kinkoph Gunter

800 East 96th Street,
Indianapolis, Indiana 46240

Outlook® 2013 Absolute Beginner's Guide

ISBN-13: 978-0-7897-5091-4
ISBN-10: 0-7897-5091-0

Library of Congress Control Number: 2013939281

Printed in the United States of America

First Printing: August 2013

Trademarks

Warning and Disclaimer

Bulk Sales

Que Publishing offers excellent discounts on this book when ordered in quantity for bulk purchases or special sales. For more information, please contact

U.S. Corporate and Government Sales
1-800-382-3419
corpsales@pearsontechgroup.com

For sales outside of the U.S., please contact

International Sales
international@pearson.com

Associate Publisher
Greg Wiegand

Acquisitions Editor
Michelle Newcomb

Development Editor
Ginny Bess Munroe

Managing Editor
Kristy Hart

Project Editor
Andy Beaster

Copy Editor
Barbara Hacha

Indexer
Lisa Stumpf

Proofreader
Dan Knott

Technical Editor
Vince Averello

Publishing Coordinator
Cindy Teeters

Interior Designer
Anne Jones

Cover Designer
Matt Coleman

Compositor
Nonie Ratliff

Contents at a Glance

Table of Contents

About the Authors

Diane Poremsky is the owner of Slipstick System's Outlook and Exchange Resource Center. She has provided support and training for Microsoft Outlook for the past 15 years. She is the author of several books and video training CDs. She also teaches online training classes. You can find her in the forums at OutlookForums.com and in Microsoft's Answers and TechNet forums.

Diane is a longtime Microsoft MVP (Most Valuable Professional) in recognition for her support of Outlook in the Microsoft forums and Internet community. She is often accused of knowing more about Outlook than many Microsoft employees.

Diane and her husband, Phil, live near the shores of Lake Erie, with their dog Henri. She spends her free time trying to keep up with the activities of her grandchildren, doing what every good grandparent does when they come for a visit: sugar them up before sending them home. She enjoys bird watching, gardening, and traveling. You can reach her at diane@slipstick.com and visit her websites at slipstick.com and outlook-tips.net. You can follow her on Twitter @dicot or @outlooktips.

Sherry Kinkoph Gunter has written and edited oodles of books over the past 20 years covering a wide variety of computer topics, including Microsoft Office programs, digital photography, and web applications. Her recent titles include *Word 2013 Absolute Beginner's Guide*, *Sams Teach Yourself Facebook in 10 Minutes*, *Easy Microsoft Word 2010*, and *Microsoft Office for Mac Bible*. Sherry began writing computer books back in 1992 for Macmillan, and her flexible writing style has allowed her to author for a varied assortment of imprints and formats. Sherry's ongoing quest is to aid users of all levels in the mastering of ever-changing computer technologies, helping users make sense of it all and get the most out of their machines and online experiences. Sherry currently resides in a swamp in the wilds of east central Indiana with a lovable ogre and a menagerie of interesting creatures.

Dedication

This book is dedicated to the memory of my parents, Ruth and Carl Cotner. I miss hearing mom ask, "Are you done with the book yet?" in our weekly phone calls.

—Diane

To my Mr. Gunter for helping to keep the swamp somewhat quiet during work hours.

—Sherry

Acknowledgments

Yes, Mom, I'm finally done writing the book. Special thanks to my husband, Phil, and daughter, Cecilia, for their support during the time I was writing the book while working full time. It was great having someone else doing the cooking and cleaning. We had very little pizza and a lot of nutritious meals this time around. Cecilia even weeded my flower beds.

To my fellow Outlook MVPs and friends on Facebook, thanks for humoring me and tolerating my whining.

To Vince Averello, my tech editor, thanks for catching all of my errors. Sometimes my fingers move faster than my brain. To Michelle, Ginny, Barbara, and Andy, thanks for everything.

Here's hoping it's the best Outlook book ever.

—Diane

Special thanks go out to Michelle Newcomb for allowing me another wonderful opportunity to write about Outlook; to development editor Ginny Munroe, for her dedication and patience in shepherding this project; to copy editor Barbara Hacha, for ensuring that all the i's were dotted and t's were crossed; to technical editor Vince Averello and project editor Andy Beaster, for offering valuable input along the way; and finally a big shout out to the production team for their talents in creating and assembling such a good-looking book.

—Sherry

We Want to Hear from You!

As the reader of this book, *you* are our most important critic and commentator. We value your opinion and want to know what we're doing right, what we could do better, what areas you'd like to see us publish in, and any other words of wisdom you're willing to pass our way.

We welcome your comments. You can email or write to let us know what you did or didn't like about this book—as well as what we can do to make our books better.

Please note that we cannot help you with technical problems related to the topic of this book.

When you write, please be sure to include this book's title and author as well as your name and email address. We will carefully review your comments and share them with the author and editors who worked on the book.

Email: feedback@quepublishing.com

Mail: Que Publishing
        ATTN: Reader Feedback
        800 East 96th Street
        Indianapolis, IN 46240 USA

Reader Services

Visit our website and register this book at quepublishing.com/register for convenient access to any updates, downloads, or errata that might be available for this book.

INTRODUCTION

Microsoft Outlook is not the most intuitive program to use, even for people who've used it before. The basics of creating a new message are the same in every email client, but Outlook has so many features and options that it's easy to be overwhelmed by it. Our goal is to help you find your way around Outlook 2013 and turn you into an Outlook power user.

If you're new to Outlook, we'll introduce you to the features Outlook 2013 offers, not only for email, but also for Calendar, Contacts, and Tasks. If you're upgrading from an older version of Outlook, you'll learn about the new features in Outlook 2013 and discover some new tricks that will help you manage your life, or at least the part that is in Outlook.

By the time you are finished reading this book, you'll be more organized than ever and on the road to becoming an Outlook expert.

What's in This Book?

Beginning with an introduction to Outlook, you'll discover the features in Outlook 2013, including the Navigation pane, the Reading pane, Search Folders, and Quick Steps. You'll learn how to set up your accounts and customize Outlook.

Outlook is unlike any other email program. It supports common Internet email accounts using POP3 and IMAP protocols, free Outlook.com accounts, as well as corporate email hosted on Exchange Server. You'll learn about the other features that make Outlook the most powerful messaging client available, such as voting, message tracking, and deferred delivery. Outlook's Junk E-mail filter automatically removes most of the spam you receive from your Inbox as it's downloaded, eliminating much of the spam before it takes over your life. We'll show you how to set up your accounts and use email in Chapters 1-6.

Although Outlook is a first-rate email client, it does more than just email. With Calendar, Contacts, and Tasks, it's also a personal information manager (PIM). You'll learn how to use these features to their fullest. Learn how to use categories to organize your contacts and calendar, and use your contacts in a mail merge. Finally, you will learn how to create recurring appointments and send meeting requests. We'll show you how to use Calendar, Contacts, and Tasks in Chapters 7-9.

And let's not forget the Social Connector—with LinkedIn and Facebook enabled, you'll see your contacts' smiling faces as you read their email messages and see your contact's LinkedIn and Facebook photos and status updates in Outlook. You can learn about the Social Connector in Chapter 10.

Integration with other Office programs and online services is important to many users. In Chapters 12 and 13, we show you how to link SharePoint lists to Outlook and use Outlook contacts in Word. You can learn how to use mail merge in Chapter 20.

Managing your email is easier when you use the tools Outlook provides: Color Categories, Instant Search, Search Folders, and Rules. Views are one of our favorite power-user features, and we'll show you how to work with the views that Outlook includes and how to create your own custom views. You'll find this in Chapters 14-17.

In Chapter 18, we'll show you how to print your email, calendar, and contacts. Learn about Outlook data files and how to back up your email, calendar, and contacts in Chapter 19.

IN THIS CHAPTER

- Learning about the various ways you can use Outlook

- Identifying new features and improvements

- Opening and exiting the program

- Acclimating yourself to the program elements

- Finding help when you get into a jam with an Outlook task or feature

1

INTRODUCTION TO OUTLOOK

Does it feel like you're going a hundred different directions at once and juggling dozens of tasks each day? Keeping track of all the details in your busy life is often a chore, whether you're at work or you're at home. How would you like to have someone always available to assist you, remind you about things you need to do, and help you manage important happenings without having to pay the assistant a salary, provide an office and phone, or carpool with the assistant? Meet Microsoft Outlook 2013. Outlook is a tailored organizational tool you can use to help your complicated life seem a bit less complicated and a lot more organized.

Outlook is a *personal information manager* program, or PIM for short. You can use it to record, track, and manage all types of personal information. Acting as both a project manager application and an email client, Outlook can help you organize appointments, plan and coordinate events, jot down notes, manage addresses and phone numbers, and track your many email messages. In short, Outlook is a powerful communications and organization tool, one that's sure to quickly become an indispensable part of your computing activities whether you use it on your computer, laptop, or tablet. In this chapter, you learn how to get started by putting the application to work for you.

Welcome to Your New Outlook

Congratulations on choosing the number one email client and personal information manager on the market today! Millions of users make Outlook their go-to program all day long. People use it to collaborate with others or to help keep themselves on track, making it an essential part of their everyday routines at home or in the office, or both. Despite its widespread popularity, many users take advantage of only a small fraction of all the things Outlook can do to make life easier. Hopefully, this book will push you out of the fraction group and into the well-informed and fully integrated group when it comes to using Outlook 2013.

You can use Outlook to

- Send, receive, and read email messages, reply to messages, forward and copy messages.

- Send file attachments, such as spreadsheets, documents, pictures, and presentations.

- Sort junk email from regular email and rid your Inbox of spam.

- Receive regular information from your favorite websites and social media networks using RSS feeds.

- Create a corporate or personal signature to appear at the bottom of every message.

- Organize and archive messages, or remove emails you no longer want to keep.

- Schedule appointments or all-day events on your calendar, and turn on reminders to sound off and alert you to upcoming activities.

- Plan and coordinate meetings with other users and keep abreast of who is attending and who is not.

- Share your schedule with other users and view their schedules as well.

- Manage tasks you need to complete, and delegate them to others.

- Record contact information for all the people in your life, from colleagues and co-workers to friends and family.

- Quickly find a message, contact, attachment, or task using tags, categories, and search options.

Those are just a few items off the top of the list, and we haven't even begun to scratch the surface yet.

Outlook Then and Now

If you're new to Outlook, it might help to know a little about its back story. Microsoft Outlook has been around for a while now, first entering the scene as a part of the Microsoft Office 97 suite of apps. Prior to this, Microsoft's time-management software was wrapped up in a program called Schedule+, and its email client was called Exchange. Office 97 merged the two to create Outlook.

Today, Microsoft Outlook is a highly recognized program and an integral part of the Office suite. Each new version of the program offers more improvements and features, and Outlook 2013 is no exception. The new Outlook sports a more modern, polished interface with a sleek ribbon full of tools and features, as shown in Figure 1.1.

FIGURE 1.1

Welcome to Outlook 2013.

Acting quite literally like a personal assistant, you can open Outlook every day and accomplish things you need to get done, from the urgent to the mundane. Outlook consists of several key components, which are called *modules* because it's more techy sounding. Here's what you can expect with each module:

- **Mail**—Use this component to manage, send, and receive email messages. You can control junk email, organize messages into useful folders, and access multiple email accounts.

- **Calendar**—Use this component to keep track of your schedule, recording appointments, specifying all-day events, and assigning reminders when a date or scheduled time approaches.

- **People**—Use this component to manage all the people you contact, including friends, family, work colleagues, clients, and the like. Keep important information, such as phone numbers and emails, at easy reach, and add to the info as you go.

- **Tasks**—Help keep your important projects and To-Do lists organized with this component, which lets you monitor a task's status, due date, and share it with other users. Whether you're working on an important office assignment, or just trying to organize your daily activities, the Tasks component can help you stay on top of it all.

- **Notes**—Use this component to jot down notes for yourself and keep track of important information, such as ideas, questions, and quotes.

The real beauty of Outlook is how well everything works together and with other Office applications (if you happen to use Word, Excel, PowerPoint, and so on). You can use the modules individually or you can use them with each other, such as turning an email recipient into a contact in your Address Book, or turning a task into an appointment on your calendar. With just a little bit of knowledge and know-how, you'll soon find Outlook is an integral part of your daily life.

NOTE In previous versions of Outlook, the collection of names and addresses you recorded were called "Contacts." Now they're calling this component "People." What's the difference? Well, they've added a lot more to the module and the amount of information collected with people in your contacts list, making it easier than ever to get in touch with people and make sure you have all the information you need. Plus, "People" sounds a lot cooler than "Contacts."

What's New?

Microsoft has made quite a few improvements to Outlook 2013. For starters, you can utilize multiple email accounts, access social network feeds, and take advantage of cloud storage using your Microsoft SkyDrive account. Sure, Outlook offers all the same great tools as before, but there's more than ever. For example, the new Folder pane area is now dedicated to displaying folder structures, and the navigation pane of old has morphed into a Navigation bar. And it's worth mentioning the sleek and simple redesign of the user interface as a whole. There's a lot to be excited about.

Here's a rundown of some of the improvements and new features:

- You can quickly reply to a message using the new inline reply feature, which lets you respond with a click directly in the Reading pane.

- The message list now displays the message subject, sender, and first line of content so you can quickly check a message at a glance.

- You can also directly access commands to flag, delete, or mark your message from the message list.

- You can use the new quick peek feature to sneak a peek at current information for your calendar, contacts, or tasks.

- The new Weather bar in the Calendar module lets you see the current weather conditions for a specified location, which is pretty handy if you want to know what the weather's doing for an appointment later in the day.

- The new People Card view shows a single contact's information gathered from multiple sources, such as social networks, Microsoft Lync, or Outlook, and you can easily initiate contact with a click.

- Outlook supports a variety of email accounts, including anything based on Exchange or Exchange ActiveSync-compatible, POP (Post Office Protocol), or IMAP (Internet Message Access Protocol). This means you don't have to have extra add-ins to connect to services such as Hotmail or Gmail.

- Quickly insert online pictures into your message body by searching for pictures among the Office Clip Art collection, your SkyDrive account, or using the Bing Image Search tool.

- You can assign a custom background design to the ribbon and title bar area of the program window to spruce things up on your screen.

- Use the new Navigation bar to easily switch between the Outlook components, and you can choose which items to appear by default.

- You can create site mailboxes to let everyone on your team access the same Outlook data for much improved SharePoint integration.

Surely that's enough to whet your appetite for more!

Things to Know Before You Get Started

If you haven't installed Outlook yet, you can prepare the way by making sure you meet all the system requirements—or at least make sure your computing device does. Your computer or tablet needs to be at least 1GHz or faster in terms of processing power, and you'll also need 1GB RAM (memory) for a 32-bit system or 2GB for a 64-bit system. You also need at least 3GB of hard disk space (storage) and a screen display of 1366×768 resolution. The installation process is relatively painless and straightforward, whether you're just installing Outlook or the entire Microsoft Office suite. An installer program takes care of the whole procedure, even migrating settings and files from a previous version of Outlook for you, if applicable. All you have to do is hang around during the ordeal and agree to the software license terms, choose whether you want to customize the installation or upgrade it, and follow any other onscreen prompts that pop up.

 NOTE   Microsoft Outlook 2013—and the entire Office 2013 suite of programs—can run on Windows 7 or Windows 8. It will not run on Windows XP or Vista. You can run Outlook on laptops, desktop computers, or tablets (with sufficient drive space and RAM). Outlook is available as a standalone program or as part of the Microsoft Office suite of productivity software. Outlook is also a part of the new Office 365, as cloud-based subscription software you can access on the Internet for a monthly fee. In addition, you can also utilize Outlook as part of Microsoft's Web Apps—browser-based versions of the full-blown software, but from within a browser window. As a new Outlook user, you can take advantage of the Outlook Web App using your Microsoft account.

Outlook 2013 fully supports touchscreen technology, so if you have a touch-enabled device, you can interact with the program using the touchscreen in addition to the regular old mouse and keyboard. For example, you can pinch to zoom on messages and calendar events, and you can hold your finger on an item to access available context-sensitive options. You can also minimize the ribbon to free up onscreen space and move around more freely.

If you haven't jumped through all the setup hoops yet, you can do so before diving into learning how to use Outlook. Basically, the setup hoops consist of a Microsoft Outlook Account Setup Wizard that greets you the first time you use Outlook 2013 and welcomes you to the program. The wizard walks you through the steps for establishing an email account and making a profile, and then hands over a lovely gift basket welcoming you to the Microsoft family. I might have just imagined the complimentary gift basket when I installed Outlook, but wouldn't it be cool if that did actually happen at the end of every software installation? Freshly baked banana muffins would make a good addition to a welcome basket, I think.

An Internet connection and a Microsoft account are extremely important for getting the most out of Outlook. A *Microsoft account* is a free, cloud-based account that lets you use SkyDrive (cloud storage), Hotmail (free email service), Skype (online video conferencing), and more. In fact, a Microsoft account gives you access to a wide range of services and tools, including productivity tools to help you manage files, and social tools that help you communicate and share with others. If you already use a Microsoft service like Hotmail or Messenger, you already have a Microsoft account, but if not, you can create a free one. The key word here is *free*.

Because you can't very well email people without an Internet connection, you definitely need a reliable way to access the Internet. Most people nab an account with an Internet service provider of some sort, whether through Wi-Fi or hard-wired with cables (like DSL or cable modems), and typically for a fee. The key word here is *fee*. It usually costs a little something to rent a larger company's Internet connection, especially if you expect it to be reliable.

After you've established an Internet connection, a Microsoft account, and installed Outlook, you're ready to start exploring the program.

WHAT'S A MICROSOFT ACCOUNT?

Everyone using Office 2013 products (including Outlook) needs a Microsoft account (also known as an Office account) to take advantage of all the new online offerings and expanded features. Given that an account is free, why not partake in all the bonuses? Your Microsoft account offers the following online services:

- Email—Outlook (yes, the same name as the program) is the official online email service, and you can use it with a Hotmail or Outlook email address, or you can use an email address you already have.

- Messenger/Skype—Use this service to send instant messages to your friends and contacts. (Microsoft is transitioning this service to Skype now, but it used to be called Messenger.)

- Calendar—Keep track of important events and appointments, and share this data with others using this web-based calendar.

- Office Web Apps—Web-based versions of the popular Office suite, including Word, PowerPoint, Excel, and OneNote.

- SkyDrive—Not only is SkyDrive an online file storage space, but it's completely integrated with Office Web Apps.

- Profile—Create a public information page about yourself for other users to view who instant message you or contact you using email.

- Windows Essentials Apps—Includes Photo Gallery (photo viewer and editor app), Movie Maker (a simple video editing app), and Writer (blog editor).

GET YOUR HEAD IN THE CLOUD

Why do they call it the "cloud?" The term comes from the way in which network engineers had to describe networks outside their own, such as the Internet, which they connected to but didn't necessarily control or know what was going on in the other networks. Real clouds are opaque, and network clouds are rather like this, too, because you can't see how all the data moves across the Internet, but it does end up somewhere on the other side via all the connections. When the engineers would diagram the various devices and connections on their networks, they would draw the Internet portion of the network as a cloud. Aren't you glad you asked now?

Starting and Exiting Outlook

You can start Outlook the same as you start any other program on your computer. If you are using Windows 7, for example, you can apply any of these techniques:

- Click the Start button and type **Outlook**; then click Outlook 2013 at the top of the Start menu.

- Double-click the Outlook shortcut icon on the desktop (if there is one).

- Click the Start button, and then click All Programs, Microsoft Office 2013, and Outlook 2013.

Figure 1.2 shows the Windows 7 Start menu with the Microsoft Office programs listed, one of which is Outlook.

FIGURE 1.2

You can start Outlook using the Start menu in Windows 7.

If you are using Windows 8, try one of these methods:

- From the Windows 8 Start screen, type **Outlook**; then from the Apps search screen, click Outlook.

- If you added a tile for Outlook on the Start screen, you can click it to open Outlook on the desktop.

- In Desktop view, you can click Outlook's shortcut icon on the desktop, if available.

In Windows 8, Outlook launches over on the desktop, which means you can minimize and maximize the program window, and the taskbar shows the open Outlook program icon.

NOTE   If you're new to Windows 8, try the *Absolute Beginner's Guide to Windows 8*, available in fine bookstores online and off. It's sure to get you up and running fast with the latest Microsoft operating system.

After you open Outlook, the first thing you see is the Mail module, shown in Figure 1.3. I'll show you how to navigate around the program window in a minute, but first let's talk about how to exit the program. Yes, I know you're not ready to quit using Outlook yet, but this is as good a spot as any to tell you how to close the window.

Minimize button ─┐ ┌─Close button

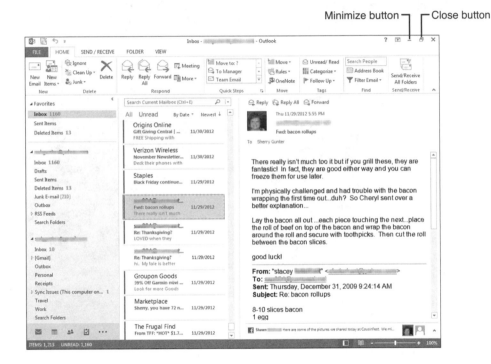

FIGURE 1.3

The easiest way to exit Outlook is to click the window's Close button.

Exiting is easy. Do any of the following:

- Click the Close icon in the upper-right corner of the program window.

- Click the Outlook icon in the upper-left corner and click Close.

- Right-click the Outlook icon on the taskbar and click Close Window.

- Click the File tab and click Exit.

As soon as you activate the Close command, Outlook closes entirely.

If you'd rather get the program window out of the way for a bit while you tackle other computer tasks, you can minimize the window; click the Minimize button.

Minimizing the Outlook window reduces it to a button icon on the desktop taskbar. To open it again, click the icon.

I highly recommend that you keep the Outlook program running in the background, even while you work with other programs. If you close it, you won't hear or see any reminders about pending appointments or emails received, thus making it difficult for your personal assistant to assist you.

Familiarizing Yourself with the Program Window

Microsoft Outlook shares a similar look and feel with all the Microsoft Office programs, including Excel, PowerPoint, and Word. The bonus in this news is that if you learn your way around one program, you can use the same techniques in another. Even if you do not plan to use any other Microsoft programs, the skills you learn in Outlook 2013 carry over into other non-Microsoft programs, too. Lots of other software manufacturers, for example, adopted the Microsoft ribbon approach to organize and present commands and features.

If you're new to using Outlook, take a few moments and familiarize yourself with the program window's many nuances, some of which are conveniently pointed out in Figure 1.4. You can learn more about using many of these elements in the next chapter.

Let's go over the various elements you see onscreen and what they're used for in Outlook:

- **Outlook icon**—Click this icon to display a drop-down menu of program window controls, such as Minimize (reducing the window to an icon on the taskbar), Maximize (enlarging the window to optimize workspace), and Close (exiting the program).

- **Quick Access toolbar**—Use this toolbar to quickly perform a common Outlook task, such as undoing or redoing an action. By default, the toolbar shows only the Undo command, but you can add other common tasks to the toolbar, such as the command for sending/receiving or printing.

- **Title bar**—Look for the name of your active account at the top of the program window, along with the name of the module you're currently viewing.

- **Ribbon**—The collapsible bar across the top of the window houses most of the commands you need to work in Outlook. Related commands are grouped into tabs, and you click a tab to view its various commands.

- **Folder pane**—This pane displays different folder structures depending on which module you're using. If it's Mail, the Inbox and subfolders appear for messages; if it's Calendar, navigation calendars appear. This pane can expand and collapse to free up onscreen workspace.

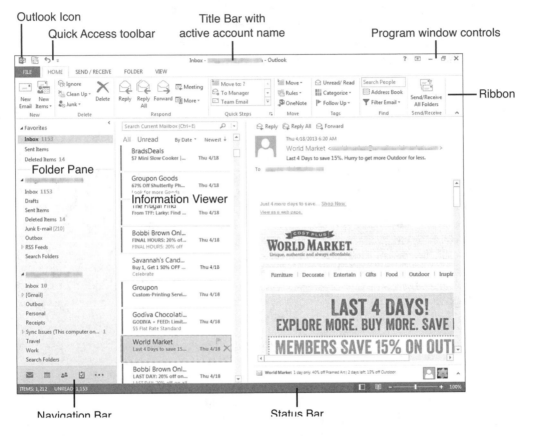

FIGURE 1.4

Familiarize yourself with the various window elements.

- **Information Viewer**—In the middle of the window you do all your work, such as viewing messages or appointments.

- **Navigation bar**—Use this bar, which can expand or collapse, to switch between Outlook components. Each icon represents a module; click an icon to view the module.

- **Status bar**—The bottom area of the window displays status information, such as the amount of messages in the Inbox, and so on.

- **Program window controls**—Use these controls to minimize, maximize, and close the program window. These same controls are also available through the Outlook icon. In addition to window controls, you see icons for accessing Help and collapsing/expanding the ribbon.

You'll learn more about using the various Outlook elements as you tackle different tasks and features. If you are new to using Outlook, however, you may benefit from understanding how the program window controls work.

Program windows are resizable, and you can minimize them to get them out of the way to tackle other computer tasks. You can resize the Outlook program window by clicking the Restore Down icon located in the program window control group (see Figure 1.5). This reduces the size of the window, as shown in Figure 1.6, and you can then drag it around by its title bar to move it. You can also click and drag a window corner to resize the Outlook window. To make it full-screen size again, click the Maximize button, which appears in place of the Restore Down button when the window is smaller in size. To minimize the window and hide it completely, click the Minimize button; click the Outlook icon on the taskbar to view the Outlook window again.

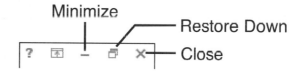

FIGURE 1.5

You can use the program window controls to control the actual window.

 TIP You can utilize window controls on all kinds of windows and dialog boxes you encounter while working with Outlook. For example, the Close button—displayed with an X—is handy for closing dialog boxes, tool palettes, panes, and the like.

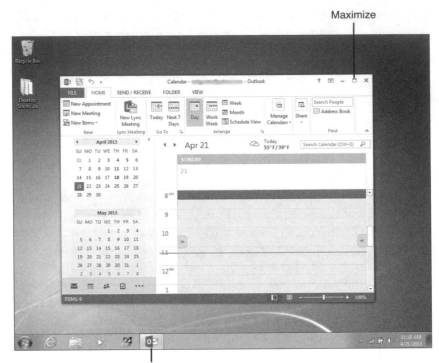

FIGURE 1.6

You can resize and move the Outlook window around the computer screen, as needed.

Finding Help with Outlook Issues and Topics

If you ever find yourself in a jam regarding an Outlook task, you can seek help through the Outlook Help feature. When activated, Help opens a special window you can use to look up topics, search online for additional resources, and generally learn more about the program or the feature you are working with at the time. With an online connection, Help taps into resources from the Microsoft Office website. Help offers tutorials, links to related topics, and a table of contents you can peruse.

To utilize Help, click the Help icon in the upper-right corner of the program window. An Outlook Help window opens, as shown in Figure 1.7. You can scroll through the featured topics, if you like. You can click a link to learn more about a subject. Help displays additional information in another window, as shown in Figure 1.8.

Help window   Help icon

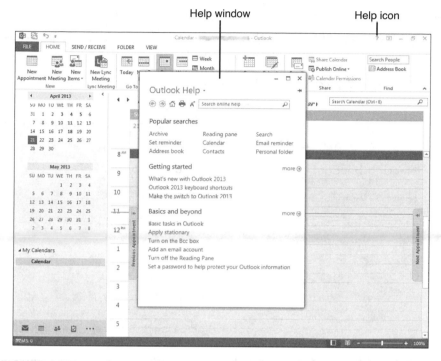

FIGURE 1.7

Help is always a click away, if you need it.

Help buttons   Search box

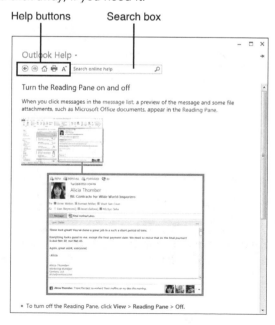

FIGURE 1.8

You can peruse the Help topics and use the navigation buttons at the top of the window to move around the topics.

After you open a Help window, you can do the following:

- Use the navigation buttons (Back and Forward) at the top of the Help window to move back and forth between topics.

- Click the little icon that looks like a house, aptly named Home, to return to the main Help window you started in.

- If you're having trouble viewing the window's type size, you can click the Text button to toggle back and forth between regular and large type.

- Need to print out a help topic? Click the Print button.

- Use the Search box to search for keywords and topics.

- To close the Help window, click its Close button (the X in the upper-right corner of the window).

 NOTE   Although the Help window offers lots of assistance in learning new commands and features, you might also open your browser window (such as Internet Explorer) and look around the Microsoft Office website (office.microsoft.com) for additional resources, forums, and other support help.

THE ABSOLUTE MINIMUM

Now you know a little more about what you can do with Outlook and how to start working with various parts of the program window, and you're about to learn a lot more in the chapters that follow. Meanwhile, here are a few items to take away from this chapter:

- Microsoft Outlook is the most famous personal information manager program on the market today.

- Outlook 2013 includes a lot of exciting improvements, including a new user interface, quick peeks, and a Weather bar.

- Outlook consists of several main modules: Mail, Calendar, People, Tasks, and Notes.

- Outlook is easy to launch, regardless of which operating system you're using.

- The program window layout is very intuitive; commands are located on the various tabs on the ribbon, the Folder pane displays your folder structure, and the Information Viewer area in the middle is where you view messages and appointments and such.

- You can use the Help feature to find help with Outlook topics and tasks, including tutorials and access to online support.

IN THIS CHAPTER

- Learn how to work with the ribbon
- Accessing the Quick Access toolbar
- Using shortcuts with context menus
- Dealing with dialog boxes
- Learn how to use the Navigation bar
- Find out how to control panes

BASIC OUTLOOK OPERATIONS

Before you jump in and start whipping up emails and appointments willy-nilly, it's a good idea to take some time and familiarize yourself with the basic methods Outlook offers to access tools, commands, and features. Learning how to find your way to the commonly used commands and features now can help you speed up your work later. Microsoft Outlook presents commands, settings, and options through dialog boxes, context menus, toolbars, and the ribbon. In many cases, you can access the same tools and features through several different avenues.

It's also a good idea to figure out how the Folder pane, Information Viewer, and Navigation bars work so you can easily maneuver around the various modules and their associated tasks. In this chapter, I'll show you how Outlook presents commands and tools for you to use, and how to control the Navigation bar and the way panes work.

Working with the Ribbon

The ribbon organizes commands and features into tabs listed across the top of the program window. If you haven't worked with the latest versions of Microsoft Office in the past few years, you may be interested to know that the ribbon replaces the menus and toolbars of old. With the ribbon format, related command buttons and features are organized into groups found within each tab. For example, if you display the Home tab, shown in Figure 2.1, you can find most of Outlook's module-specific commands, such as creating new items. If you display the Folder tab, it offers tools for working with folders. The various buttons, drop-down menus, and galleries found on the ribbon tabs are grouped under labeled headings, such as Actions or Tags, along the ribbon's expanse.

FIGURE 2.1

The Home tab on the ribbon displays various tools and features.

Now here's something rather interesting—the commands found on the various tabs change based on what module you're using. If you're working with the Mail module, for example, the Home tab shows tools related to emailing, but if you're working with Calendar, the Home tab shows commands for changing Calendar's display. Pretty nifty, eh? Just keep this in mind when you're looking for a command in a certain spot, but it's not there—you probably need to switch modules to find it again.

When you open a specific item in Outlook, such as a message window or an appointment window, the individual window has its own ribbon of tabs pertaining to the item. These tabs of commands are unique to the task at hand. If you're writing an email message, for example, the message window displays tools for formatting the message text or inserting pictures, shapes, and so on, as shown in Figure 2.2.

NOTE When it comes to software lingo, lots of terms are interchangeable. For example, commands, features, settings, and options are all basically the same thing—selections you make in the program to perform a computer task or define something. Sometimes this involves clicking or tapping a command button, such as OK or Cancel; other times this involves choosing from a variety of options to apply, such as clicking check boxes or option buttons (the tiny circles with bullets) to turn items on or off. At the very heart of it, all software programs are about taking your input, whether it's clicking/tapping buttons or typing in text, and turning it into something, such as an email message.

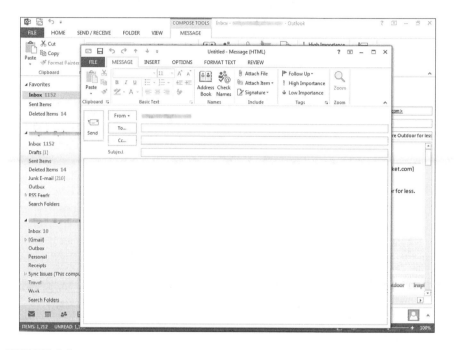

FIGURE 2.2

Individual items in Outlook have their own windows with their own ribbons.

How to Use Ribbon Elements

Using the ribbon is a fairly straightforward procedure. All you have to do is click a tab name to view its contents—or if you have a touchscreen computer or tablet, tap the tab name. To activate a command or feature, click it or tap it. Suppose you want to flag a task you create in the Tasks module. You can select the task from your list, click the Home tab (if it's not already displayed), click a follow-up flag to assign (or tap). Bada-boom, bada-bing, the flag is immediately added.

 NOTE   The ribbon appears throughout the Microsoft Office suite of programs, such as Excel and PowerPoint, and it also appears in other programs. After you learn your way around the ribbon in Outlook, you'll easily traverse the ribbon format in other programs with ease.

If you see a drop-down arrow—which is simply a downward pointing arrow icon—next to any ribbon feature, you can click it or tap it to display a menu of additional choices or options. Figure 2.3 shows an example of a drop-down menu. After the menu drops, you can click (or tap if you have a touchscreen) a selection from the menu to apply it to your document.

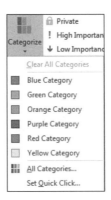

FIGURE 2.3

Drop-down menus offer a variety of selections you can make.

The ribbon also features list boxes, called galleries, as shown in Figure 2.4. You can scroll through the gallery to view selections and click or tap the one you want to apply.

FIGURE 2.4

Galleries list a variety of selections, such as Quick Steps you can apply.

You can also expand the gallery to view all the settings at one time, as shown in Figure 2.5.

 NOTE The ribbon got its name from its earliest conception idea of combining commands onto an area of the screen resembling a paper scroll-like strip. Although the ribbon doesn't really work quite like a paper scroll, it still offers easy, intuitive access to commands and features.

FIGURE 2.5

You can also open the gallery to view its contents.

TIP You may notice some groups of commands on a tab have a tiny icon in the bottom-right corner of the group. When clicked, this icon opens a dialog box where you can find additional and advanced commands. For example, if you click the Arrange group's icon found on the Calendar module's Home tab, the Outlook Options dialog box opens with more settings. You learn more about dialog boxes later in this chapter.

As for the tabs found on the ribbon, here's a rundown of the main tabs:

- **File**—This tab opens a special screen called Backstage view, with various file-related commands, such as Open & Export, Info, and Print.

- **Home**—This tab organizes all the basic commands for working with module items.

- **Send/Receive**—This tab lists commands for sending and receiving messages for your email account folders.

- **Folder**—Use the commands on this tab to control how you work with folders in Outlook, including moving items between folders or sorting folders.

- **View**—You can find all the various ways to change your view of a module's contents on this tab, including controlling panes.

In addition to these, remember that task-specific tabs may appear when you are working on a specific type of Outlook item, such as a message window or task window.

TIP If you're using a touchscreen device, such as a tablet, you can use all the common touch gestures to interact with onscreen elements, such as flicking to scroll or tapping to select. Just assume anytime I instruct you to select or click something, you can use the tap gesture to accomplish the same thing with your touchscreen.

 TIP Outlook's ScreenTips can help you quickly identify commands and what to do with them. Hover your mouse pointer over a command or tool to reveal a pop-up ScreenTip. Move the pointer away and the ScreenTip disappears. To turn ScreenTips off, click the File tab, click Options, and click the General category. Click the ScreenTip style drop-down menu and choose Don't Show ScreenTips.

Hiding and Displaying the Ribbon

There are a lot of commands available in Outlook, and placing them on various tabs on the ribbon helps keep them organized. However, it also makes the ribbon appear a bit intrusive at times because it holds so many things. You can easily hide the ribbon and get it out of the way when you're working. You can summon it back again with a click.

To hide the ribbon, double-click any tab name on the ribbon. Outlook immediately hides the entire thing except for the tab names, shown in Figure 2.6. To display the ribbon again, double-click a tab name.

If you want the ribbon to always appear locked in place, click the Pushpin icon located at the far right end. Click the same area to unlock the ribbon again.

 TIP Want to customize the ribbon? You can add and subtract commands to suit the way you work. To find customizing options, right-click an empty area of the ribbon and click Customize the Ribbon. This opens the Outlook Options dialog box to the Customize Ribbon tab, where you can add and subtract commands, create new tabs, rename tabs, or reset to the default settings.

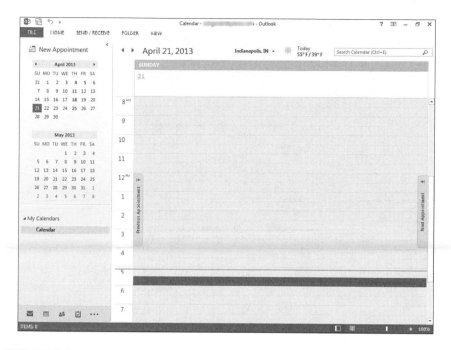

FIGURE 2.6

You can hide the ribbon to free up screen space.

Working with the Quick Access Toolbar

In the top-left corner of the Outlook program window, you'll find a small grouping of icon buttons called the Quick Access toolbar. This toolbar gives you quick access to common actions. By default, the Quick Access toolbar displays the Send/Receive All Folders and Undo buttons, as shown in Figure 2.7. For example, you can use the Undo shortcut icon to quickly undo an action.

The Quick Access toolbar camps out in the corner

FIGURE 2.7

Tucked away in the corner lurks the Quick Access toolbar.

You can also choose to display more or fewer shortcuts on the toolbar. Click the arrow icon at the end of the bar to display a drop-down menu (see Figure 2.8). Check marks next to the command names indicate the icons that appear on the toolbar. To add an icon, click the command name. To remove an icon, click it to uncheck it and delete it from the toolbar.

Click here to display the menu

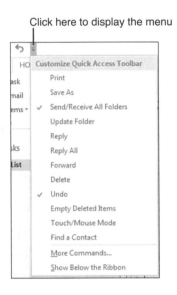

FIGURE 2.8

Use the drop-down menu at the end of the toolbar to specify which shortcut icons appear.

As you can imagine, placing shortcuts up at the top of your program window can be a time saver if you find yourself performing the same tasks over and over, such as printing an email message, and you tire of looking through the ribbon or other dialog boxes to find a command.

 TIP Want to customize the Quick Access toolbar? You can add an icon for a command you use the most or rearrange the order of buttons. Click the arrow icon at the end of the Quick Access toolbar and choose More Commands. This opens the Outlook Options dialog box to the Quick Access Toolbar tab where you can add and subtract commands.

Using Context Menus and Toolbars

Microsoft Outlook offers several ways to apply commands related to the task at hand. Called context menus and toolbars, these features pop up and display shortcut commands pertaining to the item you are working with in a document.

For example, when you select text in an email window, a mini toolbar appears near the cursor. You can use this toolbar, shown in Figure 2.9, to quickly apply basic formatting commands to the message text. If you ignore the mini toolbar and keep working, it eventually disappears. To activate a command from the toolbar, click the button.

A pop-up toolbar offers shortcuts to popular formatting commands

FIGURE 2.9

The mini toolbar offers shortcuts to common formatting commands, like Bold and Italic.

TIP You can turn off the automatic mini toolbar display if you do not find it helpful. To do so, click the File tab on the ribbon, and then click Options. The Outlook Options dialog box opens. Click the General category, then deselect the Show Mini Toolbar on Selection check box and click OK. This turns the feature off. To turn it on again, revisit this dialog box and check the box again.

If you right-click while performing a task, such as reading email, a context menu pops up listing commands related to what you're doing. For example, if you right-click a task (see Figure 2.10), the context menu includes commands for marking the task, categorizing it, sending it to OneNote, and more. To make a selection from the context menu, click the command.

FIGURE 2.10

Context menus appear when you right-click.

Dealing with Dialog Boxes

Dialog boxes are a basic part of just about every software program. Dialog boxes allow users to specify more input. Many of Outlook's dialog boxes offer more options for you to choose from before applying a feature, or present a variety of related settings all in one convenient spot. Figure 2.11 shows a typical dialog box. As you can see, it looks a lot like a form you might fill out.

FIGURE 2.11

Dialog boxes require additional input from a user before implementing a feature or action.

Dialog boxes display many of the same tools found in the ribbon, including buttons, list boxes, drop-down menus, spinner arrows, check boxes, and text boxes or *fields* in which you enter data. You can also find slider controls, tabs, and option buttons among the many dialog boxes in Outlook.

The bottom of a dialog box typically has command buttons to execute the changes or to exit the box without changing anything. Click OK to execute the settings you specified, or click Cancel to forgo the changes.

Some dialog boxes may include buttons that open additional dialog boxes. Tools and settings you find on Outlook's ribbon may open dialog boxes as well. You are sure to encounter lots of dialog boxes as you work, but once you know what to expect from them and how to enter your input, you can handle them with ease.

TIP   You can move a dialog box around onscreen by clicking and dragging its title bar.

NOTE   From time to time, Outlook presents another type of box to you, called a prompt box. It looks like a dialog box in appearance, but generally it cautions you about a task or program need and offers some command buttons to choose from—just make the appropriate selection to move on.

Working with the Navigation Bar

As you learned back in Chapter 1, "Introduction to Outlook," you can use Outlook's Navigation bar to switch between *modules*—the different parts of Outlook. By default, the bar is set to display in compact mode, as shown in Figure 2.12, which shows only icons representing each module. You can also display the bar in full mode, which shows the text-based names of the components across the bottom of the program window (just above the status bar). Figure 2.13 shows the bar with the text names displayed.

Depending on your screen display, not all icons may appear listed on the bar. You can click the bar's ellipsis to view additional icons, as shown in Figure 2.14. If you happen to collapse the Folder pane, which you learn how to do in the next section, the Navigation bar appears listed vertically (see Figure 2.14), but only if the bar displays icons instead of text labels.

Icon labels

FIGURE 2.12

Use the Navigation bar to switch between Outlook components.

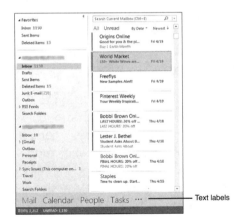

Text labels

FIGURE 2.13

You can choose to display the Navigation bar as text labels instead of icons.

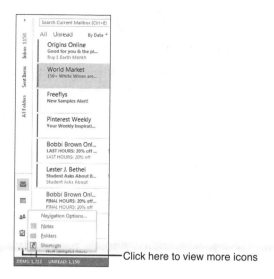

Click here to view more icons

FIGURE 2.14

If the Folder pane is collapsed, you can still view the Navigation bar, either vertically or horizontally.

You can control the display of the Navigation bar using the Navigation Options dialog box, shown in Figure 2.15. To find your way to this dialog box, use one of these methods:

- Click the ellipsis on the Navigation bar and choose Navigation Options from the pop-up menu.

- Click the View tab, click Folder pane, and then click Options.

Click here to turn icons off and text lables on

FIGURE 2.15

Control the Navigation bar display through the Navigation Options dialog box.

When you've got the dialog box open, you can do the following:

- To turn text labels on, deselect the Compact Navigation check box.

- To change how many module icons appear listed in the bar, set another number of visible items in the Maximum Number of Visible Items box.

- To change the order of module icons in the bar, adjust the display by moving module names up or down in the list.

When you finish making your changes, click OK to apply them.

Working with Panes

A common way to divide a program window into workable areas is to use *panes*. Most users are familiar with panes from Web browsing. Typically, a navigational pane appears on the left or top side of a web page with links that, when clicked, display another page somewhere off to the right or below. Outlook uses panes to divvy up areas of the window. Let's go over the various ways you can work with these panes.

Working with the Folder Pane

The far left side of the program window features the Folder pane. This pane displays different aspects of your Outlook folder structure depending on which module you're viewing. For example, when viewing the Mail module, shown in Figure 2.16, the pane displays all your email account inboxes and their subfolders.

You can expand and collapse the pane to free up onscreen workspace. Click or tap the Minimize button located in the upper-right corner of the pane, pointed out in Figure 2.16. When collapsed, the pane folds to a skinny columnar display along the left side of the program window, like the example in Figure 2.17. To expand it again, click the Expand button.

 NOTE Notice when the Folder pane is collapsed, the Navigation bar runs vertically instead of horizontally—but only if the bar is displayed in Compact Navigation mode (icons instead of text labels).

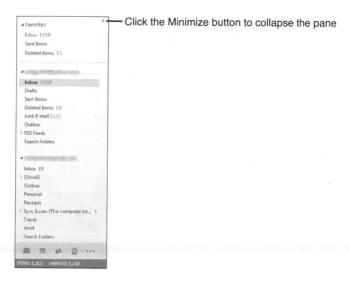

FIGURE 2.16

You can expand and collapse the Folder pane as needed.

FIGURE 2.17

The Folder pane, collapsed.

You can also control the Folder pane using the Folder pane drop-down menu on the View tab, as shown in Figure 2.18. For example, you can turn the pane off entirely by selecting the Off option. To turn it back on again, revisit the drop-down menu and choose Normal.

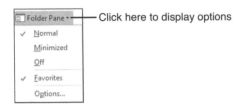

Click here to display options

FIGURE 2.18

You can also control the Folder pane through the View tab.

You can also resize the Folder pane. Just move your mouse pointer over the pane's right border and drag it to a new size, wider or thinner. You can do the same thing with any pane in Outlook; drag the pane's border to resize the pane, whether it's the Reading pane, the message list, or the To-Do bar. Figure 2.19 shows what the Folder pane looks like when it's being resized.

Click and drag to resize

FIGURE 2.19

You can also resize the Folder pane by dragging its right border.

Working with the Reading Pane

Out in the main area of the Outlook window, called the Information Viewer by Microsoft programmers, you can also control the view of the Reading pane. The Reading pane, which displays the contents of a selected message from the list, is an optional item. You can turn it on or off, or resize it. You can choose to display it to the right of the message list, at the bottom of the main area, or turn it off entirely. Figure 2.20 shows the Reading pane displayed at the bottom of the viewing area, and Figure 2.21 shows the pane turned off. The pane can be displayed in any module, but it appears by default when using Mail and Tasks.

Reading Pane

FIGURE 2.20

The Reading pane shows a selected message or file attachment.

To control the Reading pane, click the View tab and click the Reading pane drop-down arrow, as shown in Figure 2.22. Next, select a setting you want to apply. Outlook immediately changes the window to reflect your selection.

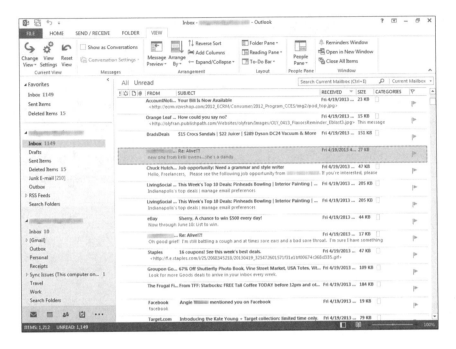

FIGURE 2.21

Look, ma, no Reading pane!

FIGURE 2.22

Control the Reading pane through the View tab.

Working with the To-Do Bar and Peeks

You can use the To-Do bar to view sneak peeks of your calendar, people info, or tasks, or all three at the same time. A *peek* is a quick glance at current content, such as your calendar. Suppose you're busy typing up a reply to an email and need to check your calendar to suggest a date. Rather than having to open the full Calendar module, you can use the peek feature to check the current month. For quick peeks, just hover the mouse pointer over the module item on the Navigation bar, as shown in Figure 2.23.

—Peek

FIGURE 2.23

Outlook's peeks let you see your calendar, a contact, or a task list at a glance.

The To-Do bar opens a full-on pane for peeks, as shown in Figure 2.24. The To-Do bar is not turned on by default, but you can summon it anytime you want it. Click the ribbon's View tab, click the To-Do bar drop-down arrow, and click which part you want to view, as shown in Figure 2.25. You can turn on just one peek or all three. A check mark next to the item's name indicates it's displayed; no check mark means the item is turned off. To turn them all off, click the Off command. To turn off individual peeks in the bar itself, you can click the peek's Close button.

 NOTE   You can also turn on a People pane to view details about a particular contact. To learn more, check out Chapter 8, "Contacts."

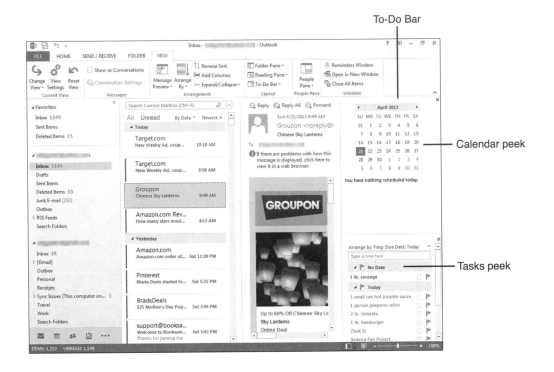

FIGURE 2.24

You can use the To-Do bar to keep different peeks in view.

FIGURE 2.25

You can control the To-Do bar through the View tab.

THE ABSOLUTE MINIMUM

This chapter introduced you to several basic Outlook operations. Here are the key points to remember from this chapter:

- The ribbon hosts all the tools and features you need to work with the various items you create in your modules. Click a tab to view its associated tools.

- Use the Quick Access toolbar in the upper-left corner to undo actions. You can also add and subtract buttons that appear on this toolbar to suit the way you work.

- You can right-click in a document to reveal task-related shortcuts via pop-up menus or toolbars.

- Use dialog boxes to enter additional settings and options.

- You can use the Navigation bar to switch between Outlook parts.

- You can choose to display icons or text labels on the Navigation bar.

- You can use the Reading pane to view the contents of a message or a file attachment.

- You can use peeks to quickly glance at your calendar, a contact, or your tasks list.

- You can turn panes on or off in the main viewing area to suit the way you like to work.

IN THIS CHAPTER

- Find out more than you wanted to know about types of email services
- Learn how to use Backstage view
- Add new email accounts and keep track of them with ease
- Change your user account's background and account photo
- Switch between user accounts

3

SETTING UP ACCOUNTS AND PERSONALIZING OUTLOOK

Outlook's Mail module is a serious workhorse, but before you can hook it up to the proverbial messaging plow, you need to make sure everything's ready to go. By everything, I mean that all your email accounts need to be connected and configured. In this chapter, you learn how to add email services and make sure Outlook can play nicely with them.

Understanding Email Services and Internet Access

If you're using Outlook at work, chances are Information Technology (IT) people or your network administrator set everything up for you. Lucky! If you're using Outlook at home or you're your own network administrator in a small office situation, you're in charge of setting up Internet access and choosing email services. If you're the boss of your own connectivity destiny, then like most people, you probably use an outside source to access the Internet. These typically include a cable, satellite, or phone company (home or wireless). Companies that offer Internet access through their giant servers and networks are called Internet service providers, or ISPs. In most instances, these types of connections encompass access to the Internet for web surfing as well as for email. Many offer dedicated storage on their servers, too, so you can back up important files. Email comes in several types of accounts:

- **POP3**—Post Office Protocol 3; this is the most popular email account type. With it, your email messages are downloaded from the server hosting your account and read and stored on your computer and not the mail server. This means you can read the messages on your computer only and the mail server keeps your email only until you download it (unless your provider has a Web mail interface).

- **IMAP**—Internet Message Access Protocol; this type of account stores your emails on the mail server without your needing to download them onto your computer. The nice thing about this setup is that you can access your messages from any computer.

- **MAPI**—Messaging Application Programming Interface; this account type is a lot like IMAP, but with more features, especially if you're running Outlook with a mail server that uses Microsoft Exchange. MAPI accounts are generally associated with Microsoft Exchange.

- **HTTP**—This is a Web protocol, and you can use your browser to log on to the site and view mail. Yahoo! Mail, Hotmail, and Gmail are examples of Web-based email services.

 NOTE Microsoft Exchange is a server that handles email and collaboration tasks popular in business settings or larger organizations. More specifically, Exchange is a server program, and it's designed to run on Windows Server products. In addition to email, it is a platform for calendaring and unified messaging, offering it a competitive advantage for businesses over standard POP3 setups. Microsoft Exchange also delivers a seamless Outlook experience across different devices. Exchange makes use of MAPI protocol, but it also supports POP3 and IMAP programs.

For a fee, ISPs offer the use of their equipment (giant servers and other computers and networks) and their connection to the Internet. Many include email as part of the package. Basically, this means you can set up an email address with them. On the downside, if you ever switch ISPs, you'll have to switch email addresses and notify everyone of the change. If this potentially poses a problem, you might consider getting an email account through a free service.

Turns out Microsoft offers email, and all you need is a Microsoft account—it's completely free. So, if you don't already have an email service, it's easy enough to set one up through Microsoft. Best of all, a Microsoft account works seamlessly with Outlook. Up until 2013, Microsoft's free perks included email through their Windows Live and Hotmail services. Users needed a Windows Live ID to sign into things like SkyDrive (cloud storage), Messenger (the instant messaging service) or Windows Phone (smart phone). You had to have another ID to use Xbox Live to play games online. Now they've merged all these into one service under the umbrella called a *Microsoft account*. The good news is if you already have an account through Windows Live or Xbox Live, you already have a Microsoft account. They're one and the same. You can use this account to access your data from any device, whether it's your Xbox, Windows Phone, or tablet, for example. You can also connect your Microsoft account to services like Facebook, Twitter, and LinkedIn.

If you don't have such an account yet, here is how to get one. Steer your web browser to www.outlook.com and click the Sign Up Now link, similar to Figure 3.1. You can then fill in a form and choose an email address, called a Microsoft account name. Figure 3.2 shows what the form looks like. You can even specify whether you want the new email account to use the outlook.com domain, hotmail.com, or live.com. Variety—it's the spice of life.

Your account name can be anything you want. Most people use their actual names or a combination of initials and such to create a unique email address. If you happen to choose something already in use by someone else, Microsoft prompts you to try another name. After you've got a Microsoft account established, you can start using it to email with Outlook as long as you tell Outlook what the account is—learn more about adding and editing email accounts later in this chapter. I'll even show you how to personalize your account with a profile picture. Yippee.

FIGURE 3.1

You can sign up for a free Microsoft account on this page; look for the Sign Up link to get started.

NOTE You can have all the free email accounts you want, but they don't do you any good if you're not connected to the Internet. To find an Internet service provider, check with your local cable or phone company. Cell phone companies also offer wireless connections you can use, such as setting up a hotspot in your house that all your household computing devices can access. It doesn't hurt to shop around for the best deal, either. If you're on the go all the time, you can also tap into free Wi-Fi services around town to surf the Internet and access your email accounts. (Wi-Fi stands for wireless fidelity, a technology that uses radio waves to provide high-speed Internet and network connections.) Just be sure to safeguard your computer when you do use Wi-Fi to prevent hacking (firewalls and virus protection, for example).

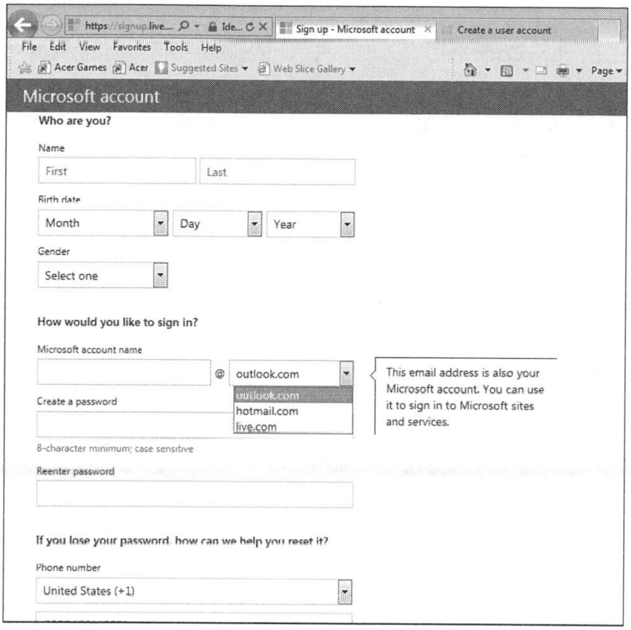

FIGURE 3.2

Signing up is simple; add your name information and choose an email address.

If you already have an email account, you're good to go and can easily associate it with a Microsoft account. I'll show you how in just a bit.

Using Backstage View

To start setting up Outlook to work the way you want, including adding email accounts or editing existing services and customizing Outlook, you need to visit Outlook's Backstage view. It's a weird name, I know, but this is what they call the screen that appears when you click the ribbon's File tab. Figure 3.3 shows an example. Some of the items listed in this window vary ever so slightly based on which module you're currently using, but the main elements stay the same. In fact, when you land in Backstage view (just click the File tab to get there), the Info page is displayed showing Account Information. You might as well familiarize yourself with Backstage view before you venture much further into Outlook. Any sort of changes to accounts or personalizing the program window are set in Backstage view.

The drop-down list at the top of the window reveals all the email accounts currently set up to work with Outlook. Click the drop-down arrow, shown in Figure 3.3, to reveal the accounts. Directly below this is a button you can use to add more email accounts to Outlook. A click of the Account Settings button, shown in Figure 3.4, reveals settings for changing account settings and social networks you connect to.

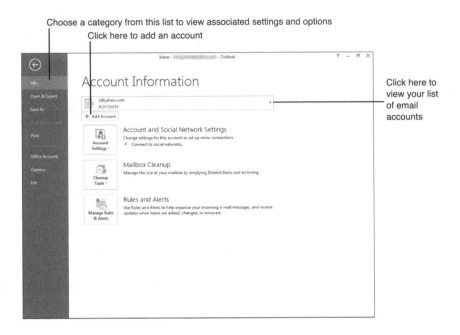

FIGURE 3.3

Backstage view lets you see the behind-the-scenes settings that operate Outlook.

The list along the left side of Backstage view categorizes things you can set or features you can access, such as printing or exporting. Each category you select has its own settings to reveal. Click the Info category anytime you want to see the Account Information screen.

The navigation arrow in the top-left corner takes you back to whatever module you were viewing.

Now that you know how to find your way to Backstage view and what to expect when you get there, it's time to fiddle with your accounts and program settings.

Click the navigation button to return to the main Outlook program window

Click here to view commands for adding accounts

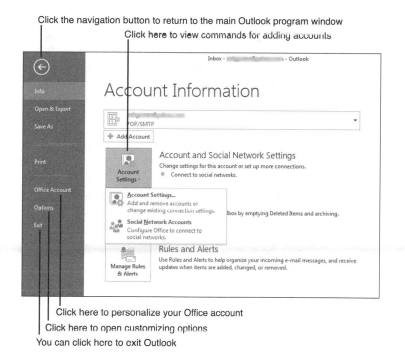

Click here to personalize your Office account

Click here to open customizing options

You can click here to exit Outlook

FIGURE 3.4

Use the Account Settings button to access account options.

Adding Email Accounts to Outlook

You can use multiple email accounts with Outlook. This is extremely convenient. You might have a work account, for example, and a home account. Rather than having to check them separately, you can tell Outlook to work with both. Perhaps you have a special email account you use when signing up for online newsletters and advertising information. Or maybe each family member wants his or her own account. You can add additional accounts to Outlook and view your emails using the Mail module.

Outlook automatically configures your email accounts for you. All you need to specify is your email address and password; Outlook takes care of the rest. On the off chance it cannot establish a connection, you may need to gather up some additional information from your ISP and manually configure the account. This can include identifying your server type, the address of the incoming mail server and outgoing mail server, and any passwords required for each. We'll go over both methods.

Automatically Configure an Account

To have Outlook automatically set up an email account, you need to switch over to Backstage view to get things started. Follow these steps:

1. Click the File tab.

2. Click Add Account.

3. The Add Account dialog box opens, as shown in Figure 3.5. Fill in your name in the first form field.

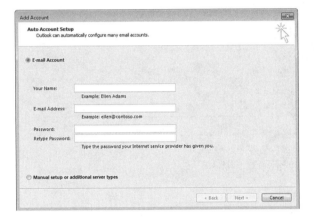

FIGURE 3.5

Use the Auto Account Setup tool to help you configure an account automatically.

4. Type in the email address for the account you want to add.

5. Type in the account's password.

6. Verify the password by typing it in again.

7. Click Next to continue.

8. Outlooks checks the network connection, finds your settings, logs on to the mail server, and then displays a congratulations prompt. Click Finish.

TIP   You can also set up a new account through the Add Account dialog box. From Backstage view, click the Account Settings button, and then click the Account Settings command. This opens the dialog box listing all of your accounts. Click the New button to display the Add Account dialog box shown in Figure 3.6.

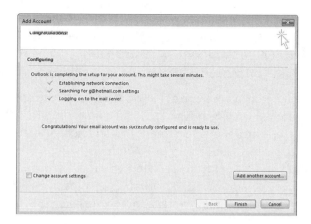

FIGURE 3.6

Outlook verifies your account and settings and logs on to the mail server.

You can now see your new email account listed in the Folder pane in Outlook's Mail module. When you click the Send/Receive All Folders button on the Home tab, Outlook checks the account for messages. Any messages received appear in the account's Inbox; click the Inbox to view the messages. Remember, each account's Inbox keeps a running list of messages received for that account.

 NOTE Uh-oh. Run into some snags? If you mistype any part of your email address or password, Outlook won't be able to complete the automatic configuration. If you run into additional problems, you can try a manual setup, which is explained in the next section.

 TIP One thing to consider when using multiple accounts is to make sure the correct account for new messages is selected before you send it off. If you're trying to keep things organized and precise, you don't want to send a business message from your personal account, for example.

Manually Configure an Account

The manual route might be right for you if you know your email provider has some preferred settings or if you decide you want to control the details about the setup. For example, you may need to ascertain a special Incoming mail server or outgoing mail server info, or special log on info. The first step in the manual process is to tell Outlook what type of email service you're adding. You can choose from a Microsoft Exchange Server (an Exchange account), Outlook.com or Exchange ActiveSync service (use this option if you have a free email through Microsoft), or a POP or IMAP service. If you're not sure, check with your email provider. They can provide you with all the pertinent info required.

After you've gathered all the correct information, you're ready to set up an account. Depending on which type of email service you're adding, different configuration steps appear. If you're adding an Exchange account, Outlook prompts you to close Outlook and use Windows Mail settings in the Control Panel. If you're adding an Outlook.com account, you must enter your server and logon information. If you're adding a POP or IMAP account, you'll need to specify the account type and the incoming and outgoing servers.

To start the process, click the File tab and click the Add Account button. So far, this is the same as having Outlook automatically configure the account. When the Add Account dialog box shows up, however, you need to click the Manual Setup or Additional Server Types option, as shown in Figure 3.7. Click the Next button to continue.

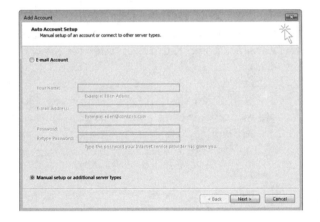

FIGURE 3.7

Choose the manual option to configure the email account yourself.

Now you're presented with the Choose Service portion of the process, as shown in Figure 3.8. Select the type of email account you're adding and click Next.

Depending on what you're selecting, different options appear. Figure 3.9 shows the POP and IMAP Account Settings you need to fill in, and Figure 3.10 shows the Server Settings fields for an Exchange ActiveSync service.

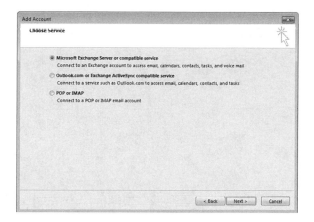

FIGURE 3.8

Specify the type of email account you're adding.

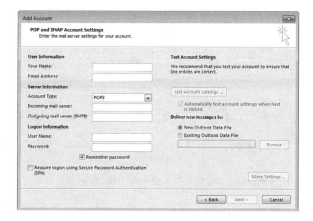

FIGURE 3.9

POP and IMAP settings.

 TIP   Click the More Settings button, if available, to add additional information.

After you've entered all the appropriate fields, you can click Next, and Outlook establishes the network connection.

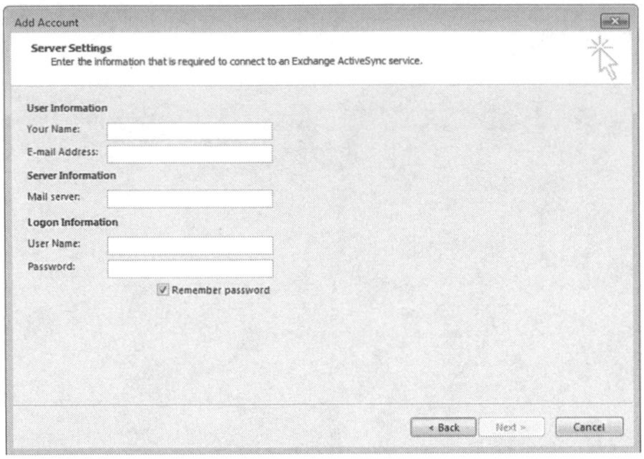

FIGURE 3.10

Exchange ActiveSync settings.

Editing Your Email Accounts

You can make changes to your email accounts through the Account Settings dialog box. This particular box keeps a list of all the accounts you're using. You can add new accounts from this dialog box, remove accounts you no longer use, or make changes to accounts. You can also reorder the way in which Outlook checks the accounts for new messages.

To access the dialog box, click the File tab to switch to Backstage view. Click the Add Accounts button, then click the Add Accounts command. A dialog box similar to Figure 3.11 appears, with the E-mail tab displayed.

From the Account Settings dialog box, you can do any of the following:

- To add a new account to the list, click the New button and follow the steps for automatically or manually configuring a new email service to work with Outlook.

- To repair an account, select it in the list and click the Repair button. This reopens the setup box containing the information about the account, which includes the same form fields you used to enter information about the email service; you can recheck the information.

- To change an account, select it in the list and click the Change button. This displays detailed information about the account, and you can make changes, such as setting a new password.

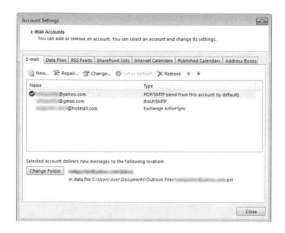

FIGURE 3.11

Use the Account Settings dialog box to make changes to your email accounts.

- To remove an account, select it and click the Remove button. Outlook warns you that you're about to delete the account; click Yes and it's gone.

- To change the default account—the account listed to send from in the new message window—click the account and click Set as Default.

- To change the order of your accounts, click the Up and Down arrows to move the selected account up or down in the list.

Personalizing Your User Account

You can do a little customizing to make Outlook your own, such as assigning an account picture and applying some design tweaks to the program window. The customizing settings you add apply only to your account. Other users who share Outlook with you can customize their own accounts.

Changing the Background and Theme

New to Outlook 2013, and the other programs in the Microsoft Office suite, is the capability to customize the program window background and theme. Changing the background only affects the very top of the program window (Title bar and ribbon tab names), but it does make you feel good choosing a design pattern that suits you. The design you choose does not spill over into the Information Viewer area, so it's more of an extra visual element for personalizing Outlook.

To change the background, click the File tab and click Office Account to view the Account settings shown in Figure 3.12. Click the Office Background drop-down arrow, as shown in Figure 3.13. Move your mouse pointer over the different selections to preview what each one looks like. Click the one you like, and it's immediately applied. To remove a background, just choose the No Background selection.

FIGURE 3.12

The Account page has a few interesting customizing options.

The Office theme is a choice between White, Light Gray, or Dark Gray, as shown in Figure 3.14. This color affects the top of the program window, too, including the ribbon.

To fully appreciate your new customizing options, click the Back navigation arrow (top-left corner) and return to the Outlook window. Now sit back and admire your tweaks.

FIGURE 3.13

Choose a background design from this menu.

FIGURE 3.14

Choose from three theme colors.

Adding and Switching User Accounts

You can add multiple user accounts to Outlook and switch between them. User accounts are called Office accounts, and you can use them across all the Office suite of programs. This is helpful if you are sharing Outlook with other users in your household, for example. You can create an account for each family member and they can customize their accounts the way they like.

To add an account, start by displaying the Account page again (click the File tab and click Office Account). Click the Switch Account link to get things rolling; Outlook opens the Accounts box, shown in Figure 3.15. If you already know the other person's email and password, you can set up the account, or the person can take over your keyboard and do it. Click Add Account to start the process by displaying the Sign In box, similar to Figure 3.16; you have to enter the email address, followed by the password. After the new account is created, it's automatically added to the user Accounts list.

FIGURE 3.15

You can switch between accounts using the Accounts box.

To switch between multiple accounts, click the Switch Account button on the Account page to display the Accounts box shown in Figure 3.15. Click the account you want to use in Outlook and you're ready to go.

FIGURE 3.16

Use the Sign In box to create a new account and sign in.

Changing Your Account Photo

The account photo is shown with all your Microsoft account activities online as well as in some of the Microsoft Office programs you use, such as Word and Excel. Surprisingly, the picture does not appear on your Outlook program window like it does in Word or Excel. However, it does appear in other users' Outlook features when it comes to you as a contact or email recipient.

An account picture can be any graphic file found on your computer, including a photograph or an illustration. To assign a picture, click the Change photo link on the Account page (see Figure 3.12). This opens your online Microsoft account Profile web page, shown in Figure 3.17. (If you're not logged on to your account, you can sign in first.) Click the Change Picture link.

From the Picture page, shown in Figure 3.18, click the Browse button. This opens the Choose File to Upload dialog box, as shown in Figure 3.19.

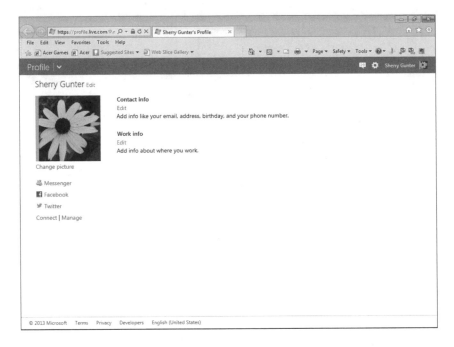

FIGURE 3.17

You can log on to your Microsoft account's Profile page to change your account picture.

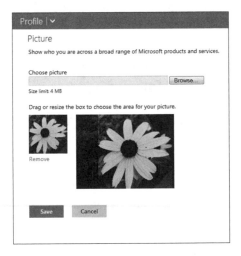

FIGURE 3.18

First you need to find the picture you want to upload, so click the Browse button.

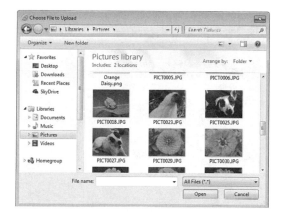

FIGURE 3.19

Next, select the image you want to use.

Navigate to the folder or drive containing the image you want to use, and select the image. Click Open to return to the Picture page (see Figure 3.20). Per the instructions there, you can drag or resize the picture box to get the best part of your picture to display as the account photo. When you have everything just right, click the Save button.

FIGURE 3.20

Position your picture the way you want it.

The Profile page now displays the new account picture, as shown in Figure 3.21. You can close out the browser window.

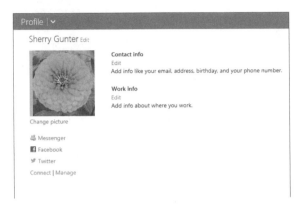

FIGURE 3.21

The new account picture now appears with your account name.

ADDING ONLINE SERVICES

You can add online services to your Microsoft account to enhance your computing experience and manage them from Outlook's Account page (see Figure 3.12). You can find services listed under the Add a Service drop-down menu on the Account page. The categories displayed may vary based on whether you are signed in under a personal, organizational, or school account.

THE ABSOLUTE MINIMUM

Now that you have control of your email accounts in Outlook, the next step is to start emailing. Before you exit this chapter, take a look at what you learned:

- There are different types of email services, but Outlook can handily accommodate them.

- You can add multiple email services to Outlook and configure them automatically or manually.

- Visit the Account Settings dialog box to manage your email services.

- You can share Outlook with others in your household and create a user account for each person.

- You can customize user accounts with photos.

- You can also customize Outlook's appearance with a background and theme.

IN THIS CHAPTER

- Composing and sending new email messages
- Retrieving and reading messages
- Replying and forwarding messages
- Deleting messages
- Working with file attachments
- Using simple message tools

BASIC EMAIL TASKS

It's high time we started emailing. You've got your email services set up and squared away, you've figured out how to maneuver around the program window with confidence, and now it's time to communicate with the outside world—or, if you work in an office, send a message to your coworker inquiring about where you're eating lunch later.

Basic emailing tasks involve composing and sending messages and receiving and reading messages. That really is the gist of it—send some, get some sent to you. Ah, but it's the subtle nuances of the activity of emailing that require explanation. In this chapter, we explore all those nuances and make sure you can handle all the incoming and outgoing communications with true finesse.

Composing and Sending Messages

You can compose a brand new email message using Outlook's Message window, a special form with special boxes for filling in special message details. Perhaps I'm overselling it a bit, but forms are a handy way to tell Outlook what to do. A Message window also offers all kinds of bells and whistles you can apply to add extra elements to your message, and you can find them dispersed among the tabs on the window's ribbon. (Yes, a Message window has its own ribbon of commands and tools, and they're a bit different from the ones found on the Mail module.) Figure 4.1 shows an example of a Message window already filled in with details.

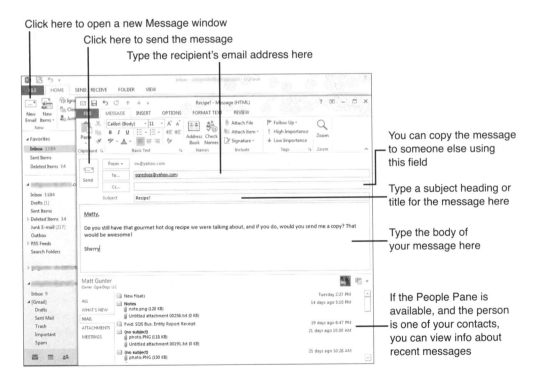

FIGURE 4.1

Here's what a typical Message window looks like.

A Message window looks a lot like the main Outlook window, with a title bar, ribbon of tools, and window controls. Naturally, the title bar tells you the name of the window; in this case, it's the Message window. As soon as you fill in a subject for the message, the title bar displays the subject as its title, too.

You can use any of these methods to open a new Message window:

- Click the New Email button on the Home tab (see Figure 4.1).

- Press Ctrl+N on the keyboard.

- Click the New Items button in any Outlook module and choose E-mail Message from the drop-down menu.

To fill out your empty form, shown in Figure 4.2, start by addressing your email. Do you know the recipient's email address? Good, then you can type it into the To field. Is the recipient already someone in your contacts list—the digital Address Book you use to store information about people you contact? If so, you can click the To button and grab the person's name from the Select Names dialog box, shown in Figure 4.3. Simply double-click the name of the person to insert it into the To field, and click OK to close the dialog box.

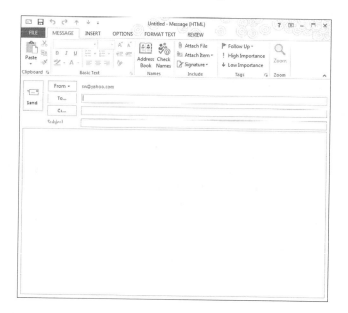

FIGURE 4.2

A blank Message form is ready for your input.

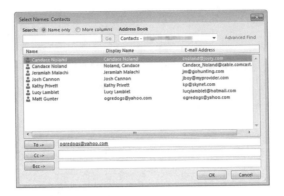

FIGURE 4.3

Use the Select Names dialog box to access your Outlook contacts list.

WHAT MAKES AN EMAIL ADDRESS?

Email addresses follow a certain format, and they're always easy to recognize; for example, bobsmith@mymail.com or johnjones@mycompany.net. If you know the parts, it's easier to understand how they work. An email address is composed of three parts: a username (typically the person's name, or variation thereof), an @ symbol (which acts as a separator), and the host or domain name (the company or organization through which persons have their email service). The dot at the end of the host or domain name is followed by two or three characters, such as us.gov or amazon.com. Those characters indicate the type of service or domain, such as government or commercial.

You really have to type addresses in accurately or your message won't make it to the intended recipient. One misplaced character can create havoc for your message in cyberspace. If a message returns to your Inbox as undeliverable, recheck your address input to see if you missed something crucial. In some instances, the email address just may not be available anymore—the person may have cancelled that account.

TIP   If you have more than one email service, you can change which one the message is sent from using the From drop-down menu at the top of the form. Click the button and choose a service.

TIP If you're on an Exchange network, you don't have to type in a full email address of the person you're sending to who's also on the network. Instead, you can just type in the person's email alias. Timesaver!

Do you need to address the message to more than one person? That's easy; use a semicolon to separate email addresses in the To field. If you use the Select Names dialog box to add names, Outlook automatically inserts a semicolon for you, even if you insert only one name from your Address Book. (To learn more about building your contacts list in Outlook, see Chapter 8, "Contacts.")

TIP If you don't quite know a person's full email address, Outlook can help you out. Type in as much as you know, and then click the Check Names button on the Message window's ribbon (look on the Message tab). This opens the Check Names dialog box and a list of possible matches you can choose from; click one and click OK.

Do you want to carbon copy someone else on the message? The term *carbon copy* is a remnant of the days in which you had to use a sheet of carbon paper inserted between two sheets of paper in a typewriter to make a copy of a memo or letter. To Cc someone, click in the Cc field and type in the email address, or click the Cc button and choose people from your contacts list.

TIP Want to send a blind carbon copy? Click the Cc button to find the Bcc field in the Select Names dialog box. To blind carbon copy is to send a copy of the message to another user without the original recipient knowing or seeing the other person's inclusion. You can also send a blind copy of a brand new message, too.

After you enter the email address or addresses, you can move on to the Subject field and type in a title or subject heading for the message. This text identifies the message content for recipients; it's a heads up regarding what the message is about. In turn, the subject title is what they'll see when they view their incoming messages. It's a good practice to keep your subject titles brief and to the point.

Finally, click in the large, empty area of the Message window to type in your message text. If you're interested in formatting the text (applying attributes such as bold, italic, different fonts, sizes, and text color) or adding other features, flip over to Chapter 6, "Advanced Email Features," to read more. Not everybody's email services can read all message formatting, so keep that in mind before you start trying to format a message like a Microsoft Word document. You can choose between three overall message formats in Outlook:

- **HTML**—This format, which is a web page format, supports text and paragraph formatting (such as bold, italic, text alignment, fonts and sizes, background colors, and the like). Most email readers support HTML, and if one doesn't, the message appears as plain text.

- **Rich Text**—This format supports more attributes than HTML, such as borders and shading. On the downside, this format is usually compatible only with Outlook and Microsoft Exchange Server. The text is converted to HTML for other email readers.

- **Plain Text**—This is the most basic of the formats; no attributes appear in plain text messages, just straight up text. This format is supported by all email readers.

You can control the message's format by clicking the Format Text tab on the ribbon, then making your selection from the Format group of buttons.

After you've completed your message, click the Send button or press F9. If you're connected to the Internet, Outlook immediately sends the message. If not, the message hangs out in the Outbox folder until you're ready to send and receive messages.

 TIP If you're piling up messages in your Outbox, you can press F9 or click the Send/Receive All Folders button on the Quick Access toolbar when you finally connect to the Internet and are ready to send.

And that's how you compose and send an email.

Reading and Replying to Messages

All the emailing activities you perform happen in the Mail module, Outlook's email component. You learned a little about how the Folder pane works in Chapter 2, "Basic Outlook Operations." That's where all the Inboxes for each email account you use are listed. That's also where your list of incoming messages piles up. To view a list of messages for a particular account, click the account's Inbox. The message list that appears shows you who sent the message and gives you a peek at the first line. You can scroll up and down to view the list of messages.

If you turn off the Reading pane, you can see more details about the messages displayed across the width of the viewing area (aka Information Viewer), such as date and time sent, message size, priority levels, or flagging. You can also see tiny paper clip icons representing file attachments. Figure 4.4 shows an example of the message list expanded.

Column labels

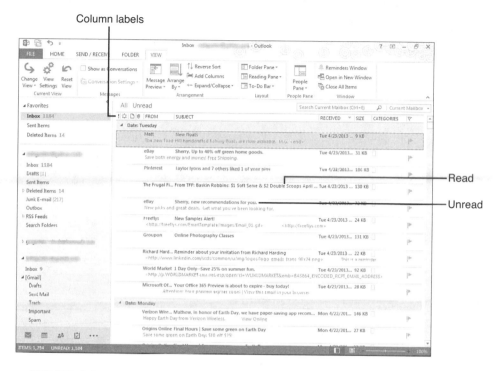

FIGURE 4.4

You can view your list of messages expanded if you close the Reading pane.

Notice that the message details are organized into columns with labels. If you want, you can resize the columns if you need to view more or less of a certain detail. Click and drag the column label's border to resize the column. You can also use the column headings to perform sorts on a particular column. For example, you can sort your list by date or sender, and so on. You might choose to sort your list alphabetically by sender name, for example, to help you see who sent you what. Outlook displays two buttons at the top of the list to view all the message or just the unread messages.

You can tell which messages are read or unread based on their appearance in the list. If they appear bold and in blue, they're unread. If they are not bold and have no color, you've read the message already (see Figure 4.4). If the Reading pane is displayed and the message list is less wide to accommodate it, a blue vertical bar on the left side of the message indicates an unread message.

To select a message, click it. This makes it active, and you can perform actions on it. To open it entirely, double-click it. This opens the message in a Message window, similar to Figure 4.5. The window is the same as the one you use to compose new messages. To close it and return to viewing your message list, click the window's Close button.

FIGURE 4.5

You can also open a message in its own window to read.

If the Reading pane is open, you can also view a selected message's content there. Figure 4.6 shows an example of the Mail module with the Reading pane displayed (the pane can be displayed to the right or at the bottom of the window—your choice). If the People pane is displayed, you can see contact information pertaining to the sender. You can reply directly in the Reading pane, which I'll show you in a bit. To toggle the pane on or off, click the View tab, click the People pane button, and choose a setting.

From the Reading pane, you can navigate messages using these techniques:

- You can scroll through longer messages using the scrollbars, or you can click the scroll arrows.

- To move up or down a long message one page at a time, press the spacebar on the keyboard. At the end of the message, press the spacebar again to open the first page of the next message.

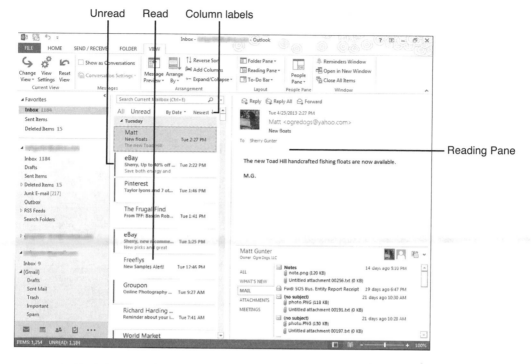

FIGURE 4.6

You can use the Reading pane to view a selected message's content.

- You can use the Zoom tool on the status bar to zoom your view of the Reading pane display; drag the slider left to reduce the size of text, or drag the slider right to magnify the text.

- Don't forget—you can choose between displaying the Reading pane on the right side of the pane or at the bottom of the pane. (Press the View tab, click the Reading Pane button, and make your selection.)

NOTE If you turn the People pane on, it appears directly below the Reading pane. The People pane displays information about the message sender, including references to previous correspondence. If you keep info about the person stored in your contacts, you can view it in the People pane. For example, if the person's contact record includes a picture, the image appears in the People pane. You can expand and collapse the People pane using the tiny arrow icon in the upper-right corner of the pane. You can also control the pane through the View tab; click the People pane button and choose Normal (expanded), Minimized (collapsed), or Off.

Checking for New Messages

You can tell Outlook to check for messages, or you can set the program up to check them automatically at a designated interval. By default, Outlook is set up to check for new email every 30 minutes.

To check for new messages manually, use one of these methods:

- Click the Send/Receive All Folders button on the Quick Access toolbar; you can do this no matter which Outlook component you're viewing.

- Click the Send/Receive All Folders button on the Home tab when viewing the Mail module (see Figure 4.7).

- Click the Send/Receive tab and click the Send/Receive All Folders button.

- Press F9 on the keyboard.

You can also click here   Click here

FIGURE 4.7

Look for the Send/Receive All Folders button to download new email messages.

Of course, you must be connected to the Internet to receive messages from your email services. That's a given.

To set up an automatic email check or to change the default setting, click the File tab to visit Backstage view, and then click the Options category. This opens the Outlook Options dialog box, as shown in Figure 4.8. Click the Advanced category, and then scroll down to the Send and Receive group of options. Click the Send/Receive button to open the Send/Receive Groups dialog box, shown in Figure 4.9. Here you can turn off automatic mail retrieval or specify a different interval for downloading messages. You can even set options for retrieving email from individual email accounts.

To turn off the default retrieval, deselect the Schedule an Automatic Send/Receive check box. You can also reset the interval to another setting, such as every 60 minutes. You can tell Outlook to retrieve mail whenever you exit the program window, too. Click Close to exit the dialog box, and click OK to exit the Outlook Options dialog box.

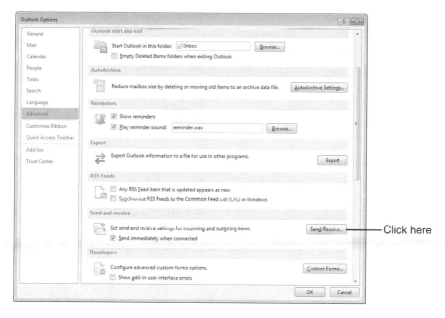

FIGURE 4.8

Access automatic email downloading through the Outlook Options dialog box.

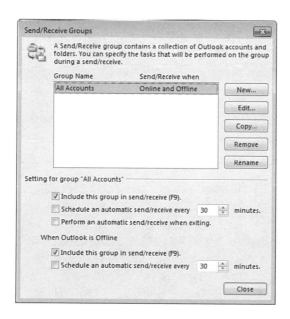

FIGURE 4.9

Use the Send/Receive Groups dialog box to set up automatic mail retrieval.

Replying to a Message

One of the niftiest aspects of emailing is the capability to send messages back and forth. You can keep replying to an original message as long as you need to, with both parties sending their responses back and forth, thus creating a conversation of sorts. By default, Outlook includes the original message content each time in the message body. New responses are added to the top of the message, and the conversation scrolls along newest to oldest.

New to Outlook 2013, you can reply directly to a message from the Reading pane without opening a Message window. With the Reading pane turned on, select the message from the list to view it in the pane, as demonstrated in Figure 4.10, and then click the Reply or Reply All button at the top of the pane. Reply sends a response to the sender, whereas Reply All sends the response to everyone referenced on the sender's list (the To field).

FIGURE 4.10

Look for message reply buttons at the top of the Reading pane.

Outlook displays mini form window fields, and you can type in your reply, similar to Figure 4.11. Outlook also automatically adds an RE: prefix to the subject title, which stands for Reply, Regarding, or Referencing (depending on whom you ask). After typing in your reply text, click Send.

Click here to pop out the reply in its own message window
Click here to send   ⌐Click here to forego the reply entirely

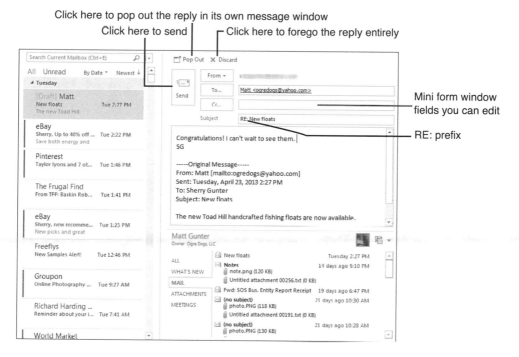

Mini form window
fields you can edit

RE: prefix

FIGURE 4.11

Type your reply directly into the Reading pane.

You can click the Pop Out button to pop out the reply into its own window, which lets you access all the additional message tools. If you decide you don't want to carry through with creating a reply message, click the Discard button to remove it.

You can also reply to a message by double-clicking it in the message list to open it in its own window, and then click the Reply or Reply All button.

Forwarding a Message

You can also forward a message to a new recipient. For example, you may want to forward a funny email you received from your coworker to your friend, or forward a message about a new product to your boss. When you forward a message, Outlook adds a FW: prefix to the subject title, which stands for Forward, naturally. Figure 4.12 shows an example.

To forward a message from the Reading pane, click the Forward button at the top of the pane. This command displays the same mini form window fields that appear when you click Reply or Reply All. You can type in any message text you want to include with the forwarded text, and click Send.

FW: prefix

FIGURE 4.12

You can also forward a message from the Reading pane.

To forward a message from a message window, double-click the message from the list and click the Forward button on the ribbon's Message tab.

Deleting a Message

You can remove messages from the list and place them in the Deleted Items folder to permanently delete later. Deleting messages as you read them can help keep your Inboxes managed. If you don't stay on top of it, the messages tend to pile up fast and create giant lists, which in turn, takes up more room on your computer. I find it incredibly satisfying to delete junky messages.

To delete a message, select it and use one of these methods:

- On the right side of the highlighted message (see Figure 4.13), click the Delete button.

- Right-click the message and choose Delete.

- On the Home tab, click the Delete button.

You can empty the Delete Items folder periodically to clean out messages. See Chapter 5, "Managing Email," to learn how to permanently delete messages.

Delete button

Delete icon

FIGURE 4.13

Look for a Delete icon when you hover your mouse pointer over a message.

 TIP If you accidentally delete a message you still wanted to see in your message list, click the Deleted Items folder in the Folder pane, select the message, and drag it back to the Inbox.

Saving Messages

Unlike some of the other Microsoft Office programs, such as Word or Excel, you don't have to worry about saving files much in Outlook. Items you create, such as messages, tasks, and contacts, are saved when you add them to the modules. You don't have to save your work before exiting Outlook, for example. However, there are occasions for saving emails, as I am about to show you.

Saving a Draft Message

If you're in the middle of composing a message and need to step away before completing it and sending it, you can save it. The Message window form has a Save button on its Quick Access toolbar which, when clicked, places the message in the Drafts folder, shown in Figure 4.14. (Each email account you work with in Outlook has its own Drafts folder.) The Message window stays open, however, so you can keep working on it. If you happen to close the window, the message still sits in the Drafts folder waiting for you.

Drafts folder

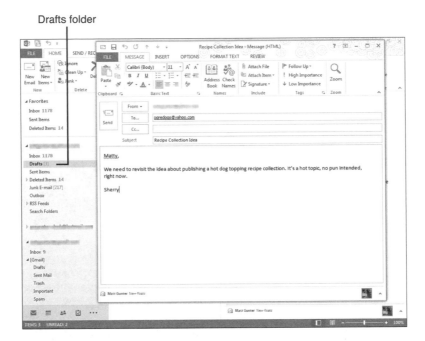

FIGURE 4.14

The Drafts folder is where your messages in progress hang out.

This feature is handy when you want to work on a message and keep it around temporarily until it's ready for sending. You can reopen it anytime and work on it more. Click the account's Drafts folder and double-click the message you want to edit. When it's finally ready to go out, click the Send button.

 TIP   If you decide not to use the draft message after all, you can delete it from the Drafts folder. Click the message in the Drafts folder list of messages and then click the Delete button. Outlook moves the message to the Deleted Items folder.

Saving a Message File

You can also choose to save an Outlook message as a message file. You might, for example, save a message to use in another program, or maybe you've written a masterful message that needs to be saved for posterity. Aside from the obvious ways to retain a message (print it out on paper), you can save it as a file on your computer or other storage device, or export it to another program.

When saving a message as a file, you have the option of controlling what sort of file format is used. You can save it in any of these formats:

- **Text Only**—The simplest of formats, this saves just the text, no formatting (attributes you assign to make the text look nice).

- **Outlook Template**—Use this option if you're creating a message template to use over again in your emailing tasks. It saves all the formatting controls and attachments associated with the message. (Learn more about formatting in Chapter 6).

- **Outlook Message Format**—The default format, this saves all the attributes and attachments, too. However, the only way to read this file type is in Outlook.

- **Outlook Message Format**—Unicode—Sort of the international flavor of file formats, this file type saves the message and attributes for easy reading with other versions of Outlook that use different languages.

- **HTML**—This saves the message as a web page, which means it can be viewed in a web browser or other programs that read web pages. When you use this option, an additional folder is also created with the file, containing support files for HTM (Hyper Text Markup).

- **MHT files**—This is the same as HTML, but without an additional folder for support files.

To save a message, use these steps:

1. With the Message window open, click the File tab.

2. Click Save As.

3. Navigate to the folder and drive to which you want to store the file (see Figure 4.15).

4. Click the File Name box and type in a name for the file.

5. Optionally, click the Save as Type drop-down arrow and specify a file type.

6. Click Save.

Outlook saves the message as directed.

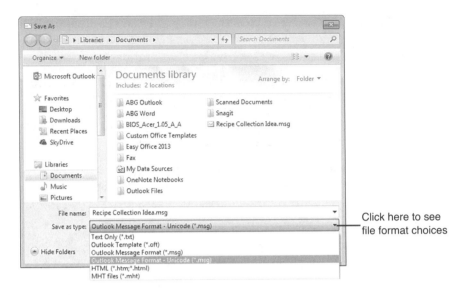

FIGURE 4.15

You can specify a file format for the messages you save as files.

Working with File Attachments

You can attach files to your emails to send to others and receive file attachments, too. *File attachments* are files created in other programs that you want to send along with a message. File attachments can be pictures, word processing documents, spreadsheets, slideshow presentations, desktop publishing documents, and so on. For example, suppose you want to send an email to a new client and include an electronic copy of your latest product list or a picture of your top-selling widget. You tell Outlook what file you want to include and it attaches to the message as a file the recipient can open and view. Or how about this—you just captured the best family portrait ever and want to send it to your aunt in California; add it to your email message as a file attachment.

File attachments increase the overall size of your email message. This is something to consider if your email service sets limits to how much data you can send. Some files are obviously bigger than others, with picture files often being the largest.

At the other end of the spectrum, you can open attachments you receive from others and save them on your computer for viewing and using. You can easily see if a message in your list has an accompanying attachment; Outlook displays a tiny paper clip icon when a message has a file attachment.

TIP Here's something nifty—you can email attachments directly from the other Microsoft Office programs. Suppose you want to send a Word document; just click the File tab, click Share, click Send Using E-Mail, then choose Send as Attachment.

Attach a File

To attach a file, follow these steps:

1. From the Message window, click the Message tab (if it's not already displayed).

2. Click the Attach File button (see Figure 4.16).

FIGURE 4.16

Look for the Attach File button on the ribbon.

3. In the Insert File dialog box (see Figure 4.17), navigate to the folder or drive containing the file you want to attach and select the filename.

4. Click **Insert**.

Outlook attaches the file. Now you can send the message when you're ready.

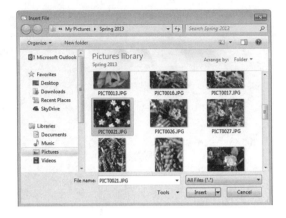

FIGURE 4.17

Use the Insert File dialog box to choose your file attachment.

If you've chosen HTML or Plain Text as the email's format, the attached file's name appears in the Attached box in the message header area, just below the subject title, as demonstrated in Figure 4.18. If the message format is in Rich Text, the attachment appears as an icon in the message body, as shown in Figure 4.19.

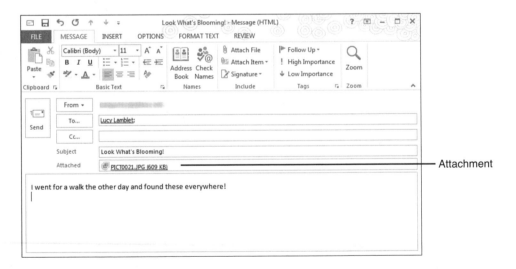

FIGURE 4.18

A file attachment shows up here.

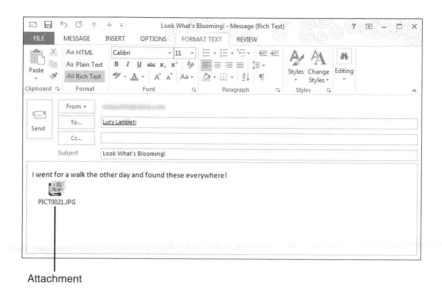

Attachment

FIGURE 4.19

Or an attachment can show up here.

Open an Attachment

When you receive a message with a file attachment (which is marked as a tiny paper clip icon in your message list), you can choose to view the attachment in several ways. You can preview some types of files, such as PDF files, Word documents, and Excel workbooks, in Outlook's Reading pane. Figure 4.20 shows an example of what this looks like. Click the attachment and instead of showing the message text in the Reading pane, a preview of the attachment fills the area, and an Attachments tab appears on the ribbon. To switch back to the message content again, click the Show Message button on the Attachments tab (see Figure 4.20) or click Message in the Reading pane's header area.

To open a file attachment in its own program-appropriate window, double-click the file attachment. Depending on the file type, a program window opens to view the file.

To save the attachment onto your computer and work with it later, right-click the attachment and choose Save As. You can then navigate to the folder or drive you want to save to and activate the Save command.

Click here to return to the message text

Attachment tab ─┐ ┌─ You can also click here to return to the message

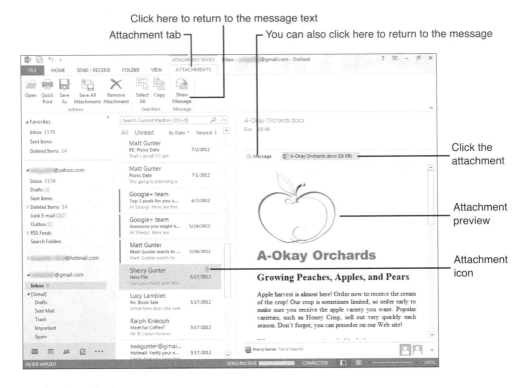

Click the attachment

Attachment preview

Attachment icon

FIGURE 4.20

You can preview an attachment directly in the Reading pane.

NOTE Outlook may prompt you about viewing attachments from unsafe sources. This is a precaution against computer virus and hacking. If you trust the source, you can continue with the preview. If not, stop to run a virus check using your computer's virus protection software.

Using Simple Message Tools

To close out this chapter, I'll show you some basic features for working with your messages, particularly as you read them. In Chapter 6, you can learn about advanced features, such as formatting controls, automating replies, adding signatures, and such. For now, though, let's talk about some of the tools you can use to process messages in the message list.

Marking Messages as Read or Unread

As you're working with messages in the list, Outlook lets you know which messages are read and which ones are unread. Learning to ascertain which ones you've read already can help you eliminate wasted time reviewing unimportant messages. Every new message that arrives in your Inbox (or Inboxes, if you're using multiple email accounts) is marked with a blue vertical line and bold blue header text. This indicates that the message is unread. As soon as you open it, or preview it for a margin of time, Outlook marks the status as read, indicated by the lack of the blue vertical line.

Occasions may arise when you want to mark a read message as unread to remind yourself to view the message again. Or you might want to mark an unread message as read so you don't have to stop and view (maybe it's another joke email from your Uncle Roger that you're trying to avoid).

To change the message status, use one of these methods:

- Click the blue vertical bar to mark the message as read (see Figure 4.21).

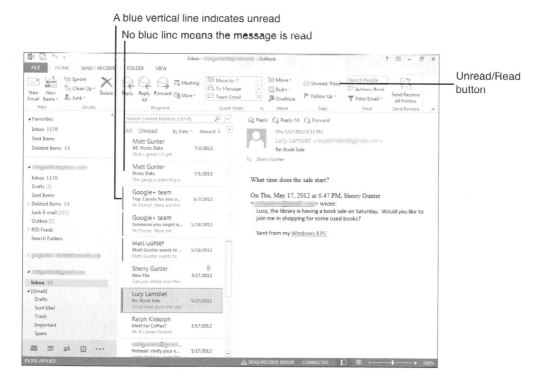

FIGURE 4.21

Marking messages as read and unread can help you review which messages require your attention.

- Right-click the message and choose Mark as Unread or Mark as Read.

- Select the message, and on the Home tab, click the Unread/Read button.

- Press Ctrl+Q to mark a selected message as read.

- Press Ctrl+U to mark a selected message as unread.

- To mark everything in a folder as read, right-click the folder name and choose Mark All as Read.

You can also mark groups of messages by selecting the group first before applying a new status.

Flagging Messages

You can flag a message with a reminder so you'll revisit the email later to address it or take care of a task. Flagging is a great tool to help you stay on top of things you need to do or people you need to reply to with haste. Any messages you flag are added to your Task list. (See Chapter 9, "Tasks and To-Do's," to learn more about working with tasks in Outlook's Task module.)

You can flag messages with dates and reminders. For example, if you want to tell yourself to deal with the message the following day, choose the Tomorrow flag. If you want to assign a reminder, choose the Reminder option and fine-tune the start and due dates.

To flag a message, use one of these techniques:

- Hover the mouse pointer over a message until you see a Flag icon (see Figure 4.22); click it and choose how you want to mark the message.

- Right-click the message and choose Follow Up; then click a flag.

- Click the Home tab, click the Follow Up button, and then click a flag.

To remove a flag, hover over the flag icon in the message list and click it to turn it off.

Categorizing Messages

You can color code your messages to help you determine actions you need to take on them. Outlook offers six preconfigured category colors, and you can rename them to suit your own workflow or create new ones. You can learn more about using categories in Chapter 14, "Using Color Categories," but for now, you learn how to apply them to your messages.

Flag icon   Follow Up button

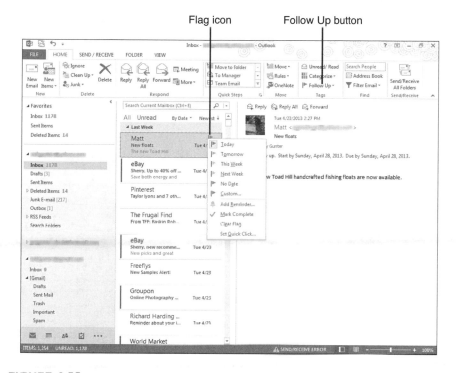

FIGURE 4.22

Flagging messages marks them so you'll return to the message and take care of it.

Select the message you want to categorize, then click the Categorize drop-down arrow on the Home tab. Click a color category and Outlook immediately assigns it to the message, adding a color box to the listed item and adding a color bar to the message content, as shown in Figure 4.23. The first time you use the feature, Outlook may prompt you to give the color category a unique name. You can do so then, or you can change it later (see Chapter 14).

You can also right-click a message in your list and choose Categorize, and then specify a color.

Click here to assign a color category

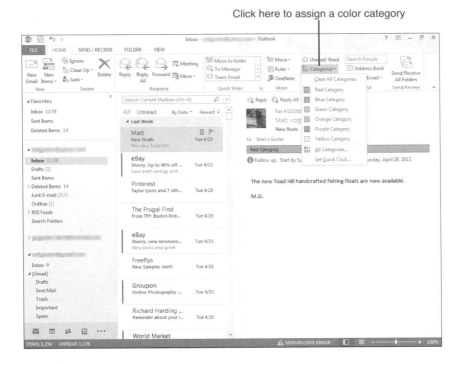

FIGURE 4.23

Color coding messages also helps you identify messages for actions.

THE ABSOLUTE MINIMUM

By this point, you're launching all kinds of communicative missives out into cyberspace and receiving plenty of correspondence in return, even if it is just ads for miracle weight loss pills. At the very least you now know the following:

- You can compose new email messages using a special form for filling out the recipient's email address, assigning a title, and typing in message text.

- The Message form window includes its own unique ribbon of message-related tools.

- You can send a message directly from the Message window by clicking its Send button.

- To check for new email messages and send any existing ones waiting in the Outbox, click the Send/Receive All Folders button.

- You can read messages for any Inbox or folder by displaying the contents as a message list.

- If you turn on Outlook's Reading pane, you can use it to read message contents.

- You can reply and forward messages directly from the Reading pane, or open them in their own Message window to enter message text.

- You can save a message you're working on in the Drafts folder and return to finish it later.

- You can attach files you create in other programs to send along with your email message.

- You can preview file attachments in the Reading pane, or open them in their native programs.

- You can flag and categorize messages to help you manage tasks and keep on top of things you need to do.

IN THIS CHAPTER

- Organizing messages into folders

- Automating your Inbox with Quick Steps

- Sending incoming email to different folders for easy organizing

- Stopping junk email from reaching your Inbox

- Archiving old messages so they don't languish in your mail folders

- Learning how to look for a message in a haystack

5

MANAGING EMAIL

As your email messages start piling up, you eventually need to plan out ways to manage them or your Inbox is going to seem like it's bursting at the seams. Thankfully, Outlook makes it easy to choose how you want to organize and store messages. In fact, this is where Outlook puts the word "manage" in personal information manager and kicks it into high gear.

Although it may be tempting to let messages turn into a mountain in your Inbox, don't. You can opt for a variety of handy methods for dealing with them efficiently:

- Store messages in special folders so they stay neat and tidy (OCD people are going to love this one).

- Delete messages you don't want to keep so your Inbox isn't clogged.

- Archive messages to move older messages out of the way, yet keep them available if needed again.
- Thin down your incoming deluge of messages by creating rules to sort email.
- Weed out junk mail before it even makes it into the Inbox.
- Route messages to the right places using Quick Steps.

In this chapter, you'll learn essential techniques for keeping ahead of your email stack.

Organizing Messages with Folders

In case you haven't noticed yet, every message you receive for a particular email service appears in the account's Inbox folder listed over in the Folder pane. You're not stuck using just your Inbox to contain your messages. You can use the folder structure hierarchy to organize and manage email into logical containers. In the same way you use folders to organize files on your computer, you can use folders in Outlook to store and sort email messages.

Each email account includes a set of default folders, one of which is the main Inbox for the account where your messages tend to pile up. Other folders may include Drafts, Sent Items, Deleted Items, Junk E-mail, and Outbox. (These may vary depending on your email service.) Most of the preexisting folders are self-explanatory based on their names alone, but you can also add more folders to help you better organize your messages. For example, you may want to keep all your departmental emails in a folder labeled Sales Department, or all of your business correspondence in a folder labeled Clients. You can create as many folders as you need, even for temporary projects and tasks.

 TIP   You can learn more about using folders to organize other Outlook items in Chapter 15, "Using Folders." Meanwhile, in this section, we'll focus strictly on using folders for email messages.

Making a New Email Folder

Follow these steps to create a new folder:

1. With the Mail module displayed onscreen, click the Inbox folder under the email service you want to add a folder to (see Figure 5.1).

2. Click the Folder tab on the ribbon.

3. Click the New Folder button.

New Folder button

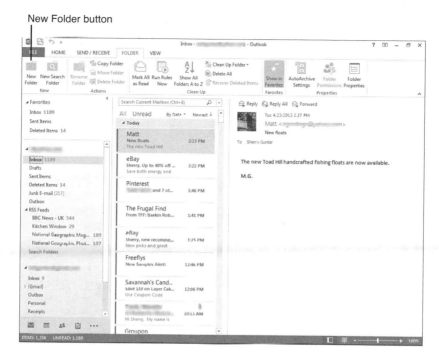

FIGURE 5.1

Start by choosing which email account you want to add a folder to.

4. Outlook opens the Create New Folder dialog box, as shown in Figure 5.2. Type a name for the new folder in the Name box.

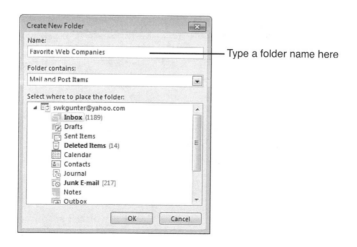

Type a folder name here

FIGURE 5.2

Use the Create New Folder dialog box to make new folders.

5. Leave the other settings intact (Mail and Post Items is selected in the Folder Contains box, and the Inbox you selected in step 1 is highlighted in the Select Where to Place the Folder list box).

6. Click OK.

Outlook adds the new folder to the Folder pane, similar to Figure 5.3. Now you can start moving messages to the folder as needed.

New folder

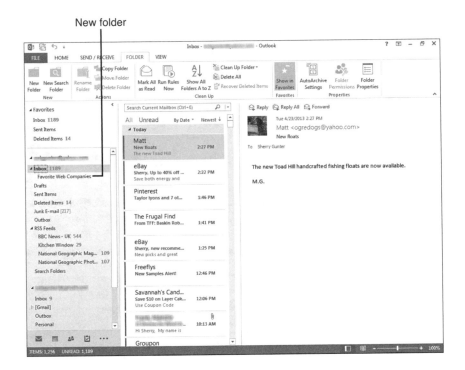

FIGURE 5.3

Outlook adds the new folder to the list.

TIP You can also right-click the Inbox name and choose New Folder from the context menu that pops up; then type in a new folder name directly without using the Create New Folder dialog box.

TIP Adding folders is a key part of using some of Outlook's other message management features, such as rerouting incoming emails to designated folders. Sometimes it helps to plan out ahead of time what types of folders you might need later, such as a work project or important client you're corresponding with. You can always remove folders you no longer need and archive any old messages.

Moving a Message to Your New Folder

To move a message to a folder, you can drag and drop it in place. You can also use this method:

1. Click the title of the message you want to move.

2. Click the Home tab.

3. Click the Move button.

4. Select the name of the folder where you want to place the message (see Figure 5.4).

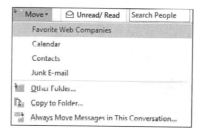

FIGURE 5.4

Use the Move menu to move selected messages around in your folder structure.

If the folder you want to use isn't listed in the Move menu, click the Other Folder option and use the Move Items dialog box to choose your folder.

Working with Folder Contents

While we're on the subject of folders, let's go over the ways you can work with them, view their contents, and purge contents you no longer want to keep.

- To view any folder in your Folder pane, click the folder name. The Mail module immediately displays a list of contents, and if the Reading pane is displayed, you can view entire messages.

- To rename a folder you've added yourself, click its name twice and type in a new name, or right-click it and choose Rename Folder.

- To remove a custom folder, right-click it and choose Delete Folder (see Figure 5.5).

FIGURE 5.5

Oh, that handy right-click menu— it's a time-saver.

- To move the folder, right-click the folder name, choose Move Folder, and then choose where to move it.

- You can copy a folder. Right-click the folder name and choose Copy Folder, and then tell Outlook where to copy it to.

- To remove a message from a folder, right-click it and choose Delete or press the Delete key, or click the Delete button on the Home tab. So many deletes. As soon as you activate a Delete command, Outlook moves the message to the Deleted Items folder.

- To empty out your Deleted Items folder, right-click the folder name and choose Empty Folder. A prompt box appears, telling you that you're about to delete stuff forever. Click Yes to make it happen.

- To clean out your Junk E-mail folder, right-click the folder and choose Clean Up Folder. A prompt box appears, warning you that you're about to move messages to the Deleted Items folder; click Clean Up Folder to proceed.

TIP Your Sent Items folder keeps a copy of all the emails you send. This feature is turned on by default, which makes it a nice safeguard in case you need to find a message later.

You can learn more about working with Outlook folders in Chapter 15, including how to manage other data types in them.

Routing Messages with Quick Steps

You can use Outlook's Quick Steps feature to perform multiple actions on your email messages with just one click. For example, you might want to flag a message for follow up later *and* move it to a special folder. Rather than do the two actions separately, why not do them at the same time? That's where Quick Steps come into play.

Outlook stores Quick Steps in the Quick Steps gallery on the **Home** tab when you're using the Mail module. You can scroll through the gallery to view them or expand the gallery to view all of them at once. Outlook even includes a few preset Quick Steps you can take advantage of:

- **Move To**—If you find yourself moving messages to the same folder over and over, designate it as the Move To folder and use this Quick Step to immediately relocate messages.

- **To Manager**—This opens a message form that's automatically preset with a designated recipient, such as your manager (hence the name), along with the forwarded message.

- **Team Email**—Use this Quick Step to send a new message to everyone on a team. All the member's email addresses are saved and preloaded in the form window, ready to go.

- **Done**—This marks the selected message as read, completed (with a Mark Complete flag), and moves it to a designated folder—three things at once.

- **Reply and Delete**—This one opens a reply form to send back a reply and also moves the original message to the Deleted Items folder.

To practice using one of the default Quick Steps, you can try out the one that moves messages. While viewing your Inbox messages in the Mail module, select the message you want to dispatch (click it or tap it to select it). Next, make sure the Home tab is displayed and click the Move to: ? Quick Step from the Quick Step gallery, as shown in Figure 5.6. If the Move to: ? option isn't in view, scroll through the gallery to locate it.

FIGURE 5.6

Use the Quick Steps gallery to apply automated tasks to your messages.

When you activate the option, the First Time Setup dialog box appears, similar to Figure 5.7. The same box opens for some of the other Quick Steps the first time you use them. That's because you need to specify people or folders first so Outlook can carry out the actions. To designate a folder to move the selected message to, click the drop-down arrow and specify a folder name.

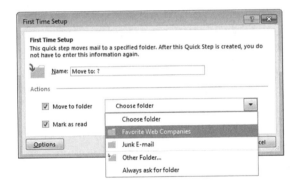

FIGURE 5.7

Use the First Time Setup dialog box to tell Outlook which folder to move messages to.

The Mark as Read check box is also conveniently selected. You can leave it checked if you want to consider the message read; uncheck it if you want to move it and treat it as not read yet.

Finally, click the Save button. Outlook saves the folder name as your designated folder and adjusts the Quick Step name accordingly. The next time you want to move a message, click the option listed in the Quick Steps gallery, and Outlook takes care of the relocation for you. You can use the Quick Steps gallery on the Home tab to make your selection, or you can right-click the message, choose Quick Steps, and then choose the name of your step.

TIP   Need to make a folder? Back up to the previous section to learn how to add folders to your Inbox to organize messages.

As you can imagine, you can create different Quick Steps to handle various ways you want to process email messages. You can move, copy, and delete messages, change their status from read to unread, assign categories and flags, generate automatic message responses, turn them into appointments, and so on. You can assign as many actions to a Quick Step as you want.

To build a custom Quick Step, choose the Create New option from the Quick Steps gallery. This opens the Edit Quick Step dialog box, shown in Figure 5.8, and you can choose actions, folders, even type out ToolTip text to pop-up to remind you what the step does when you hover the mouse pointer over the Quick Step name. Yes, those Microsoft people have thought of everything.

FIGURE 5.8

Build your own Quick Steps with the tools in this dialog box.

You can open the Manage Quick Steps dialog box (see Figure 5.9) to make changes to actions associated with Quick Steps or remove Quick Steps you no longer want. From the Quick Steps gallery, select the Manage Quick Steps option to display the dialog box. Choose which Quick Step you want to edit, then click the Edit button to make changes to the associated actions, or click the Delete button to remove it entirely from the list. You can also duplicate a Quick Step and tweak it slightly to create a new step. Go wild and make Quick Steps for everything—it's fun.

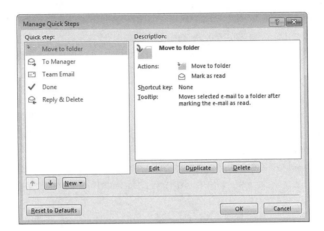

FIGURE 5.9

Manage your Quick Steps from this dialog box.

 TIP What? Don't like the order of your Quick Steps in the gallery? Reorder them in the Manage Quick Steps dialog box. Use the arrow buttons to reposition how a step is listed in the bunch.

Managing Incoming Messages with Rules

How would you like to set a few rules for your email messages, such as telling all the emails from a certain friend to go jump in a Boring folder, or put all the messages from your boss into a Do This Now folder? You can set rules in Outlook that help you sort through your email and put them in special locations, among other actions. Rules can help you move, copy, delete, reply to, forward, and redirect your email. You can choose from Outlook's preset rules or create brand new ones. Are you ready to lay down the law? Let's break out the rule book.

You can build rules with help from Outlook's Rules Wizard, a step-by-step process for creating a rule (click the Advanced Options button in the Create Rule dialog box to summon the wizard for help). However, one of the easiest ways to build a rule is to grab an example of an existing message you want to create a rule for, such as an email from a certain person that you always want routed to a certain folder, and build on it. With the Mail module displayed, follow these steps:

1. Select the message you want to turn into a rule.

2. Click the Home tab.

3. Click Rules (see Figure 5.10).

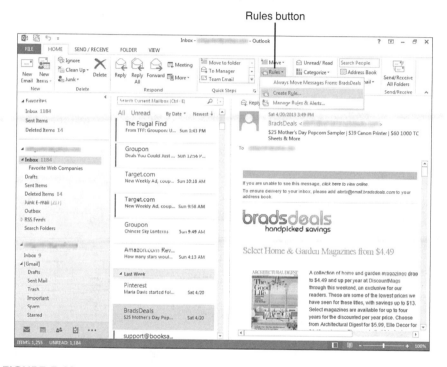

FIGURE 5.10

Activate the Rules menu to find the Create Rule command.

4. Click Create Rule to open the Create Rule dialog box, shown in Figure 5.11.

5. Use the conditions check boxes to set the criteria for the email. You can specify messages from that particular sender, identify subject matter to recognize, or who the message was originally sent to, for example.

6. Under the Do the Following group, choose what you want Outlook to do when it encounters these same message types in the future, such as moving them to a specified folder.

7. Click OK and the rule is set for any incoming messages resembling the criteria you specified.

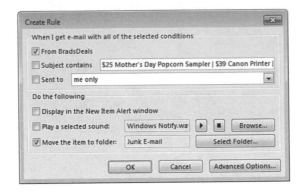

FIGURE 5.11

The Create Rule dialog box is the place to set criteria for a message rule.

8. Outlook asks if you want to run the rule immediately. Click the check box and click OK to do so, or click OK to exit without running the rule yet.

You can manage any rules you create with a little help from the Rules and Alerts dialog box, shown in Figure 5.12. To find your way to this box, click the Rules drop-down arrow on the Home tab and choose Manage Rules and Alerts. You can also access the box through Outlook's Backstage view; click the File tab, click Info, and then click Manage Rules and Alerts.

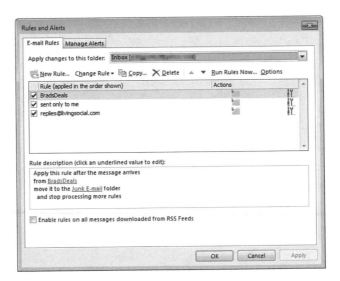

FIGURE 5.12

Manage your rules with the Rules and Alerts dialog box.

- To turn off a rule, deselect its check box.
- To remove a rule, select it and click the Delete button.
- To edit a rule, select it and choose Change Rule, Edit Rule Settings.
- To add a new rule, click New Rule.

When you finish with rules, click OK to exit the dialog box.

Controlling Junk Email

Junk email is a broad term covering advertising emails, unsolicited bulk emails, spam, or just about anything sent to your email address without your consent. Billions of spam emails are sent daily, and they're not always just about advertising something. Spam email can also be criminal in nature, generated by hackers and "phishers" trying to steal your identity or personal information for nefarious reasons. Thwarting junk email from reaching your Inbox requires some filtering on Outlook's part. Although it can't catch everything all the time, Outlook's filtering tools do a pretty good job of sorting out the bad stuff and placing it in a special folder marked for such unworthy messages.

You can even fine-tune the sensitivity settings to low or high to suit your needs. Choose from the following options:

- **No Automatic Filtering**—This setting means there's no filtering happening at all. Junk mail can flow freely into your Inbox.
- **Low**—Some junk mail still gets through, but the worst of it is tossed away.
- **High**—The most ruthless setting; nothing gets through, sometimes not even legitimate emails (be sure to check the Junk E-mail folder periodically to see if anything important gets tossed in by mistake).
- **Safe Lists Only**—This setting allows only emails from specified companies and individuals (from your safe recipients list) to make it into your Inbox. You have to identify senders first in a special Safe Senders list (sort of like a guest list for your email, and only the invitees make it into the party).

In addition to setting a filtering level, you can also choose to go ahead and permanently delete junk email when it's found, disable links in suspected phishing messages, or display a warning prompt for suspicious domain names for a heads up.

To adjust your junk mail settings, follow these steps:

1. From the Mail module, click the Home tab. If you have more than one email service, select the account's Inbox first.

2. Click the Junk drop-down arrow, shown in Figure 5.13.

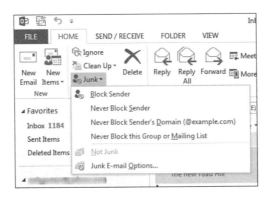

FIGURE 5.13

Look for the Junk drop-down menu on the Home tab.

3. Click Junk E-mail Options. The Junk E-mail Options dialog box opens to the Options tab, as shown in Figure 5.14.

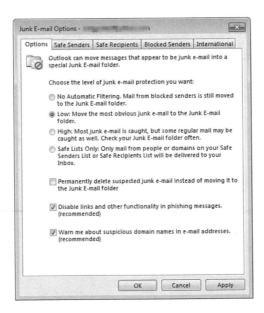

FIGURE 5.14

Set any junk email protection levels in this dialog box.

4. Click a protection level.

5. Click OK.

You can also help Outlook identify junk email by pointing it out when you find it in your Inbox. Right-click the icky message from the list, click Junk, then choose the Block Sender option.

If you find the filter dumping legitimate messages into the Junk E-mail folder, display the folder's contents (click the folder name in the Folder pane), right-click the message from the list, and choose Never Block Sender or Not Junk (see Figure 5.15).

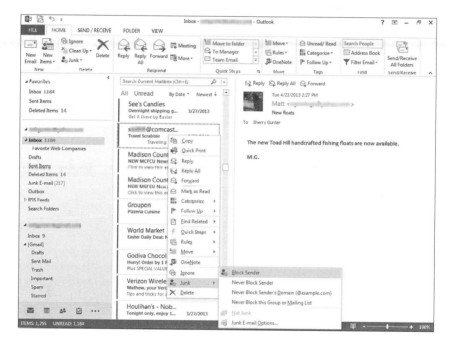

FIGURE 5.15

Un-junk a legitimate message using the right-click menu.

   TIP   If you're concerned Outlook might identify email messages from someone as junk, like the weekly family updates from Uncle Marvin, you can add the individual to your Safe Recipient's list. From the Junk E-Mail Options dialog box (see Figure 5.14), click the Safe Recipients tab and click Add, and then type in the user's address.

Archiving Messages

Sure, deleting old messages is a great way to clean out your Inbox, but sometimes you need to hang on to your messages for posterity, or in case you need to refer to them again to recall an exchange. You can archive messages, sort of like putting them into storage, but without the mothballs or monthly rental fee.

You can archive manually or automate the task. Outlook's AutoArchive tool is perfect for taking care of archiving tasks in the background without any help from you. You can set different archiving tasks for different folders. For example, you can instruct the tool to automatically archive messages in your Inbox that are older than 3 months and move them to a special archive folder.

By default, Outlook is set up to archive messages to a file named archive.pst. You can specify another location for your archive files as well as specify more descriptive filenames.

Manually Archive Messages

If you're doing a little folder cleaning, you can manually archive messages. For example, you might be wrapping up a work project and need to put all the email messages associated with it into an archive file.

To manually archive messages, follow these steps:

1. Click the File tab.

2. Click Info.

3. Click Cleanup Tools (see Figure 5.16).

4. Click Archive to open the Archive dialog box shown in Figure 5.17.

5. Click the folder you want to archive.

6. Choose a cutoff date, such as items older than 6 months.

7. Choose an archive file location (click the Browse button, navigate to the location, and specify a more descriptive filename), or use the default filename and locations.

8. Click OK, and Outlook archives the messages.

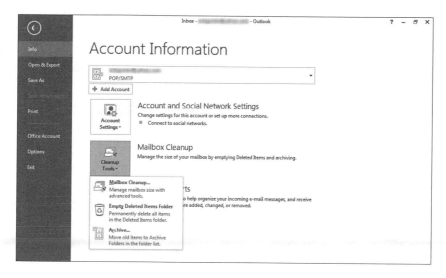

FIGURE 5.16

Use the Backstage view to find your way to Outlook's cleanup tools.

FIGURE 5.17

Use the Archive dialog box to manually archive old messages.

Setting Up Automatic Archiving

You can instruct Outlook to perform automatic archiving for you. You can set automatic archiving for individual folders or the Inbox in general. To set up automatic archiving, follow these steps:

1. Select the folder or subfolder you want to archive, such as your Inbox or an old project folder.

2. Click the Folder tab.

3. Click the AutoArchive Settings button.

4. Outlook opens the Junk E-mail Properties dialog box to the AutoArchive tab of tools, as shown in Figure 5.18. Click Archive this folder using these settings option.

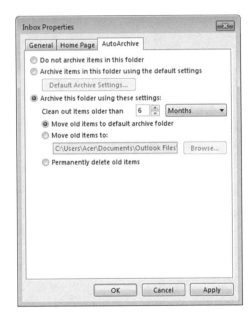

FIGURE 5.18

Use the AutoArchive feature to automatically archive old messages.

5. Specify the age of the messages, such as older than 3 months.

6. Specify a location for the archived file, or use the default location.

7. Click OK.

Each folder can have its own archiving settings, which is handy if you don't want some folders tampered with, but others are good to square away.

 TIP Want to check out how much room is being consumed in your Inbox? Switch over to Backstage view (click the File tab) and click the Cleanup Tools button, then click Mailbox Cleanup. This opens the Mailbox Cleanup dialog box. Click the View Mailbox Size button to check out how much room is taken up by your messages in the various folders. Based on what you see, you may decide you need to clean up some folders and archive old messages.

Searching for Messages

As your digital stack of email grows, so does the inevitable need to search through them for a particular message. If you're worried that searching for a message may be like looking for a needle in a haystack, don't sweat it. Outlook has tools you can use to look for messages. In fact, Outlook taps into the Windows Search technology, which means you can even search for Outlook items from the Windows Start menu (Windows 7) or using the Windows 8 search screen.

 TIP You can learn more about searching for Outlook items in Chapter 16, "Using Search."

Conducting a Quick Search

When you select an Inbox to view in the Mail module, a search box appears at the top of the list, much like the one found in Figure 5.19. You can click in the box and type any keyword or words you want to search for, whether it's a name, subject title, or a word within the message body. As soon as you start typing, Outlook starts searching. Any matches are listed, newest emails first, similar to Figure 5.20. Outlook also opens a Search tab on the ribbon with additional search tools you can access and apply.

Search box

FIGURE 5.19

Use the search box at the top of the message list to search for messages in that particular Inbox or folder.

You can narrow the search by adjusting the keyword or words you search for, or by tweaking the search criteria, such as searching subject lines or recipient names. To add search criteria, select among the Refine group of tools on the Search tab and then type in your refining keyword or words in the search box, similar to Figure 5.21. You can also click the drop-down arrow on the search box to change which folder or Inbox you search.

When you finish with your search, click the Close Search button on the Search tab.

 TIP Performing a sort can help you find messages by subject, name, or date. To perform a quick sort, click the sort category at the top of your message list, such as Subject or From. If you turn off the Reading Pane, you can view more sort categories.

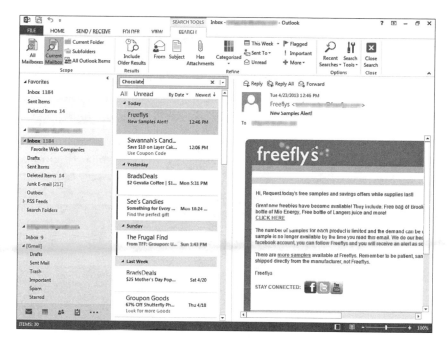

FIGURE 5.20

Outlook displays possible matches and opens a Search tab of tools.

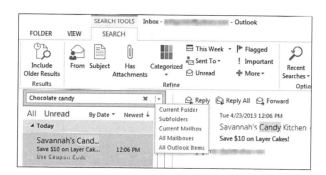

FIGURE 5.21

Use the Refine group of tools to refine your search further.

Making Search Folders

You can use Outlook's Search folders to speed up searching tasks. A Search folder gives you a spot to look for certain kinds of messages regardless of where they're actually located. It's rather like a catalog of messages pertaining to a set of criteria. Search folders can save you quite a bit of time and energy otherwise searching through a vast amount of messages. Plus, after they're established, Outlook keeps your Search folders up to date.

Outlook offers several preset Search folders you can use. For example, the Mail Flagged for Follow Up folder shows only messages you've flagged, whereas the Unread Mail folder shows only messages you haven't read yet.

To create a custom search folder, click the New Search Folder button on the Folder tab. The New Search Folder dialog box opens, similar to Figure 5.22. Choose the type of Search folder you want to add. If you're making a custom folder, click the Choose button to fill in any additional information required by the type. When you finish filling out details, click OK.

FIGURE 5.22

The New Search Folder dialog box.

To search your Search folder, click the folder name and a list of messages immediately appears. To exit the folder, click the Inbox again.

See Chapter 16 to learn more about searching in Outlook.

THE ABSOLUTE MINIMUM

Now you know how to manage and organize your vast pile of accumulating email messages. In this chapter, you learned the following:

- You can use Outlook's folder hierarchy to organize messages in an orderly fashion; just add new folders when you need them and move messages around.

- Use Outlook's Quick Steps to perform multiple actions on your messages, such as sending particular ones to a certain folder and flagging them with priority status.

- You can use message rules to direct the flow of incoming email, such as sending messages from your colleague to a project folder or sending routing messages from your brother-in-law to an Avoid Reading folder.

- Turn on Outlook's filtering tools to stop the flow of junk email to your Inbox.

- You can archive older messages to get them out of the way, yet keep them available if you need to refer to them again.

- You can search for a message using the Search box at the top of the message list, easy-peasy.

6

ADVANCED EMAIL FEATURES

By now, you're probably starting to notice the plethora of tiny tool buttons hanging out in the Message form window, and perhaps you're already clicking them to see what happens. Or maybe you're wondering about that strange toolbar that pops up when you select text in a message. Outlook has many extra features you can use to spruce up your email messages, automate replies, and take your emailing tasks to the next level. For example, did you know you can automatically insert a digital signature at the bottom of all your emails that includes contact info or a company name and number? Or did you know you can embed pictures to enhance your messages? I'm going to show you some exciting tools you can use to expand your Outlook email knowledge beyond the basics.

Formatting Your Messages

If you're interested in making your message text look a little more polished or downright eye-popping, you can tap into Outlook's formatting tools. *Formatting*, also referred to as *attributes*, includes commands you can utilize to change the appearance of your text and its layout in the message body. You might be familiar with formatting tools in other programs, such as Microsoft Word or PowerPoint; the same tools are available in Outlook. For example, you can bold text to add emphasis, change the font and size, and control the alignment of text across the message page.

You can find basic formatting controls ready at the click on the Message tab in any Message form window, as shown in Figure 6.1. You can also gain quick access to basic formatting commands using the pop-up toolbar, called the mini toolbar. It appears when you select text in the message and hover near the top of the selection area, as shown in Figure 6.2. Ignore the toolbar and keep working if you don't want to activate any tools, and the toolbar fades away.

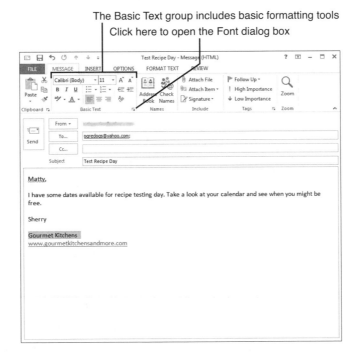

FIGURE 6.1

Look for formatting tools on the Message window's Message tab.

Mini toolbar

Matty,

I have some dates available for recipe testing day. Take a look at your calendar and see when you might be free.

Sherry

Gourmet Kitchens
www.gourmetkitchensandmore.com

FIGURE 6.2

You can also use the mini toolbar to quickly assign basic formatting commands.

For an even greater selection of formatting tools, click the Format Text tab, shown in Figure 6.3. This tab includes styles (preset formatting you can apply), indentation controls, and more. Formatting tools are arranged logically into groups on the tab; the Font group displays font-related commands, and the Paragraph group displays paragraph-related tabs, for example.

Format Text tab

FIGURE 6.3

Display the Format Text tab to view more formatting controls.

To apply formatting to message text, start by selecting the text. Selecting text in Outlook works the same way as selecting text in other programs. Drag across the selection, or double-click and triple-click to select words and sentences, respectively. To apply a formatting command, click the tool. For example, to make text bold, on the Message or Format Text tab, click the Bold button, or on the mini toolbar, click the Bold button. Outlook immediately bolds the selected text.

You can also right-click and choose Font or Paragraph to open dialog boxes of commands for formatting text and paragraphs.

Formatting is a personal preference. You decide how fanciful your messages need to look. Just keep in mind that too much formatting can distract from your message and make it difficult to read. The best approach is to use formatting wisely, just as you would in a document you create in Microsoft Word. Whether you use a little formatting, a lot, or none at all, at least you know that the formatting tools are there if you need them.

Recall from Chapter 4, "Basic Email Tasks," that Outlook offers three email formats you can apply to your messages:

- **HTML**—A web page format supported by most email readers. It allows text and paragraph formatting (such as bold, italic, text alignment, fonts and sizes, background colors, and so on).

- **Rich Text**—A step beyond HTML, this Outlook/Exchange Server email format supports more attributes than HTML, such as borders and shading.

- **Plain Text**—Supported by all email readers, this format is simple, basic plain text.

To change the email format for a message, click the Format Text tab and choose an option from the Format Group of tools. To change the default format for all your messages, open the Outlook Options dialog box (click the File tab and click Options). Under the Compose message group of options, click the Compose Messages in This Format drop-down arrow and choose a format.

You can apply Office themes and color schemes to your messages using the tools found on the Options tab in the Message form window. You can even set a background color for the message page.

 TIP For quick formatting while you type, try a keyboard shortcut for any of the big three basics: bold, italic, or underline. Press Ctrl+B for bold, Ctrl+I for italic, or Ctrl+U for underline.

NOTE Don't overlook Outlook's reviewing tools. You can use them to check a message for spelling errors before sending it out into cyberspace. Check out the Review tab in the Message form window for tools such as language and translation, research, grammar, and a thesaurus.

Setting Priority and Sensitivity Options

One way to add urgency or attention to an email you send is to assign a priority level. Priority levels come in three settings: High, Normal, and Low. Normal is the default setting, so you don't have to specify it when creating a regular old message. When you assign High status, for example, the recipient can immediately determine how important the message is and the urgency of a timely response. With High priority, Outlook adds a red exclamation point to the message that's visible in the recipient's email Inbox.

To assign a priority level to your message, click the Message tab and choose a priority level in the Tags group of tools, as shown in Figure 6.4. Click the High Importance button to assign High priority level, or click Low Importance to mark the message as low-level priority. You might set low priority in your office environment to help your coworkers or boss recognize the message as lower in the chain of importance.

Assign a priority level using these buttons

FIGURE 6.4

You can find two of the three priority levels available as buttons on the Message tab.

In the lower corner of the Tags group, if you click the Message Options button, you can open the Properties dialog box shown in Figure 6.5. From here, you can click the Importance drop-down arrow and choose a priority level.

While you're looking at the Properties box, you can also use the controls found within to set a sensitivity level for a message. Click the Sensitivity drop-down arrow (see Figure 6.5) and choose a setting. Like the priority level setting, Normal is the default sensitivity setting. You can also set Personal, Private, or Confidential. Be warned, however, that these settings don't necessarily protect your email message from prying eyes; rather, they just alert the recipient regarding the nature of the message. If you use Outlook in an office or corporate setting, check with your administrator concerning any policies for confidential emails.

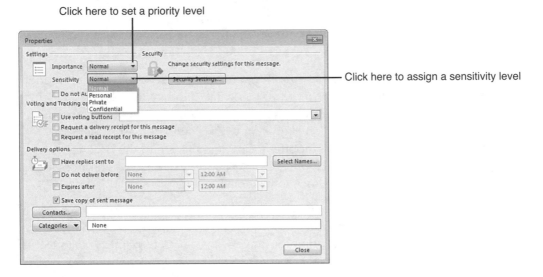

FIGURE 6.5

The Properties dialog box offers all three priority levels in a drop-down list of options.

Using Quick Parts

To help you build better, faster emails, you can save text you type in repeatedly with your messages into reusable blocks, called *Quick Parts*. Microsoft's Quick Parts feature is available throughout the Office suite and is used to insert all kinds of elements, such as headers and footers, salutations for letters, page numbers, and so on. In fact, you can turn any piece of text you use over and over into a building block and keep it in your Outlook Quick Part library, ready to use at a moment's notice.

To turn text into a building block, follow these steps:

1. Select the message text you want to turn into a Quick Part.

2. Click the Insert tab.

3. Click the Quick Parts drop-down arrow.

4. Click Save Select to Quick Part Gallery. This opens the Create New Building Block dialog box, as shown in Figure 6.6.

FIGURE 6.6

Create your own Quick Parts using this dialog box.

5. Type a name for your building block.

6. Optionally, fill out any additional details you want to save along with the text element.

7. Click OK to save the building block.

Anytime you want to add your building block to a message, click the Quick Parts drop-down menu on the Insert tab and choose your item from the gallery, as shown in Figure 6.7.

FIGURE 6.7

Choose your Quick Part from the gallery.

To remove a Quick Part you no longer need, display the Quick Parts drop-down menu, right-click the Quick Part, and choose Organize and Delete. This opens the Building Blocks Organizer, as shown in Figure 6.8. Select your Quick Part and click the Delete button to remove it. You can also use this dialog box to view a list of all your Quick Parts and manage them.

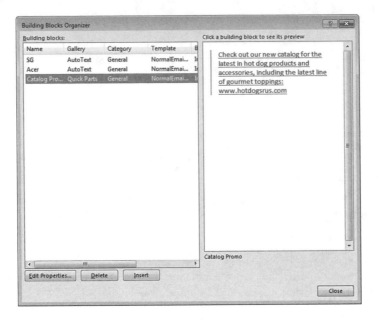

FIGURE 6.8

Use the Building Blocks Organizer to view and edit your Quick Parts.

Adding Signatures

A digital signature is a portion of text you add to the end of every email message, a salutation of sorts that uniquely identifies you as the sender. Some people use signatures to include company information, such as the name and web address, whereas others use signatures to include contact information, such as addresses and phone numbers. It's not uncommon to see signatures with famous quotes, logos and graphics, and sales information. You can instruct Outlook to add a default signature to every new message you create, or you can choose to add one manually when you need it.

To create a signature, follow these steps:

1. On the ribbon, click the File tab.

2. Click Options to open the Outlook Options dialog box (see Figure 6.9).

3. Under the Compose messages group, click the Signatures button to open the Signatures and Stationary dialog box shown in Figure 6.10.

Click to display the Mail options

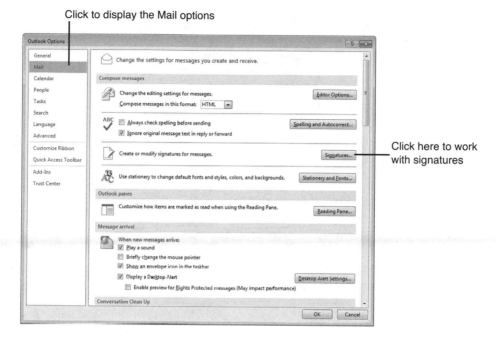

FIGURE 6.9

Use the Outlook Options dialog box to start access signatures.

Click here to start a new signature

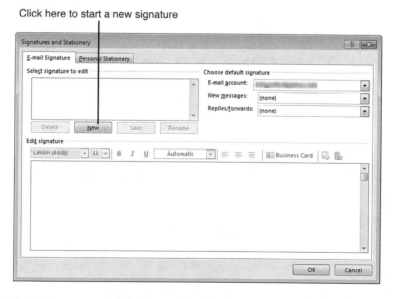

FIGURE 6.10

You can add and edit signatures with this dialog box.

4. Click New to open the New Signature dialog box (see Figure 6.11).

FIGURE 6.11

Type a name for your signature.

5. Type in a name for the new signature.

6. Click OK.

7. Type in your signature text and format it any way you want using the formatting tools (see Figure 6.12). You can change text color, make text bold or italic, or set a different font or size.

Use the formatting tools to spruce up your signature

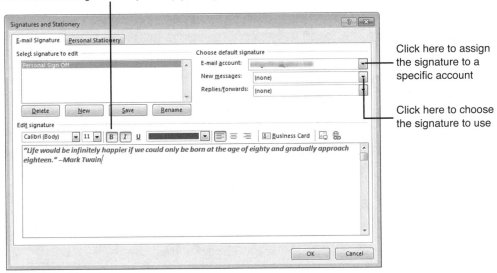

FIGURE 6.12

You can add and edit signatures with this dialog box.

8. Click OK.

9. Click OK again to close the Outlook Options dialog box.

The next time you compose a new email message for that particular account, Outlook automatically inserts the signature into the email's message body as shown in Figure 6.13.

Outlook inserts the signature automatically

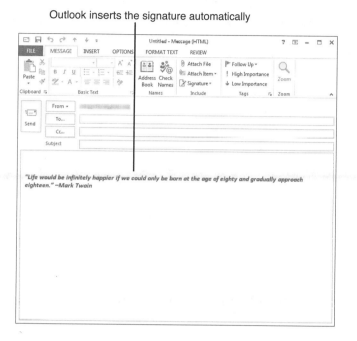

FIGURE 6.13

Open a new message and your signature is inserted.

To edit signatures or assign new ones to your accounts, reopen the Signatures and Stationary dialog box and make your changes. You can delete signatures, edit existing signatures, or change which accounts they're associated with.

Controlling Replies, Forwarding, and Receipts

You can control how Outlook handles replies and forwarding with the options found in the Outlook Options dialog box. By default, Outlook is set up to include the original message text in any replies. You can change this. For example, you may prefer to send the original text as an attachment instead.

To open the Outlook Options dialog box, click the File tab and click Options. Next, click the Mail category and scroll down to the Replies and Forwards group of tools, as shown in Figure 6.14. Click the When Replying to a Message drop-down list and make your selection. You can make similar changes to how the message text is handled when forwarded. Click OK to exit the dialog box and apply the changes.

Change how the message's original text is handled

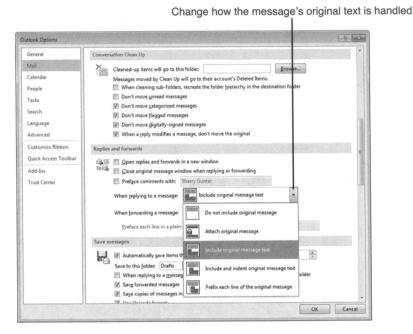

FIGURE 6.14

Control how replies and forwards appear using these options.

You can also request delivery receipts or read receipts with your messages. When you activate these features, the recipient's email server generates a response when the person receives or views the email message. This can help you keep track of whether someone has read your message. You can also assign a delivery reply to another email address, or a day or time for delivery, or even a delivery expiration. It's starting to sound like Outlook turns you into a delivery control hub. These particular tracking controls appear in the Properties dialog box for the Message form window. Check out Figure 6.15 to view them.

 TIP To view additional tracking options, open the Outlook Options dialog box; click File, Options. Click the Mail category and scroll down to the Tracking group of tools to view additional settings for receipts.

Click here to request a delivery receipt

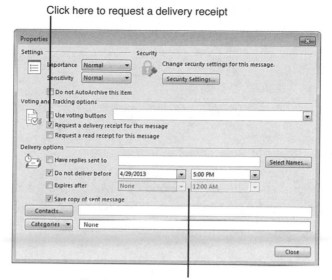

Use the delivery options to customize delivery

FIGURE 6.15

The Properties dialog box has delivery options

NOTE Outlook also offers several tools for sending automatic replies and forwarding emails if you're using Microsoft Exchange Server. For example, if you're getting ready to go on vacation, you can set up Outlook to send automatic replies to incoming messages to let people know you're out of the office. If you don't use an Exchange account, you can use Outlook's rules to set up out-of-office replies. To learn more about creating rules, see Chapter 5.

Inserting Other Items into Messages

You can insert pictures into your messages, essentially embedding them. This process is a bit different from attaching a picture file to the message. With an embedded picture, it appears in the message body. Picture options are offered on the Message form window's Insert tab, shown in Figure 4.16. Outlook lets you embed several types of pictures:

- **Pictures from File**—Use this option to insert pictures stored on your computer.

Picture tools

FIGURE 6.16

Use the Insert tab to embed pictures in your messages.

- **Online Pictures**—Activate this option to insert clip art pictures, pictures you search for using Bing Search, or pictures from your SkyDrive (cloud) account.
- **Draw a Shape**—Draw your own original shapes using the drawing tools.

Inserting a Picture

To insert a picture from your computer, follow these steps:

1. Click the Insert tab.

2. Click the Pictures button.

3. The Insert Pictures dialog box opens (see Figure 6.17). Navigate to the folder or drive containing the file you want to insert.

FIGURE 6.17

The Insert Pictures dialog box.

4. Click the picture filename.

5. Click Insert.

Outlook inserts the picture in the message body (see Figure 6.18) and displays the Format tab. You can resize the picture and adjust its formatting. The Picture Tool's Format tab offers lots of tools you can use to work with pictures, including cropping, controlling text wrap around the picture, and artistic effects you can apply.

Format tab

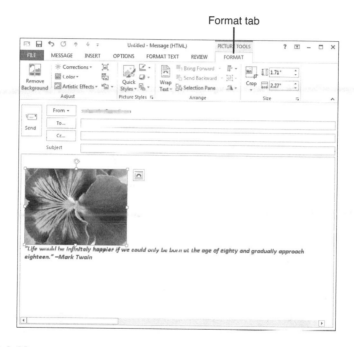

FIGURE 6.18

Ta-da! The inserted picture.

 TIP You can also double-click the filename in the Insert Pictures dialog box to insert a picture.

To resize a picture, click and drag a corner handle on the picture.

Inserting Online Pictures

If you click the Online Pictures button on the Insert tab, you can choose from three online sources for pictures. You can search for a clip art picture from the Microsoft Office website, look for an online picture using the Bing search engine, or grab a picture you're storing on your SkyDrive account. You can do all three from the Insert Pictures box (see Figure 6.19)

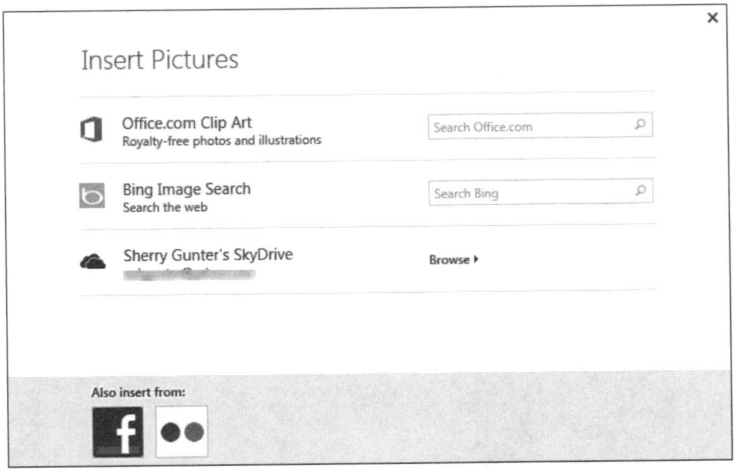

FIGURE 6.19

The Insert Pictures box.

To search for a clip art picture from the Microsoft Office website, click the Office. com Clip Art search box and type in a keyword or words for the type of picture you're looking for, then click Search or press Enter. The dialog box displays a list of matches, similar to Figure 6.20. If you find one you like, click it and click Insert.

Outlook places the picture in your message, and like a picture you insert from your computer, the Picture Tools Format tab appears with tools for editing the picture.

To locate a picture online, click in the Bing search box and type a keyword for the type of picture you want to find; press Enter. A list of possible matches appears, and you can choose one to add.

To insert a picture from your SkyDrive account, click the Browse button and navigate to the folder containing the picture you want to download. Select it and click Insert.

After you've inserted a picture, you can edit it or format it as you like.

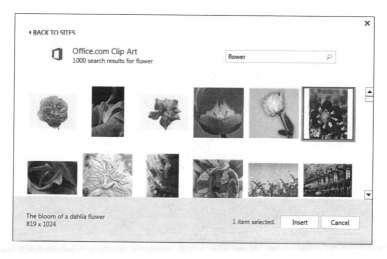

FIGURE 6.20

Choose a picture to download.

Inserting Shapes

You can also draw your own artwork in the form of shapes using the Microsoft AutoShapes collection. On the Insert tab, click the Shapes button (see Figure 6.21) and choose a shape to draw from the gallery. After you select one, click and drag the shape to the size you want in the message area, similar to Figure 6.22.

Outlook places the picture in your message, and like a picture you insert from your computer, the Drawing Tools Format tab appears with tools for editing the shape, including adding a fill color, changing the shape outline, or adding text to create a logo or graphic.

TIP You can also insert a screenshot of your own computer into your messages. For example, you might take a snapshot of a gaming screen to share with a friend. Make sure the window you want to capture is not minimized, then activate the Screenshot button on the Message form window's Insert tab and click the screenshot you want to use.

FIGURE 6.21

The Shapes gallery.

FIGURE 6.22

Draw your own shapes in your messages.

The Wonderful World of RSS Feeds

RSS feeds (Really Simple Syndication) is a technology that allows web content to be converted into a feed that is viewed as message posts. You can receive RSS feeds for blogs, podcasts, news, and so on. You can use Outlook to check the latest updates of your favorite RSS feeds. Feeds you subscribe to appear in the RSS Feeds folder in the Mail component.

You can conduct a web search to find popular RSS feeds to try if you don't already have a few favorites. Many of your favorite sites may already offer them. You need the RSS feed location, or URL, to connect to the feed.

To subscribe, use these steps:

1. Click File.

2. From the Info tab, click the Account Settings drop-down arrow.

3. Click Account Settings.

4. The Account Settings dialog box opens; click the RSS Feeds tab (see Figure 6.23).

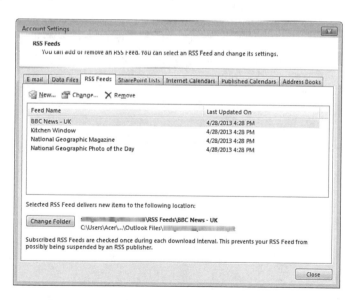

FIGURE 6.23

The Account Settings dialog box is your gateway to signing up for RSS feeds.

5. Click New.

6. Type in the RSS Feed address (see Figure 6.24).

FIGURE 6.24

You need to know the RSS feed web address to subscribe.

7. Click Add.

8. The RSS Feed Options dialog box appears with a general name for the feed already assigned (see Figure 6.25). Click OK to continue.

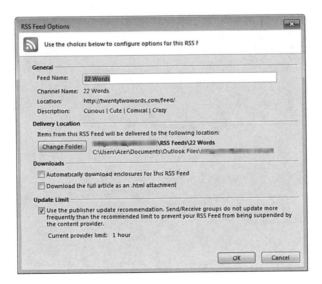

FIGURE 6.25

Details about the RSS feed you're subscribing to are listed here.

9. The RSS Feed is added to the list box; click Close.

10. Click the Send/Receive tab.

11. Click Send/Receive All Folders to update the latest posts.

12. Click the RSS Feeds folder in the Folder pane to view the RSS feed subfolders to which you are subscribed (see Figure 6.26).

RSS Feeds folder   RSS messages

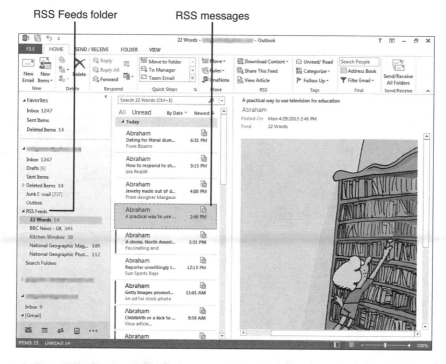

FIGURE 6.26

View your RSS feeds in the RSS Feeds folder.

13. Click the folder you want to open.

14. Click the message you want to view.

15. The Preview pane displays the message.

There are oodles of RSS feeds you can subscribe to, including YouTube channels and social media sites.

NOTE If you no longer want to subscribe to an RSS Feed, reopen the Account Settings dialog box to the RSS Feeds tab, select the Feed Name, and then click the Remove button.

THE ABSOLUTE MINIMUM

In this chapter, you learned about more email options you can use to improve your messaging. Here's a few highlights:

- You can take advantage of the formatting tools in your Message form window to make your text look nice.

- You can assign priority levels and sensitivity settings to messages to help alert the recipient to a message's importance.

- Use Quick Parts to speed up repetitive text entry in your messaging tasks.

- Add unique digital signatures at the end of your messages to personalize your emails.

- You can request receipts to verify the recipient has received or read your email.

- You can embed pictures in your messages, including pictures found on your computer or your SkyDrive account.

- You can subscribe to your favorite RSS feeds directly in Outlook and read the latest updates from the RSS Feeds folder and your Reading pane.

7

USING THE CALENDAR

If you're like most people, you probably check your calendar daily, even if it is just to remember what day it is. You typically turn on your computer daily as well. Why not combine the two activities? Meet Outlook's Calendar component. You can use Calendar to keep track of your appointments, dates, and other scheduled events with ease. With a digital calendar, you don't have to worry about making room on your wall or desk for a regular calendar ever again—although admittedly you will miss the monthly picture of cute kittens or scenic places you'll never visit. The beauty of a computer-based calendar, though, is you can view everything at a glance or with a quick click. Plus, if you have a laptop or tablet, your calendar can go where you go.

Sure, Outlook's Calendar offers a handy way to view your daily schedule, but it does a lot more. You can view multiple calendars and synchronize dates; you can schedule meetings with others, email your calendar, and even publish it online. You can also set up reminders to alert you to an upcoming appointment, prioritize calendar items with tabs, and set recurring appointments.

Displaying Your Calendar

Most calendars you're used to come in a variety of paper formats, such as a wall calendar you flip through month by month, a desk calendar that displays each day as a tear-away page, a blotter calendar that covers your desk and collects coffee spills, or pocket calendars you keep in your purse or briefcase that let you flip through daily or weekly pages. With Outlook's Calendar tool, you have all these formats in one convenient spot—your computer. To get started, click the Calendar icon at the bottom of the left pane, as shown in Figure 7.1. (By the way, this pane is always called the Folder pane, whether you see folders listed there or not, and you can hide and display it as needed. To learn more, flip back to Chapter 1.)

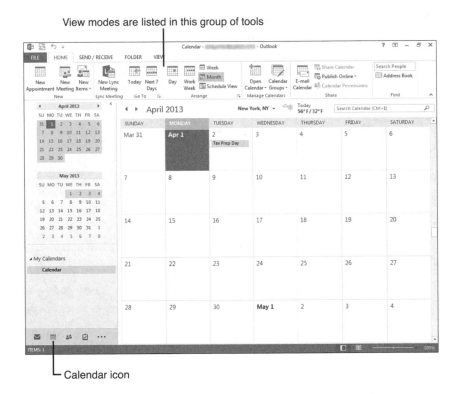

FIGURE 7.1

Outlook's Calendar displays your calendar by weekly, monthly, or daily view. In this example, the Month view is displayed.

When you switch over to Calendar, Outlook presents you with a default view mode that lays out your digital calendar in an easy-to-read design. Depending on how you want to view your information, Calendar offers several view modes you can toggle between:

- **Day**—Displays a single day on the calendar with times listed in hourly increments and subdivided into half-hour increments. (You can change the increments to suit your needs.)

- **Week**—Displays a week view of your calendar, starting with Sunday and ending with Saturday.

- **Work Week**—Also displays a week of your calendar, but from Monday through Friday.

- **Month**—Displays a full month of days.

- **Schedule view**—Displays your schedule in a horizontal layout, handy for viewing multiple calendars for scheduling meetings with other users.

View modes are available in two places. The ribbon's Home tab displays the five view modes in the Arrange group of tools, as shown in Figure 7.1, whereas the View tab lists them in the Arrangement group of tools, as pointed out in Figure 7.2. Why two spots? Probably for convenience. Keeping the view modes easy to access with a click can help you shorten the time you spend looking for controls among the various tabs. To switch between view modes, click the view you want to display. For example, to see your calendar in Month view, click the Month button.

View modes are also listed in this group of tools

FIGURE 7.2

You can also find view modes listed on the View tab.

   TIP Do you have a different set of days for your workweek instead of the traditional five? No problem. You can customize your calendar's workweek display. Click the File tab and click Options to display the dialog box. Next, click the Calendar category of options. Under the Work Time heading, choose which days constitute your workweek. You can also change the work hours for your Day and Week views, or even change the default first day of the week. After you make your adjustments, click OK to apply the changes.

In addition to the view modes, you can also activate a sneak peek mode and check your calendar from any Outlook component using a pop-up display. To do so, hover your mouse pointer over the Calendar icon located at the bottom of the Folder pane, as shown in Figure 7.3. The sneak peek lets you know if you have any appointments or meetings scheduled for the day, and it clues you into the current date.

FIGURE 7.3

You can also sneak a peek at your calendar using the Calendar icon.

Navigating Your Calendar

As far as navigating goes, different view modes offer different ways to interact with your calendar. Let's take a look at the many ways to get around Outlook's Calendar.

Methods of navigating the Calendar vary slightly between the different view modes. In Month view, for example, your calendar is presented as a grid of date squares, looking like a monthly paper calendar you might hang on the wall. To select a date in Month view, click it. When you do this, you can immediately start typing in event information (an event is an all-day activity, such as a birthday or anniversary). Calendar always displays the current date marked in bold, as shown in Figure 7.4.

TIP   If you want to set an appointment and include details such as the time and location, you can double-click the date and fill out the appointment form. Learn more about setting appointments coming up shortly in this chapter.

You can view the previous and next month's calendars in miniature in this pane
Click these buttons to move backward or forward month by month

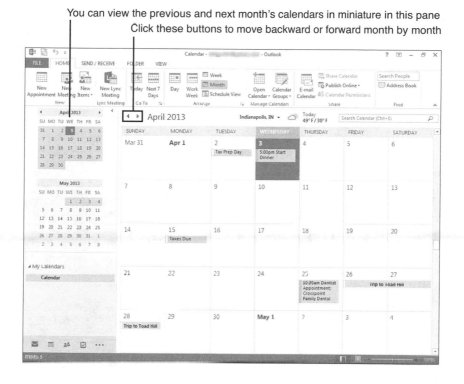

FIGURE 7.4

You can navigate between months using the navigation arrows.

To move back and forth between months, you can click the navigation arrows at the top of the calendar. Click Back to move back a month in the display, or click Forward to move forward a month in the display. You can also use the scrollbar on the far right of the program window to move between months.

The Folder pane that appears on the left side of the program window displays miniature calendars of the previous and next months, which is extremely helpful when you want to see past and previous dates. Click the navigation arrows at the top of the Folder pane to move back and forth among the months. Click a date on the miniature calendar to view it in Day view.

TIP You can hide and display the Folder pane using the Expand and Minimize arrow in the upper-right corner of the pane. Click the arrow icon; the arrow icon points left for minimizing the pane, and it points right for expanding. You can also click the View tab and click Folder pane, Normal to fully display the pane again.

Speaking of the Day view, your schedule appears in hourly increments, as shown in Figure 7.5. The same is true in Week and Work Week view—see Figure 7.6. Not only are the hours listed for the entire day, but they are divided into half hours with the help of a dotted line. Each day starts at 12 AM at the top and ends at 11:59 at the bottom. Use the scrollbar to move up and down the time slots. The same as in Month view, you can use the navigation arrows at the top to move from day to day or week to week. Notice the Folder pane stays the same as in Month view, displaying the months before and after the current date you're viewing. You can click a date on the miniature monthly display to jump to it in Day, Week, or Work Week view.

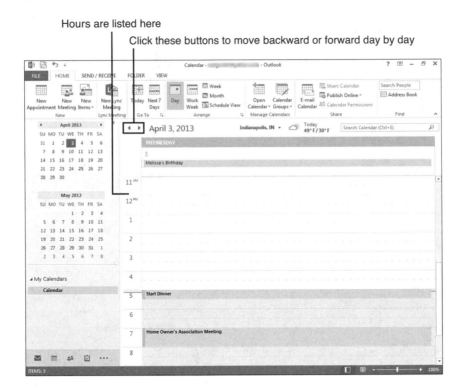

Hours are listed here

Click these buttons to move backward or forward day by day

FIGURE 7.5

Day view shows a day's worth of your schedule.

Hours in your day are listed here

Click these buttons to move backward or forward week by week

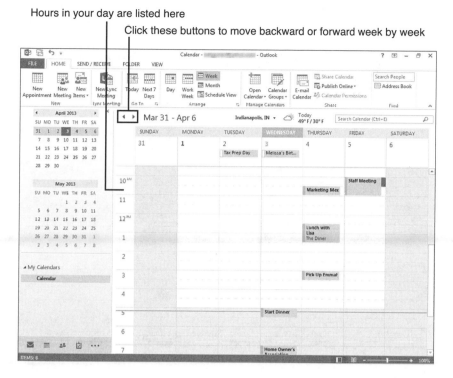

FIGURE 7.6

Week and Work Week views display your entire week in hourly increments.

The same navigation arrows are available in Schedule view, as shown in Figure 7.7. Rather than a vertical listing of hours in your day, however, Schedule view shows the times listed horizontally across the screen. That's because Schedule view is designed specifically for viewing two or more calendar schedules, such as your colleagues', so you can arrange meeting times to accommodate everyone's convenience.

If you're viewing two or more calendars, you can see them listed in the Folder pane, including any multiple calendars you're using on your computer. To view another calendar in the list, click its name.

TIP You can use the Search box at the top of the calendar to search for keywords used with appointments, meetings, and events on the calendar. Click in the box and type what you're searching for and press Enter. Outlook opens the search results in a Search tab. Click Close Search to exit the feature and return to what you were doing.

Navigation arrows

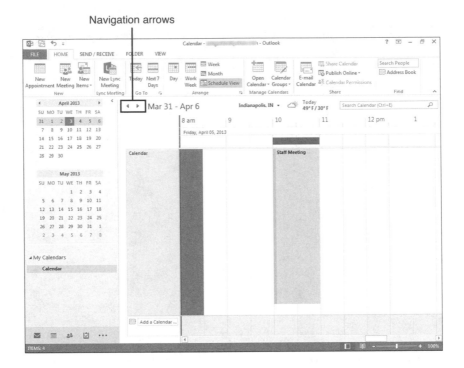

FIGURE 7.7

Schedule view shows your day in a horizontal arrangement for comparing schedules with others.

 TIP Do you like shortcuts? You can use keyboard shortcuts to switch views in Calendar. All of these involve simultaneously pressing the Ctrl key and the Alt key, followed by a number:

Press Ctrl+Alt+1 to display Day view.

Press Ctrl+Alt+2 to switch to Work Week view.

Press Ctrl+Alt+3 to switch to Week view.

Press Ctrl+Alt+4 to switch to Month view.

Press Ctrl+Alt+5 to switch to Schedule view.

Navigating to a Date

What about those times you need to jump to a specific date and it's not currently showing onscreen? To help you with such tasks, the Home tab offers a group of tools under the heading Go To. For example, to always return to the current date, click the Today button, pointed out in Figure 7.8. To jump to the next seven days, click the Next 7 Days button and Outlook immediately switches the display to show the next seven days in the calendar in Day view.

FIGURE 7.8

Use the Go To tools to jump to dates.

To jump to a date, click the Go to Date icon, shown in Figure 7.8. When clicked, this opens the Go to Date dialog box (see Figure 7.9). Type in the date and press Enter or click OK. Calendar immediately whisks you to the date.

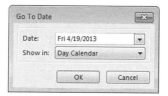

FIGURE 7.9

Use the Go to Date dialog box to jump to a date.

 TIP You can always navigate to a specific date using the miniature calendars shown on the Folder pane. Use the navigation arrows to locate the month; then click the date.

Changing the Weather Display

While we're still examining Calendar's layout, let's talk about the weather information you see at the top of the calendar area. The Weather bar displays the day's forecast for your area based on information from the iMap Weather site (www.iMapWeather.com), as shown in Figure 7.10. As you might already conclude, you need an online connection to make this feature work properly. When you hover your mouse over the forecast, a pop-up box of additional information appears, including the wind speed, humidity level, and chance of precipitation. This is very handy stuff if you're planning an outside activity for the next day or so. Of course, you have to indicate your own particular geographical area to see your local forecast.

FIGURE 7.10

The Weather bar gives you handy forecasts.

The Weather bar can remember up to five locations, and it keeps them handy in a drop-down list for future use, as shown in Figure 7.11. To view a forecast, display the list and click the location.

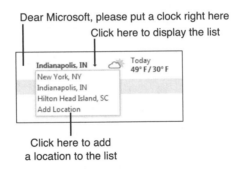

FIGURE 7.11

Choose a location from the drop-down list.

To add your own location to the list, follow these steps:

1. Click the Weather location options drop-down arrow.

2. Click Add Location.

3. Type in your city and state, or city and country.

4. Press Enter when finished.

The Weather bar reflects the new setting. Now, if they'd just incorporate a clock next to the weather bar, I'd leave this open on my computer screen all day long!

To remove a city from the list, display the drop-down menu again and move the mouse pointer over the city you want to delete. Click the X next to the name, and it's removed from the list.

TIP   Tired of the weather? You can turn the Weather bar off. Click the File tab and click Options to open the Outlook Options dialog box, then click the Calendar category. Scroll to the bottom of the box and look for the Weather options. Deselect the Show Weather on the Calendar check box to turn the feature off. You can also switch from Fahrenheit to Celsius. Click OK to apply your changes.

Recording Events and Appointments

Ready to start adding your own stuff to your calendar? The true heart of Outlook's Calendar component is its capability to manage your busy schedule. You can add both events and appointments, and there's a distinction between the two. *Events* are all-day activities, whereas *appointments* earmark both a date and a time on your schedule. You can use a form, which appears as a separate window of tools, options, and fill-in-the-blanks, to include details and specify whether it's an event or an appointment you're recording. The form is the same whether you're creating an event or an appointment, but the outcome differs depending on whether you check one particular box.

Recording Events

It's incredibly easy to add an event. As mentioned, *events* are all-day activities, such as a conference, trip, birthday, or anniversary. As such, Outlook displays events a little differently from a scheduled appointment (which occurs at a designated time in the day). In Month view, events appear highlighted in a color bar on the date, whereas in Day, Work, and Work Week view, the event appears at the top of the schedule, also in a color bar. Figure 7.12 shows an example of an event.

The simplest way to record an event is to type it in directly on the calendar. To add an event in Month view, click the date on the giant calendar display and type in your event title, such as **Bob's Birthday**, **Sales Conference**, or **Author Appreciation Day**. Press Enter and the event is added.

You can use the same method to add an event in Work Week or Week view, but click the day's date at the top of the schedule and type in the event name, similar to Figure 7.13.

Event   Event

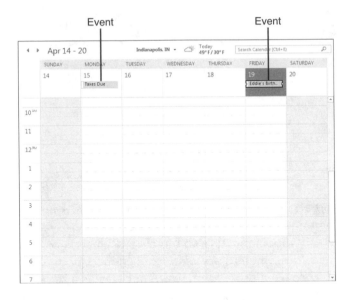

FIGURE 7.12

Events appear as headlines on your calendar.

Click here and type in your event name

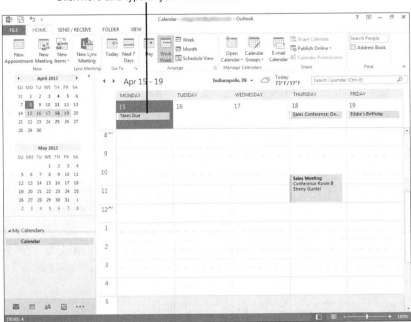

FIGURE 7.13

In Week or Work Week view, the event appears as a header at the top of your schedule.

To add an event in Day view, navigate to the date and click the area at the top, just below the day's date (see Figure 7.14). Type in an event name and press **Enter**.

Click here and type in an event name

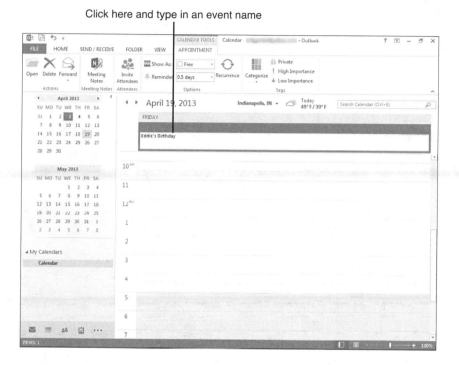

FIGURE 7.14

In Day view, the event appears as a header at the top of your schedule.

You can add multiple events to a single day, or make an event span as many days as you need. For example, your sales conference may cover three days of the week, or a vacation may require seven days. If an event requires more details, such as a location or multiple days, you can open the form window I was telling you about earlier and add more information.

To utilize the form method of recording an event, double-click the date. If you're viewing your calendar in Day, Week, or Work Week view, double-click the date at the top of the view, not a time slot in the schedule. By default, the All Day Event check box is already selected for you in the form, as pointed out in Figure 7.15. This indicates that the item is an event and not an appointment. If you deselect this check box, the item becomes an appointment.

Click here to save the item
Click here to remove the event
The Event tab has all kinds of tools and features you can assign

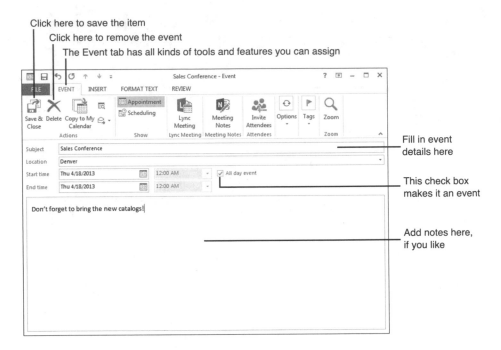

Fill in event
details here

This check box
makes it an event

Add notes here,
if you like

FIGURE 7.15

Use the form window to add more details to an event.

You can tap into additional features and tools found in the form window's tabs to customize an event. To fill out the details, click in a form field and type away. Everything's optional. For example, type a name for the event in the Subject box or a location for the event in the Location box. When you type in a subject, the form window's title bar changes to reflect the event's name.

If the event spans several days, choose a start and end date. The large notes area lets you jot down any additional notes about the event, such as **Don't forget to pick up my tux before leaving town for the wedding.** When you finish, click the Save & Close button.

Anytime you want to view information about a particular event, hover your mouse pointer over it to see a quick peek of details, such as whether a reminder is set (learn more about reminders coming up). If you click an event, the Appointment tab appears on the ribbon with tools for setting reminders, recurring status, or tagging the event with priority settings.

TIP   To quickly expand an event from one day to two or more, hover over the left or right edges of the event name in Month, Week, or Work Week view, and then click and drag across the other days you want to include.

TIP   You can also use the Event form window to remove the event; open the form window and click the Delete button on the Event tab to remove it from the calendar. Or, for a quicker delete, right-click the event name and choose Delete.

If you want to create a recurring event—one that happens with regularity, such as a birthday, anniversary, or tax day—you can assign it recurring status using the event form window (see Figure 7.16). With the Event form window open, click the Options button on the Event tab and click Recurrence. This opens the Appointment Recurrence dialog box, shown in Figure 7.17.

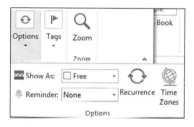

FIGURE 7.16

Look for reminders and recurrence settings in the Options list.

To change the recurrence pattern, choose how often the event appears on the calendar, then fine-tune the settings based on the type of pattern you choose. For example, if you're setting a weekly event, like "Half Price Tuesday" or "Carpool Day," you can specify which day of the week the event always occurs. Click OK to save your changes.

TIP   You can also set recurring status using the ribbon's Appointment tab. Click the event from any calendar view to display the tab. Then click the Recurrence button to open the Appointment Recurrence dialog box.

If you ever need to remove a recurring event, open the event's form window again and display the Recurrence dialog box, this time clicking the Remove Recurrence button.

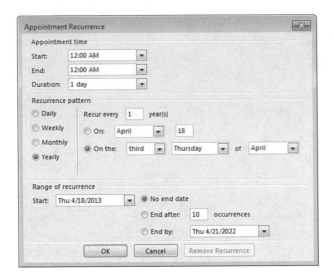

FIGURE 7.17

Use the Appointment Recurrence dialog box to set up a recurring event.

 NOTE The Calendar component does not show any holidays. You can add them though, with a few easy steps. Click the File tab and click Options to open the Outlook Options dialog box. Click the Calendar category and scroll down to the Calendar Options group. Click the Add Holidays button. Specify a country and click OK. Outlook then populates your calendar with the appropriate holidays.

Recording Appointments

Do you need to schedule an appointment? *Appointments* in Outlook are any item you add to your calendar that require a designated date and time. For example, dentist or doctor appointments, lunch dates, meetings, a project deadline, or a chosen time to take your medications—you get the idea. Anything that you need to jot down for a specific date and time in your daily life can be an appointment in Outlook.

You can use a special form to fill out appointment details and save it to your calendar. You can use a variety of methods to summon the Appointment form window:

- Click the New Appointment button on the Home tab.

- Double-click a time slot in Day view.

- Double-click any time slot in Week or Work Week view.

- Double-click any date in Month view, but deselect the All Day Event check box.

- Right-click the calendar and click New Appointment.

- Press Ctrl+N.

Like the Event form window, the Appointment form window, as illustrated in Figure 7.18, offers all the same tools and options. Yes, it's actually the same window, but with a different name at the top (and a tab name changes to Appointment instead of Event). If you click the All Day Event check box, the form becomes an Event form, but if the box is unchecked, the window is the Appointment form.

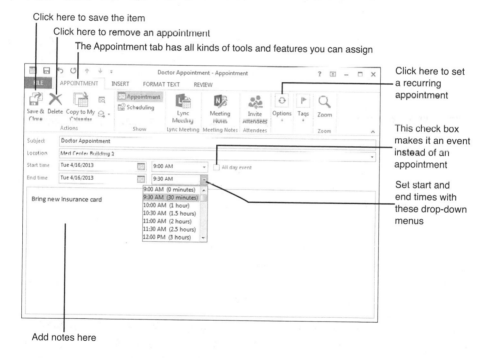

FIGURE 7.18

Use the Appointment form window to create a scheduled appointment.

You can fill out as many details about the appointment as you need. For example, click in the Subject box and type in a title or description of the appointment. Assigning a title can help you quickly see what type of appointment it is from any of the calendar views. Brief titles work best, such as **Staff Meeting** or **Dentist Appointment**. When you type in a subject, the form window's title bar changes to reflect the new title.

If your appointment needs to specify a location to help you keep track of where you need to be, click in the Location box and include information such as a conference room number, address, building, restaurant, street, or city.

Next, specify a start and end date and time for the appointment. To change the date, you can type directly into the fields, or click the tiny calendar icon at the end of the box and choose a date from the pop-up calendar. If you already double-clicked the correct date you wanted for the appointment, Outlook displays the date in the Start Time and End Time boxes.

You can set both a start time and an end time for the appointment to specify a duration. To change the time, click the time drop-down arrows and choose a time from the list, or just type the time directly into the boxes. By default, time is listed in increments of 30 minutes, so you can set an appointment for 11:30, for example. If you want to use 15-minute increments, type the time in directly, such as **11:15 AM**. If you're sharing your calendar information with others, the appointment time appears as "busy" in your schedule.

You can type up any notes about the appointment in the wide-open notes area. For example, you may want to jot down items you need to bring to the appointment, such as an insurance card your dental office may require, or information about what you're going to do at the appointed time.

When you're finished filling out appointment details, click the Save & Close button. Outlook closes the form and adds the appointment to your calendar, as shown in Figure 7.19. The time span you indicated when setting a start and end time show up as a block of light-blue color.

To revisit the appointment details at any time, double-click the appointment to reopen the form again. For even quicker details, you can also hover your mouse pointer over the appointment in your calendar to see a quick peek. Also, when you select an appointment, which just takes a click, Outlook displays an Appointment tab on the ribbon. This tab is the same as the Appointment tab in the Appointment form window. You can use the tools to help you work with the appointment, such as setting a recurrence, tagging it, or setting up a reminder.

Appointment

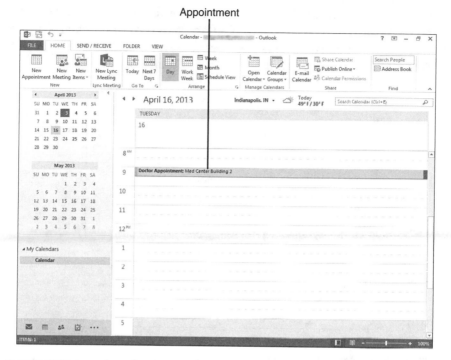

FIGURE 7.19

Behold, the appointed time and place.

TIP   You can quickly print out your appointment's details to take with you or hang up on a bulletin board for a reminder. Right-click the appointment and choose Quick Print from the pop-up menu.

If you need to move an appointment, you can click and drag its left edge and drop it where you want it in the schedule, whether it's a new time slot or a new date.

Setting Reminders

If you need some help remembering appointments and events, you can assign a reminder. When you set a reminder, Outlook displays a pop-up alert box, similar to Figure 7.20, telling you that it's time for the appointment or event and even plays a special sound. You can set reminders as far out as a week before the appointed date, or you can set a reminder to appear 5 minutes before the appointment. You decide how much lead time you need. The only caveat to reminders is that you need to have Outlook open and running in the background on your computer system; otherwise, you won't hear or see the reminder alert until the next time you open the Outlook program window.

FIGURE 7.20

Here's what a reminder alert looks like.

By default, Outlook automatically adds a 15-minute reminder to your appointments, but no reminder is added to events, so if you want one, you'll have to add it. Here are several ways to handle reminders:

- To add a reminder from the form window, click the Options button and choose when you want to be reminded by clicking the Reminder drop-down arrow and making a selection.

- To add a reminder to an existing appointment or event already on your calendar, click the item to display the Appointment tab on the ribbon. Next, click the Reminder drop-down arrow and make a selection.

- When the reminder alert appears, you can choose to turn it off by clicking the Dismiss button, or you can put it off for a little longer using the Snooze button, just like your alarm clock. You can even specify when you want to be reminded again.

Setting Up Meetings

Using Outlook's emailing capabilities and contacts list, you can set up meetings with other people and keep track of who is attending and who is not. You can view other users' calendars and schedule meetings at the most convenient time for everyone. For example, if you have a sales meeting with Joe on Friday, and you know Joe's email address or he's already one of your Outlook contacts, you can create an email invitation to let Joe know about the meeting. A great thing about this is that you can do all of it from within the Calendar component's screen.

Sending Out an Invite

To create a meeting and send out an invite, you can use the Meeting form, a special window for both emailing a message and scheduling the meeting on your calendar. Figure 7.21 shows an example of the form window, which looks hauntingly like the other form windows used to create events and appointments. Turns out a meeting is just like an appointment, but it involves more people and emailing features.

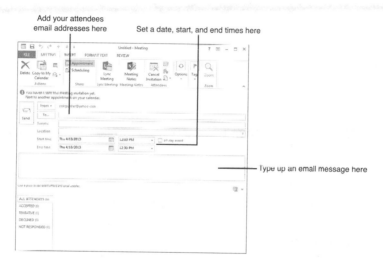

FIGURE 7.21

Use the Meeting form to set up a meeting date and email the attendees.

Follow these steps to create an invite:

1. Click the New Meeting button on the ribbon's Home tab.

2. Add the email addresses for the people you want to invite. If they happen to be Outlook contacts, you can click the To button and specify attendees from your address book.

3. Type in a title for the meeting in the Subject field.

4. Type in a location for the meeting.

5. Indicate a start and end date and time for the meeting.

6. Type in your email message text.

7. Click Send.

Outlook sends the email and adds the meeting to your own calendar.

Tracking Invites

You can keep track of people who respond to your meeting request or manage their attendance using the Tracking feature in Calendar. You can find the tool on the Meeting tab, a special tab that appears when you click a meeting on your calendar. The tab, shown in Figure 7.21, offers tools to help you manage the meeting, including adding or removing attendees, canceling the meeting, or following up with additional emails.

To open the Tracking feature, click the Tracking button, pointed out in Figure 7.22. You can use the list box area to make changes to the status of your attendees. Click the Response box to display a drop-down menu and choose whether the person has accepted, declined, is tentatively coming, or you've received no response (None). The tabs at the bottom of the window also let you see the status for a particular response at a glance.

You can use the tools found in the Meeting window's Tracking display to send out more emails, such as a reminder or date change, or cancel the meeting entirely. Here are a few actions you can take:

- To email a particular person in the list, hover the mouse pointer over the person's name and click the Email icon that appears.

- To email everyone, click the Contact Attendees button on the window's Meeting tab.

- To cancel the meeting and email everyone, click the Cancel Meeting button on the Meeting tab.

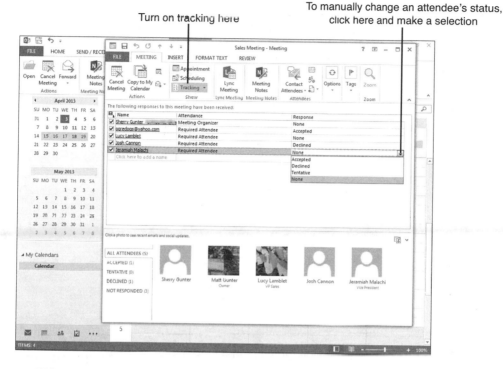

FIGURE 7.22

Use the Tracking feature to manage attendance for your meeting.

- To invite more attendees, click the Forward button and email others.

- Another way to invite someone else is to type the person's name at the bottom of the list. Outlook prompts you to save the changes and send the user an invite.

- To view your original invitation, click the Appointment button on the Meeting tab.

To reopen the Meeting window anytime, double-click the scheduled meeting on your calendar.

 TIP If you use Microsoft's OneNote program, you can create meeting notes and share them with others. Click the Meeting Notes button on the Meeting window's Meeting tab.

Sharing Your Calendar

The Calendar component offers several ways to share your calendar with others. An obvious way is to email it. You can do this directly from the Calendar component. You can choose which part of your calendar to include, such as a range of dates, the current date, and so on. Outlook then places the specified calendar portion in an email window, similar to Figure 7.23, which you can then address and add any additional message text. Your calendar appears not only in the message area, but also as a file attachment.

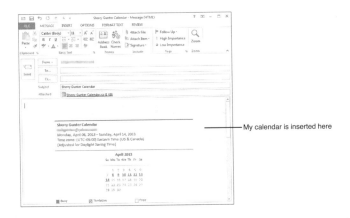

My calendar is inserted here

FIGURE 7.23

Share your calendar via email.

To email your calendar, click the Home tab and click E-mail Calendar. The Send a Calendar via E-mail dialog box appears, as shown in Figure 7.24. A message window opens with the calendar included. Now you can fill in the rest of the information to create your email message.

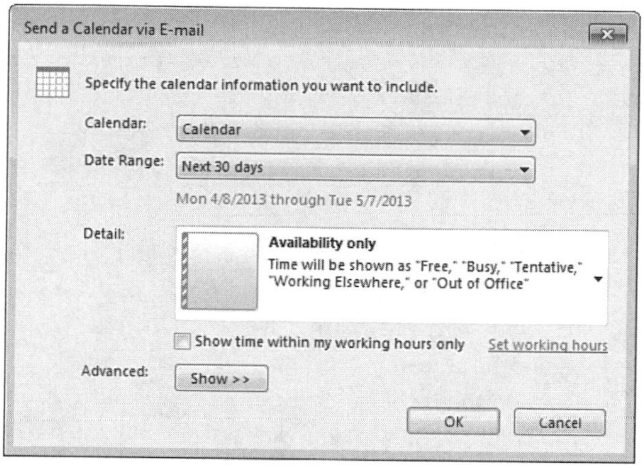

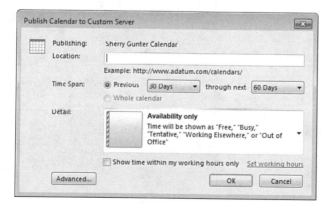

FIGURE 7.24

Use this box to specify which dates to include.

To publish your calendar online, you first need to know the WebDAV server address—that's a server that supports Web Distributed Authoring and Versioning protocols. Check with your server administrator to find out the details, but if you're good to go, click the Publish Online drop-down arrow on the Home tab and click Publish to WebDAV Server. The Publish Calendar to Custom Server dialog box opens, as shown in Figure 7.25. Type in the web address for the location of the server and choose the date range you want to publish. Click OK to post the calendar online.

FIGURE 7.25

Use this box to specify which dates to include.

TIP You can print out your calendar to share with someone. Navigate to the section you want to print, then click the File tab and click Print to display the options. You can choose a style to print, such as daily or monthly. When you've got everything ready to go, click the Print button.

NOTE You can save your calendar to another folder or drive, or export it as a file. For example, you might save it on a USB flash drive to share it with a colleague. To save your calendar to another location, click the File tab and click Save Calendar to open the Save As dialog box. Navigate to the folder or drive you want to save to and click Save. Calendars are saved in the iCalendar Format (ics).

To export a calendar, click the File tab and click Open & Export. Choose an export action and follow the onscreen prompts to complete the process.

THE ABSOLUTE MINIMUM

Now you know how to manage your busy schedule with a little help from Outlook's Calendar component. To sum it up, here's what you learned in this chapter:

- You can use Calendar's view to see your schedule by month, week, workweek, or day.

- You can use the new Weather bar to see the forecast at a glance for your location.

- An event is an all-day activity on your schedule, such as a birthday or conference, whereas an appointment is a designated time slot on your schedule.

- You can use special forms for recording details for events and appointments you add.

- You can also set a reminder alarm to go off as an appointment nears, but make sure Outlook is up and running in the background in order for the reminder to do its job.

- Set up meetings with other users by coordinating a date and sending out an email invitation, and then track the responses to manage attendance.

- Share your calendar with others directly through email, or publish it to a server that supports calendar formats to share your schedule online.

8

CONTACTS

Contact management is one reason many people choose Outlook over other email clients. Not only can you store email addresses, phone numbers, and mailing addresses in contacts, but you can also store personal information such as your contacts' birthdays, anniversary dates, and spouses' or children's names.

You can use contacts as an email addresses book, or to address letters in Word. Smartphones and tablets can synchronize their address books with Outlook contacts. This chapter shows you how to create and manage your contacts.

People Hub

The first time you open Outlook 2013's People module, you'll see a list of your contacts along with their photos, and clicking on a contact displays the contact's details in the reading pane. This view of your contacts is called the People Hub. It's a new view and may be confusing the first time you use it, especially if you used Outlook previously. When you double-click on a contact, it opens a contact card; however, while you can edit some fields in a contact card, you can't edit the contact photo or see attachments in the Notes field.

Each contact in the People Hub displays data from all sources Outlook links together. For example, if you have an Outlook contact for a person, and are friends on Facebook and LinkedIn, contact information from all three sources is displayed on one contact card in the People Hub. The contact card includes links to each data source, and you can edit the Outlook contact from the People pane (see Figure 8.1).

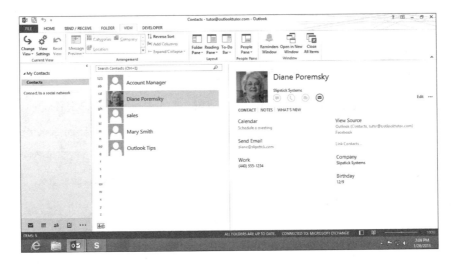

FIGURE 8.1

Outlook 2013's new People Hub. Click the blue links to create a new meeting, send email to the contact, or view the full contact.

When a modem, Skype, or Lync is installed, you can initiate a call to the contact from the contact card.

Editing Contact Cards in the People Hub

To edit an Outlook Contact from the People Hub, click Edit in the contact card or right-click the contact in the People list and choose Edit Contact.

When you click the Edit link in the Reading pane, you can edit the contact in place. If you double-click the contact (or right-click and choose Edit contact), the contact card opens in a new window. Edit the fields or click the plus sign icon to add more fields to the card. When you are finished, click Save (see Figure 8.2).

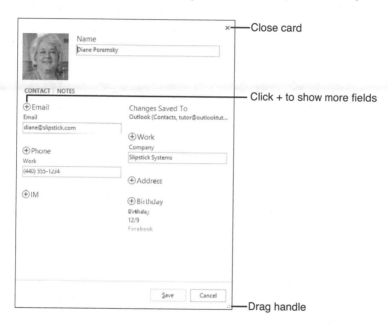

FIGURE 8.2

Edit a contact in the contact card.

You can drag the contact card to reposition it on the screen, or you can resize the card by dragging the resize handle in the lower-right corner. The contact card remains open until you click the X to close the card.

If you need to edit the full contact, click Cancel, and then click the links under the View Source heading to edit the Outlook contact. You can also view the contact's Facebook, LinkedIn, or SharePoint profile by clicking links on the contact card.

Linking Contacts

If you have more than one contact for a person, you'll see all of their contact details together in one contact card. Outlook tries to be helpful and automatically links contact records it identifies as belonging to the same person. If Outlook gets it wrong or you want to link other contacts, such as linking contacts for a husband and wife, you can manually link (or unlink) contacts using the Linked Contacts dialog box.

To open it, click the Link Contacts hyperlink to open the Linked Contacts dialog box (see Figure 8.3). When you hover over a contact, an x is visible on the right. Click it to unlink the contact.

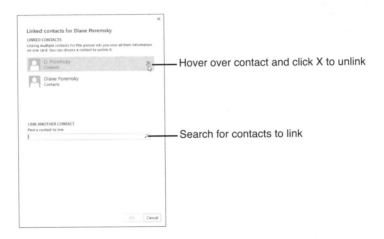

FIGURE 8.3

Link or unlink contacts using the Linked Contacts dialog box.

To link a contact to the current contact, type a contact's name in the Link Another Contact field and search for more contacts to link to this contact.

Creating Contacts

Before you can use contacts to address email or letters, you need to create some contacts. When you are viewing the Contact folder, you can click the New Contact button or use the Ctrl+N keyboard shortcut.

You don't need to view a contacts folder to create a new contact. You can do it from any Outlook folder, using the Ctrl+Shift+C keyboard shortcut. If you prefer using the mouse, click New Items, and then click Contact to open a new, blank contact form. Fill in the fields, click Save, and then click the Close button. The contact is saved to the default Contacts folder (see Figure 8.4).

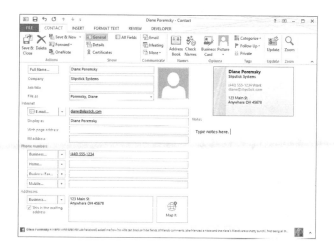

FIGURE 8.4

An Outlook contact form contains fields for email addresses, phone numbers, and mailing addresses.

The General page of the contact form includes fields for your contact's name, the employer, three physical addresses, 19 phone numbers, three email addresses, notes, websites, and IM addresses. You can also add photos or images to a contact, which display on email messages from the contact.

The business card displays the contact's name, address, and phone numbers. It can be customized to include a business logo or image.

The Details page (see Figure 8.5) is opened by clicking the Details button. It contains fields for additional information, including the contact's manager and assistant names, and the Internet Free/Busy publishing location. Personal information, such as the contact's birth date, anniversary, and spouse's name, is also entered on the Details page. Recurring events are automatically created in the calendar when you enter the birth date and anniversary of a contact.

NOTE   When birthday or anniversary dates are entered on the Details tab, Outlook automatically adds these events to your calendar. If you don't want these events created on your calendar, enter the dates in the Notes field instead.

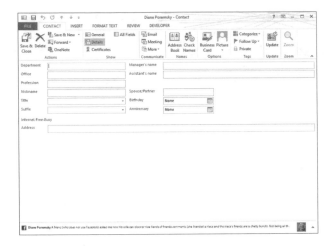

FIGURE 8.5

The Details page has fields for office and personal information.

In addition to the Contact form, Outlook 2013 also uses a contact card to display your contacts. Contact cards display contact information when you move the cursor over an email address in Outlook. The contact cards display the contacts in a simpler card format; however, not all contact fields are available on contact cards.

Creating a Contact

You can create contacts by using two different contact interfaces: the full featured contact form or the simpler contact card.

To create a new contact using the contact form, follow these steps:

1. Open a contact by clicking on New Items on the Home tab, and then Contact.

2. Enter your contact's name.

3. Fill in the other fields as needed.

4. On the Contact tab, click on Picture, and then Add Picture to add a photo or image.

5. Click the Details button.

6. Enter the birthday and anniversary dates.

7. Click Save & Close when you are finished.

Although you can create a new contact by opening a new contact form and typing in the contact information, you can also create contacts for people who send you email messages. When you use this method, the name and email address fields are filled in automatically.

1. Select a message.

2. Right-click a name and email address in the From, To, or CC field.

3. Choose Add to Outlook Contacts.

4. Fill in the desired fields.

5. Click the plus sign (+) to add email, phone, and address fields.

6. Drag the lower-right corner to resize the form.

7. Click Save when you're finished.

When you click Save, the contact is saved to your Contacts folder. The contact card remains open onscreen. Click Close to close it. If you want to add a contact photo or an attachment, click the link under View Source to open the full contact form (see Figure 8.6).

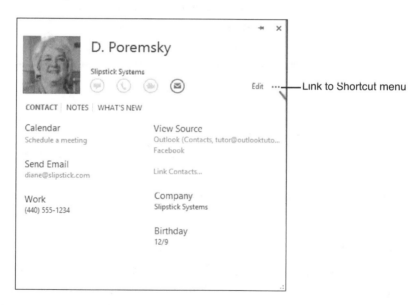

FIGURE 8.6

A completed contact card; open the full card by clicking the Outlook (Contacts, email address) link under View Source.

Click the ellipsis (. . .) to add the contact to the People Peek Favorites or to link the contact to other contacts. You may have additional options listed, including adding the contact to LinkedIn, Facebook, or other social networks. If you have Skype or Lync installed, you can link the contact to those services and tag a contact so you are alerted when they come online. If Business Contact Manager (BCM) is installed, you can add the contact to BCM from here.

TIP If you want to create a contact for someone who sent you an email, and the email message contains their mailing address or other information you want to keep with the contact, drag the email message to the Contact button in the Navigation pane. A new contact is created using the sender's name and email address; the message body is added to the notes field on the contact.

Create New Contacts from the Same Company

When you need to create several contacts from the same company on the Contact tab, click Save & New, and then select Contact from the Same Company. This opens a new contact form with the company name, business address, and phone number fields from the first contact. If you customized the business card, the new contact will have the same customization (see Figure 8.7).

Add the new contact's name and email address, and then click Save & Close.

FIGURE 8.7

Use New Contact from the Same Company to create contacts from the same company.

Customizing Contacts and Business Cards

Outlook 2013's contact form contains two image fields, one for a picture of the contact and one in the business card for a picture or company logo. You don't need to insert a contact photo or image, but if you do, the image displays in the message header in the Reading pane or opened message.

In addition to adding an image or logo to the business card, you can control which contact fields display on the business card, the text size, color, and position (see Figure 8.8).

FIGURE 8.8

Customize contacts and their business cards using images and logos.

 TIP The photo looks better if you crop and resize it using an image editor, such as Paint. You'll want the image cropped close to the person's head and sized to approximately 96×96 pixels.

Adding a Contact Picture

To add a photo to the contact, open the Contact. Double-click the Picture icon, or from the ribbon select Picture, Add Picture. Select the photo or image you want to use for the Contact's photo. Click Save & Close.

That's all there is to it. If you want to change the photo, repeat the process and select a new image.

Customizing Business Cards

Each business card can be customized with a different image and text formatting. If you want to apply a similar business card layout to every contact, you need to edit each one individually. You can't easily change the default layout, and you can't apply it to existing contacts.

Follow these steps to customize a Contact's business card:

1. Open the Contact.

2. Double-click the business card to open the Edit Business Card dialog box (see Figure 8.9).

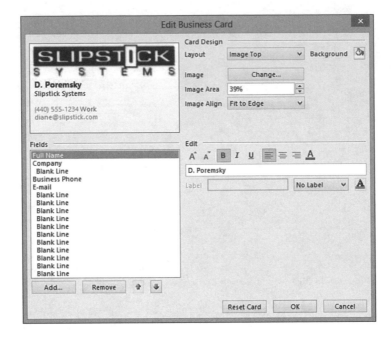

FIGURE 8.9

Use the Business Card editor to customize the business cards.

3. The business card in the upper left displays the current card layout.

4. Use the Card Design options on the right to change the size, alignment, and location of the contact picture or replace it with a different image. You can also add a background color.

5. Add, remove, or rearrange the contact fields that display on the card in the Field section in the lower left.

6. Select a field and use the Move Field Up and Move Field Down buttons to reorder the fields, or click Remove to delete the field. Changes are reflected immediately in the business card.

7. Click the Add button to add additional contact fields to the card.

8. Customize the formatting of the selected field on the right side of the Edit section. If the data in any field is incorrect, you can edit it in this dialog box and changes are updated in the contact and the business card.

When you're done editing the business card, click OK to save the change and return to the contact. If you don't want to keep the changes, click Reset. This removes all customizations and restores the default business card.

NOTE   If you want to use a new business card layout for your contacts, you can publish a custom form and set the form as the default for new items, or you can use a VBA macro to apply the format of one card to other cards. See http://slipstick.com/bizcards for more information.

Using Contact Groups

If you send messages to the same group of people frequently, you can create a Contact Group. When you send a new message to the group, you'll select the Contact Group instead of each address individually.

Creating a Contact Group

Use these steps to create a new Contact Group.

1. Open the Contact Group form by using the New Contact Group button or by pressing Ctrl+Shift+L.

2. Type a name for your Contact Group in the Name field.

3. Click the Add Members button and choose From Outlook Contacts (see Figure 8.10).

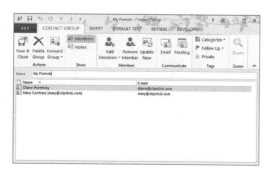

FIGURE 8.10

Create a new Contact Group.

4. Double-click each address that you want to include in the group, or select the contacts and click the Members button to add the names to the Members field.

5. Click OK when you are finished selecting names to return to the contact group.

6. To add addresses of people who are not in your contacts folder, go to Add Members and select New Email Contact and enter the name and email address.

If you have a list of addresses in Excel or Notepad, you can add your contact group in one step. The list needs to be comma or semicolon separated or have one address per row.

1. Copy the list of email addresses.

2. Click the Add Members button and choose From Outlook Contacts.

3. At the bottom of the dialog box, paste the list in the Members field and press OK.

4. If you want to add notes about this contact group, click the Notes button.

5. Save and close the group when you are finished.

You can send email to the group or create a meeting invitation by clicking the Email or Meeting buttons on the contact group form, but it's usually easier to select or type the group address in the To, CC, or BCC field of an email or meeting request.

After addressing a message with the contact group, you can click the plus sign beside the group name to expand the list and see the individual names.

If you need to remove a member from the Contact Group, select the name or address and click the Remove Member button on the ribbon.

Don't click the large X icon labeled Delete Group unless you want to delete the entire group. Surprisingly, this happens a lot. If you make this mistake, find the group in the Deleted Items folder and drag it back to the Contacts folder.

 NOTE Select more than one name at a time by holding down the Shift or Ctrl key as you select names. You can double-click names to add them to the Members field.

When you update a contact with a new email address, any groups the contact belongs to are not automatically updated. You'll need to click the Update Now button to update the contact group. Repeat this for every contact group the contact belongs to (see Figure 8.11).

Click Update Now to update the Contact Group

FIGURE 8.11

Choose the Update Now button to update the Contact Group with new addresses.

Using Categories to Send Group Mail

Because member addresses are not automatically updated when their contact is updated, it's often better to send group mail using Categories. Assign categories to the group members, and then select them using the Category arrangement.

You can send an email to a group of contacts using categories. Following are the steps.

1. Assign a category to each contact who belongs to the group.

2. Switch to the View tab, click Change view, and then click List.

3. In the Arrangement section, select Categories.

4. Click the category group name (see Figure 8.12).

5. Switch to the Home tab, and in the Communicate section, click the Email button.

A new message addressed to every contact in the category opens.

The benefits of using this method are that the group is dynamic, the addresses are always current, and deleting a member is as easy as removing the category from the contact. This is good for mailing lists where the contact group membership changes frequently. You can also use the list in a mail merge.

The benefits of using a Contact Group is that it's easier to put the group in the CC or BCC field, and you can begin the message from any folder or easily add the group to a reply. If your group membership is stable and rarely needs editing, a contact group works well.

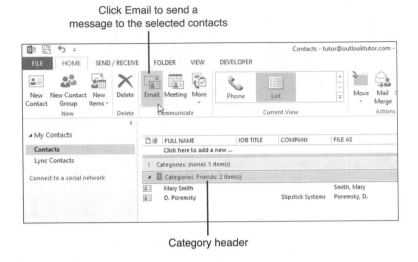

FIGURE 8.12

Select the Category header, and then click the Email button to send a new message to the contacts in that category.

Auto-Complete List

When you start typing a name or address into the To field, Outlook offers suggestions. This is called the auto-complete list. When a name is not yet on the Auto-Complete list, Outlook attempts to resolve the name against one in your address book, underlining it with a red squiggle or straight black line.

Using the Auto-Complete List

Every time you send a new message or reply, the address is added to the Auto-Complete list. The Auto-Complete list is limited to the last 1,000 addresses you sent email to. Although this is enough for most users, Outlook removes the older, least used addresses from the list when the list hits 1,000 addresses. When you open a new message, you can address it by typing the first couple of letters into the address field and selecting the address from the Auto-Complete list.

Sometimes the Auto-Complete list contains old addresses that are no longer used or mistyped addresses. You can delete these when they come up, either by selecting them with the arrow keys and pressing the Delete key or using the mouse to click the x on the right (see Figure 8.13).

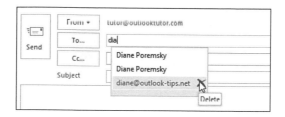

FIGURE 8.13

Select addresses in the auto-complete list to address new email or delete them by clicking on the x.

If you don't want to use auto-complete, you can disable it in File tab, Options, Mail. Look in the Send messages section for "Use Auto-Complete list to suggest names when typing in the To, CC, and BCC lines." If your auto-complete list has a large number of "bad" names, you can empty the list from this dialog box as well (see Figure 8.14).

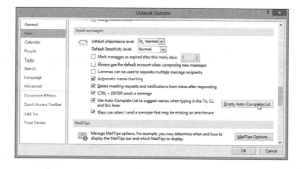

FIGURE 8.14

Empty your auto-complete list or disable it in the Outlook Options dialog box.

Auto-Resolution

When you type a name in the To or CC field and Outlook doesn't find a match on the auto-complete list, it resolves it against the contacts in your address book. When it finds multiple names, it underlines the name with a red squiggle. Right-click the name and select the address you want to use. After you've resolved the name once, you'll be offered this name the next time you type that name (see Figure 8.15).

If auto-resolution offers you the wrong addresses, type a space or semicolon after the name, and Outlook underlines the name in red, allowing you to pick a different name from the address book.

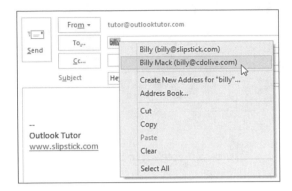

FIGURE 8.15

Outlook resolves names to the address book if they aren't on the auto-complete list.

NOTE   You don't need to type a contact's full name for Outlook to resolve it; you only need the first few letters of the first or last name and Outlook will find matches in the address book.

Using the Contact Data

After you enter the contact information and save it, you don't have to open the contact to use the information it contains. You can use commands on the Contact folder's Home tab or by right-clicking on the contact and selecting commands from the context menu to interact with the contact data. You can send messages, make calls, or schedule meetings with the selected contact.

Some of the menu items work only when one contact is selected, whereas other commands, including Email and Meeting buttons, open a message or meeting request addressed to all the selected contacts.

When the contact is open, you can view the contact's web page or view its address on a map at Bing.com.

From the Home tab, you can automatically use the contact data for the following actions:

- Send an email message to the contact.

- Create a meeting request addressed to the contact.

- Assign Tasks to the contact.

- Call the contact using one of the phone numbers entered on the contact form.

- Create a new contact using the company information from the selected contact.

- Share your contacts with co-workers (this requires Exchange Server).

- Open a co-worker's contacts folder that was shared with you (requires Exchange Server).

Using the Address Book

When you click the To or CC button when addressing a message, you are using the Address Book. The Address Book doesn't contain its own list of addresses; it displays all your contacts that contain a valid electronic address, which can be either an email address or a fax number.

Open the Address Book by clicking the Address book button on the Home tab. You can also open it using the keyboard shortcut Ctrl+Shift+B.

Click on Tools, and then Options menu to access Address book options. In this dialog box, you'll choose the order addresses are resolved in when you type partial names. You can also choose which address list is shown first when you click the To button (see Figure 8.16).

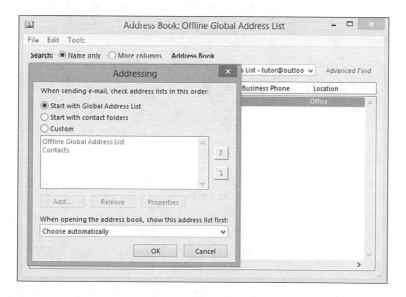

FIGURE 8.16

Configure the order Outlook searches address books and which address list is shown first in the Addressing dialog box.

Your choices are the following:

- **Start with Global Address List (Exchange Server accounts)**—If you send more email to co-workers than contacts, you'll want to check names against the Exchange Server Global Address List (GAL) first.

- **Start with contact folders**—When most of the email is sent to your contacts, you'll want the contact folders listed first.

- **Custom**—You choose the order Outlook uses. Select the address list and use the arrow button to change the order.

This dialog box is also where you choose which address book is shown first when you click the To button or open the Address book.

Changing Contact Options

Outlook 2013 limits the options you can configure. The most important options for most users are the default Full Name and File As order. These settings affect how you enter contact names and how they are filed (see Figure 8.17).

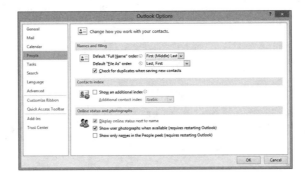

FIGURE 8.17

Click on Options and then People to open the Outlook Options dialog box to change options such as Full Name and File as Order.

These settings affect how addresses are sorted in the Address Book and Contacts folder. To change these options, click File, click Options, and then click People to open.

Choose from the following options for the Full Name and File As Order:

- **Default "Full Name" Order**—Choices include First (Middle) Last; Last First; First Last1 Last2. When you use either of the First Last formats, you can type the last name first if you use a comma separator. When you set it for Last First you do not need to use a comma between the last and first names.

- **Default "File As" Order**—Choices are Last, First; First Last; Company, Last, First (Company) and Company (Last, First).

- **Check for Duplicates When Saving New Contacts**—This checks the first and last name fields for matches. If Outlook finds an exact match, you'll be given the chance to merge the contacts or create a new one (see Figure 8.18).

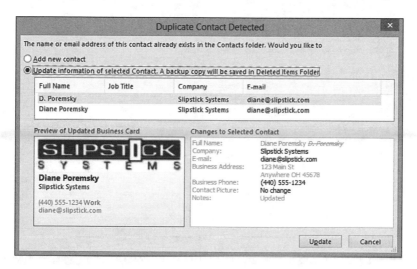

FIGURE 8.18

Outlook will warn you if a contact with the same name already exists. Compare the records and choose which record you want to keep.

- **Show an Additional Index**—This adds another index, in one of several languages, to the People and Card view. The index can also be enabled or disabled by clicking the globe icon at the bottom of the Index column.

- **Display Online Status Next to the Name**—When Lync or Skype is installed, the status of your contacts is shown beside their name in the Reading pane and open messages.

- **Show User Photographs When Available (requires restarting Outlook)**— When a contact includes a photo, it's displayed in the Reading pane or open message, to the left of the subject field.

- **Show only names in the People Peek (requires restarting Outlook)**.

One additional dialog affects your contacts and address book—the Address Book dialog in File, Account Settings, Address Book tab. Double-click Microsoft Outlook Address Book to open the options dialog and change how your contacts display in the address book. You can show contacts in First Last order or use the File As format as set on each contact (see Figure 8.19).

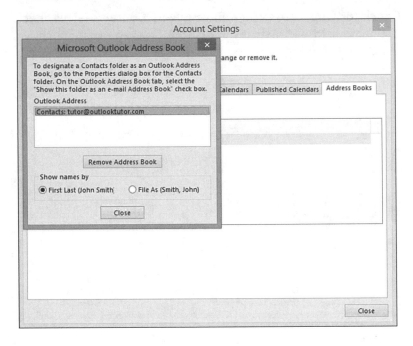

FIGURE 8.19

Use the Microsoft Outlook Address Book dialog box to change the sort order in the address book.

If there are contact folders you don't want to see when you click the To button, you can remove them from this dialog. Or you can right-click the Contact folder you don't want to use as an address book and choose Properties, click the Outlook Address Book tab, and then deselect the option Show This Folder as an E-mail Address Book. If you change your mind and want to use the Contact folder as an address book, re-select it on the Outlook Address Book tab.

Searching for Contacts

When you have hundreds of Contacts, it's usually easier to search for a contact than it is to look through the folder. There are two ways to search for contacts: using the Search People field at the end of the Home tab or using Search Contacts (press Ctrl+E) in the Contacts folder.

When you use Search People, the search results contain matches for the first, middle, or last names or company name. Search Contacts searches by more fields and you can use criteria to limit the search results.

When you know part of the contact's name but aren't sure of the spelling, use initials or the first letters contained in their name. For example, in my Contacts list, entering "j b" or "j bar" will return the contacts for Jessie Bartee, Jim Barman, and Raja Abartish.

Using the People Pane

You can view mail, meetings, and attachments sent by the contact on the People pane at the bottom of messages or contacts (see Figure 8.20). The People pane displays only mail, meetings, or attachments from the person, not messages you sent to them or other Outlook items. You can open, reply, or forward messages from the People pane, but you can't delete items.

FIGURE 8.20

Email, meetings, and attachments from the selected person are listed in the People pane.

If you have a social networking account, such as LinkedIn or Facebook, you can sign in to your account and see updates and the profile picture of contacts or people who send you email.

Using Views

When you have a large number of contacts, using views to limit the contacts that are visible is often necessary to find and manage your contacts. Among the things you can use filtered views for are

- Selecting contacts for mail merge
- Changing some contact fields
- Limiting the display to contacts that meet specific conditions
- Controlling the layout for printed lists

The default views include

- **People**—This is a new view that displays linked contacts.
- **Business Card**—Displays the business card.
- **Card**—A card layout that displays basic contact data, including all addresses and phone numbers.
- **Phone**—A list view that includes the phone number fields. Use with the Arrangements to change how this view is grouped.
- **List**—Use the Arrangements to change how this view is grouped.

List views include these default arrangements:

- **By Company**—Groups contacts by company.
- **By Category**—Groups contacts by category.
- **By Location**—Groups contacts by country as selected in the Address field. Click the Business, Home, or Other button to see the Country/Region selector.

Card, Phone, and List views have in-cell editing enabled, enabling you to make changes to visible fields without opening the contact for editing. In most cases, when you group contacts by a field, you can drag contacts to other groups to change that field for the contact. This is helpful when you need to change a field used by many contacts, such as when a company name changes or when you're categorizing contacts.

The default views are customizable, or you can create custom views. To change the current view, go to the View tab and click the View settings button. Select Change View, Manage Views to create new views. You can apply the current view to other Contacts folders from the Change View button.

 NOTE You can use custom views to control the fields that are included in a printout. Create a view that has all the fields you want included in a printed list, select File, Print, and choose the table style printout. The printout will include only the fields shown on the screen.

Edit Contact Data Using Views

Making changes to multiple records can seem like a daunting task, but depending on the field that must be changed, Outlook can make the changes for you. This method works with most editable fields.

Create a group by view for the field that needs to be changed, and drag the contacts that need to be changed to the other group.

Changing the Company Name Field

When a company changes its name, you need to update the records to reflect the new name (see Figure 8.21). Follow these steps:

1. Switch to the View tab.

2. Expand the Change View button and select List.

3. In the Arrangement section, select Company.

4. If the list is not grouped by company, click Reset or right-click the Company field and choose Group by this field.

5. Edit one contact so the company name field is correct.

6. Select the group with the old company name and drag to the group with the new company name.

When you are finished changing the company name, click the Reset View button to restore the default view.

FIGURE 8.21

Use Group By views to change fields without typing. Drag contacts between groups to change the value of the field.

The People Peek

The People Peek is a new Outlook feature that works like this: when you hover over the word People, a window pops up that lists your Favorite contacts. If you use Lync, your favorite Lync contacts will be listed here as well.

To add a contact to the People Peek, right-click a name or email address in a message or right-click a photo in the People Pane and choose Add to Favorites (see Figure 8.22).

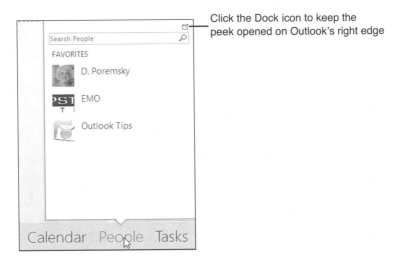

Click the Dock icon to keep the peek opened on Outlook's right edge

FIGURE 8.22

Add your favorite people to the People Peek.

Hover over the entries on the Favorites list to view the contact card and start an email, instant message, or phone call.

To remove a contact from the Favorites list, right-click the contact and choose Remove from Favorites.

Dock the people peek on the right edge of Outlook by clicking the dock icon in the open peek.

NOTE When a peek is docked, it is docked in all folders of the current item type. For example, if you dock the peek to a mail folder, it will be docked in all mail folders but not in the Contact folder.

THE ABSOLUTE MINIMUM

In this chapter you learned

- How to use the new People Hub and contact cards. You learned how to create and edit contacts using either contact cards or the full contact form.

- How to configure your contacts options and address book settings.

- How to use the people pane, instant search, and views to find and view your contacts and activities.

- To use the People Peek for your frequently used contacts.

USING TASKS AND TO-DO'S

Tasks and to-do's help you organize and prioritize your work. With reminders set, you won't forget what is on your list. Both Tasks and To-Do's display in the Task peek, so you always know what needs your attention.

What is the difference between a task and a to-do? Tasks are, well, tasks. They are created using a Task form and saved in a Tasks folder. To-Do's are messages that are flagged for follow up. Both Tasks and To-Do's are shown in the To-Do List and in the Task Peek.

Although tasks have a lot in common with appointments, they serve a different purpose. Typically, you'll use tasks to track events you need to get done but don't need to do at a specific time, such as 2 p.m. Tasks can be open-ended with no start or due date, or you can set start and due dates.

Creating Tasks

Some events and to-do's can be entered as either calendar or task items, but for the most part, you'll want to create tasks for items that don't have a set time to be completed. You can set a due date or leave the task open-ended.

To open a blank task form from anywhere in Outlook, select New Items, Task or press the keyboard shortcut of Ctrl+Shift+K.

 NOTE Windows 7 and 8 have a cool time saving feature called Jump List, where shortcuts to files are added to the menu that is shown when you right click on a program icon on the task bar. Outlook added shortcuts for new items to the Jump List for you. The Jump List makes it easy to create new tasks when you are working in other programs. Simply right-click the Outlook icon on the taskbar and choose New Task.

You only need to complete the Subject field for your task and save it. But in most cases you'll also want to include a Due Date, and you might want to include a Start Date and Reminder Time, or assign Categories. As you work on the task, you can update the Status and % Complete fields.

How to Create a Task

Now that you know a little about Tasks, you can create a task of your own.

1. From any folder in Outlook, select New Items, Task or press Ctrl+Shift+K.

2. Enter a subject for your task (see Figure 9.1).

3. Using the Tab key, navigate to the Start Date field and type or select a start date.

4. In the Due Date field, type or select a due date.

5. Select a Priority, if desired.

6. Select the Reminder field and choose a date and time. The default reminder date is the due date. The default reminder time is set in Task Options (see Configuring Task Options later in this chapter). You can choose a different reminder time if desired.

 NOTE Tasks use the default reminder sound set in File, Options, Tasks, but you can assign a different reminder sound to any task by clicking the Sound icon to the right of the reminder time and selecting a new sound.

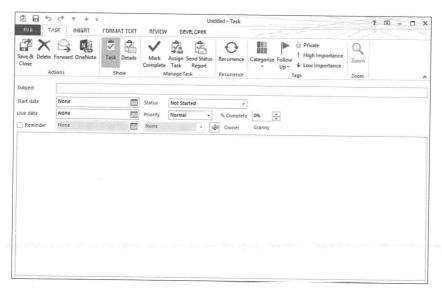

FIGURE 9.1

The task form needs only a few fields completed: Subject, Start Date, Due Date, and Reminder time. As you complete the task, you change the % Complete and Status fields.

It's much easier to type the dates in the date and time fields than to use the date and time pickers when you know the shortcuts to use. In addition to the usual short date format of 12/25 or 12/25/10, you can use natural language phrases and other shortcuts. Among the available shortcuts are 1d (for 1 day), 2w (for 2 weeks), 10 or 10a for 10 a.m., and 235 or 235p for 2:35 p.m. The date fields accept natural language words, which enable you to type such phrases as **next christmas**, **tomorrow**, and **week from friday** and have Outlook enter the correct date in the field. These fields are not case sensitive and you can use lowercase letters for holiday and day names, as I used in my examples.

 NOTE You can use the following abbreviations for dates: d for day, w for week, mo for month, and y for year. Times can be entered using numbers only; a or p is not required for times entered during working hours. To subtract from a date, use **before**, as in **2 days before**.

Outlook can set the due date based on the start date. For example, to create a task that starts next Friday and is due 2 days later, enter **next friday** in the Start field, and then press Tab to go to the Due Date field and enter **2d**.

NOTE Outlook can calculate the start date of a task from the due date. For example, if you want to create a task due in 42 days and it needs to be started 5 days before it's due, you'd tab to the Due Date field and enter **42d**, and then use Shift+Tab to return to the Start field. Type **5 days before** in the Start Date field and tab out. Outlook correctly calculates the dates in each field.

More Ways to Create Tasks

In addition to creating tasks "from scratch" with a new task form, you can drag or copy email messages to the Task folder, or type into the Type a New Task field at the top of the Tasks or To-Do List folders, or in the Task Peek. You can also flag email messages to make To-Do's.

If you want to create an actual task from an email message, rather than flagging it as a to-do, drag the message to Tasks in the Folder bar at the bottom of the Outlook window. This opens a new task form with the Task subject filled in, and the message text in the task's body. Complete the other task fields as needed and save the task.

The Move, Move to Folder, or Copy to folder command also creates a task when you select the Task folder as the destination. The Move command is on the Home tab. You can also use the Move command when you select a message in a list and right-click to display the context menu.

TIP I generally recommend using Copy to Folder; using Move to Folder inserts the email message as an attachment and deletes it from your Inbox.

Using the Type a New Task Row

At the top of the Task list in some views is an empty row with the words "Click here to add a new Task". The Task Peek has a similar row. This is the Type a New Task row and it is great for quickly adding simple tasks to your task list (see Figure 9.2). After you type in the Task Subject, the due date and reminder time are set on the task, based on your Quick Click flag options. You can right-click the task and choose a different flag to change the due date and reminder.

NOTE Calendar, Contacts, and Notes can also have a row at the top of the list views. If you are using a List view and don't see it, you need to select Allow in-cell editing and Show "new item" Row in the Other Settings dialog. Switch to the View tab, click View Settings, then click the Other Settings button. In-cell editing is near the top of the dialog.

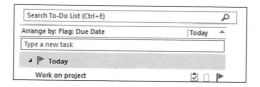

FIGURE 9.2

Create a new task using the Type a New Task Row in the To-Do List folder or Task Peek.

Using the Type a New Task row to create a quick task is simple. The task saved automatically when you press Enter or click somewhere on the screen.

1. Click in the Type a New Task field.

2. Type the subject for your task and tab out of the field.

3. The task uses the Quick Click flag due date and reminder time. Right-click the flag field and select a different flag to change the due date and reminder time.

When you need to fill in more fields in the task, double-click in the Type a New Task field to open a new task form. When you open a new task using this method, the Due Date field is set to the Quick Click default.

When the Reading pane is turned off, the New Item row is identified as Click Here to Add a New Task. You can complete any or all of the fields shown in the view.

 NOTE If you don't want the New Item row in your Tasks folder, you can turn it off in View Settings. Switch to the View tab and choose View Settings. Click Other Settings and remove the check from the Show 'new item' Row option.

 NOTE The Quick Click Flag is the gray flag that is visible when you move your mouse over a message and at the far right in some views. When you click on the Flag it sets a Follow up flag due Today. If you want to change the default to another date, right click on the flag and choose Set Quick Click. You can choose from Today, Tomorrow, This Week, Next Week, No Date, or Custom. This week and Next Week set the due date to your last work day of the week, which for many people is Friday.

Completing Tasks

As you work on the task, you can change the % Complete field to reflect how much work you've done toward completing the task. Although it's not necessary when working on your tasks, if you're working on a shared task or you are assigned a task by someone else, updating the % Complete field helps others gauge how much you have left to do. The list contains 25, 50, 95, and 100, or you can type any whole number into the field.

You can also set a status for the task, choosing from the following:

- Not Started

- In Progress

- Completed

- Waiting on Someone Else

- Deferred

When the % Complete field is changed, and the Status field is on the default of Not Started, the Status updates to In Progress or Completed. Status selections are unchanged when another status is selected and the % Complete field is updated to anything except 100% Complete, at which time the status changes to Completed.

When the task is complete, you can mark it complete using one of several methods. You can do this from the reminder window, from an open task, or in the Tasks folders:

- To mark the task complete in the reminders window, do not click the Dismiss button; this removes only the reminder. Instead, right-click the task and choose Mark Complete (see Figure 9.3).

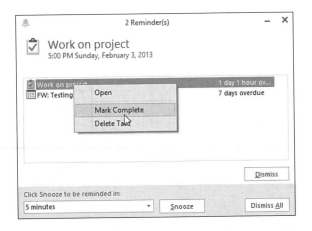

FIGURE 9.3

Right-click a Task Reminder and select Mark Complete.

- On opened tasks, click the Mark Complete button on the ribbon or set % Complete to 100.

- In the Tasks folder or To-Do bar, you can click the Flag, click in the Complete column (if shown in the view), click the Mark Complete button, or right-click the task and choose Mark Complete.

Entering Task Details

The Details page (Figure 9.4) contains fields useful for billing purposes: hours worked, mileage, and billing information. You'll need to fill in these fields yourself; only the Completed date is set for you. The Total Work and Actual Work fields use the Work Hours setting in Options, Tasks to calculate the days worked. For example, if you have the work hours set to the default of 8 hours per day and 40 hours per week, when you enter 12 hours in the work field, Outlook converts it to 1.5 days.

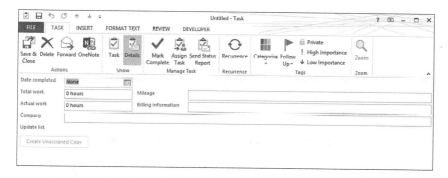

FIGURE 9.4

Use the Details page to record or review hours worked and other billing information.

The Create Unassigned Copy button is available only when you send a task request, use it to create an unassigned copy of the task on your task list.

Recurring Tasks

When you need to repeat a task over several days or weeks, you can create a recurring task and Outlook generates the next task in the series when you mark the task complete.

NOTE When you have recurring tasks with reminders, do not dismiss the reminder in the Reminder window, because this will turn the reminder off for future tasks in the series. Snooze it instead or mark the task complete to remove it from the Reminder window.

Create a Recurring Task

1. From an open task form, click the Recurrence button on the Home ribbon or press Ctrl+G to open the Task Recurrence dialog (Figure 9.5).

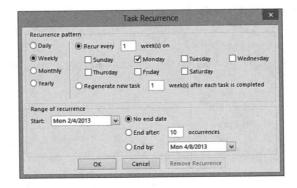

FIGURE 9.5

Use the Task Recurrence dialog box to create recurring tasks. Recurring tasks must fit a pattern; you cannot use this dialog to create tasks that don't fit a pattern.

2. Select the desired recurrence pattern. Choices are Daily, Weekly, Monthly, or Yearly.

3. Select the frequency. When you select the Recur Every option, the next task is generated as soon as you mark the previous task complete. With Regenerate New Task After Each Task Is Completed, the next task is not generated until the period of time passed.

4. Select a start date for the recurrence range and an end date. It's highly recommended that you always set an end date. For long-running tasks, I recommend ending recurrences at the end of each year and re-creating the task at the beginning of each new year.

5. Save and close the task when you're finished.

6. When the task is completed, mark it complete to generate the next occurrence.

Using Task Requests

You can assign new or existing tasks to another Outlook user. They'll receive the task by email and can accept or decline the assignment.

When status updates are enabled, each time the recipient updates the status of the task, updates are sent back to you, and the copy of the task in your Tasks folder is updated.

 NOTE   If either you or the recipient aren't using Exchange Server, many times the task updates are sent as plain-text messages, not rich text, and your copy of the task isn't updated automatically. When this happens, you'll receive a message containing the task fields and you have to update the task status yourself.

Creating a Task Request

When you are ready to assign a task to someone else, you'll follow these simple steps:

1. On the ribbon, to open a new Task Request (see Figure 9.6), click the New Items button, and then click the Task Request button or press Ctrl+Alt+Shift+U. You can also click the Assign Task button on an open task to convert the task to a Task Request. If you change your mind, click the Cancel Assignment to convert the task request to a regular task..

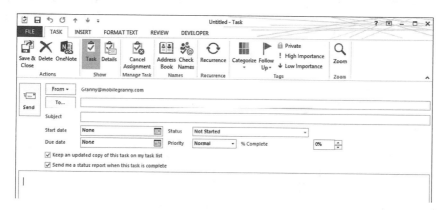

FIGURE 9.6

Create a task request to assign tasks to other people.

2. Enter the recipient's name in the To field. Although you could send the task to several people, you will not receive updates when the task request is sent to more than one person.

3. Enter the subject, start and end date, and priority.

4. Select Keep an Updated Copy of This Task on My Task List if you want the task added to your task list. If this is selected, updates the recipient makes will be reflected on your copy.

5. Select Send Me a Status Report When This Task Is Complete. With this enabled, you'll be notified by email when the task is completed.

6. To create an unassigned copy of the task in your Task list, click the Details button, and then click Create Unassigned Copy.

Click the Send button when you're finished creating the task.

After receiving the task, the recipient can either Accept or Decline it by clicking the appropriate button in the Reading pane or opened task. If the task is declined, you can take ownership of the task again by clicking the Return to Task List button.

Accepting a Task Request

When someone sends you a task request, you need to accept or decline it.

1. When a task request arrives in your Inbox, you can accept or decline it either by clicking buttons in the Reading pane or on an opened message (see Figure 9.7).

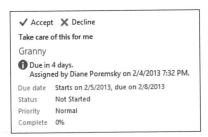

FIGURE 9.7

Click the Accept or Decline button in the Reading pane when you receive a task assignment.

2. If you accept the task, a dialog box displays this message: "This task will be accepted and moved into the Tasks folder. Do you want to edit the response before sending it?"

3. When you decline the task, a dialog comes up with this message: "This task will be declined and moved into the Deleted Items folder. Do you want to edit the response before sending it?"

4. Choose Edit the Response Before Sending if you want to add a message to the response before sending. An email message form will open for you to type a note.

5. Send the Response Now will send the acceptance or decline immediately.

After you accept the task, it's added to your task list; when you decline a task, it's moved to your Deleted folder.

Viewing Tasks

There are several ways you can view your tasks:

- In the Tasks folder
- In the Task Peek (see Figure 9.8)

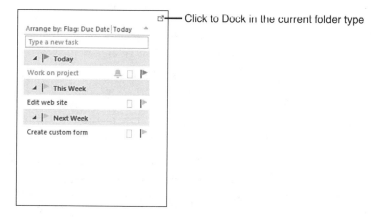

FIGURE 9.8

Hover over the word Tasks to display the Tasks Peek. Click the Dock icon to pin it open.

- Using the Daily Task List in the Calendar (see Figure 9.9)
- On the Outlook Today page

Daily Task List button

Right click to change

Minimize or Normal (open) toggle

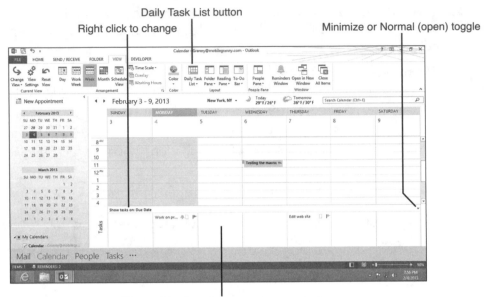

Click and begin typing to create a new task

FIGURE 9.9

Current tasks are shown under the date when you view your calendar in the day or week view.

The task list in the Task Peek displays tasks from all Tasks folders in your profile and all flagged messages, contacts, and other Outlook items.

When the peek is docked, you can resize the task section by pulling the separator up or down.

You can display your tasks in the Daily Tasks List at the bottom of the day or week calendars. The Daily Tasks List is not available in the monthly view.

If the task list is not visible on the day or week calendars, switch to the View tab and expand the Daily Task List button; then select Normal. Click the icon on the right side of the Daily Task list to minimize the list, and click it again to restore it.

Although the task list does not say Type Here, you can create new tasks by typing in the daily task list.

The task list supports two views: Show Tasks by Start Date or Show Tasks by Due Date. You can hide Completed tasks in either view. Right-click the bar separating the task list from the calendar to change the order or show/hide completed tasks. The view can also be changed from the View tab by clicking Daily Tasks List, and then clicking Arrange By.

The Outlook Today screen lists the Tasks that are due today or overdue. You can mark Tasks complete from the Outlook Today screen or open a Task by double clicking on a task in the list. This screen shows only the Tasks in your default mailbox or .pst file. The To-Do List shows the tasks in all folders.

Customizing the Task or To-Do List View

If you don't like the predefined views in the Tasks folder or To-Do list, you can customize the views or create a new view.

You can change the views from the View ribbon by following these steps:

1. Select a different view from the Change View button.

2. Choose View Settings to open the customize view dialog. Many of the options are on the ribbon.

3. Click the Reset button to reset the view to the default.

4. To view the first 1 to 3 lines of a task's Notes field, expand Message Preview and select Off, 1, 2, or 3 lines.

5. Change how the tasks group by selecting a different arrangement. The available arrangements vary based on the selected view and may include Categories, Start Date, Due Date, Folder, Type, or Importance.

6. Click the Reverse Sort button to change the sort order.

7. Add additional columns (Task fields) to the view.

8. Click Expand/Collapse to expand or collapse the groups in the view.

Customizing the Task Peek View

Unlike other folders, the Tasks Peek has only one view. You can customize the view, but you can't create additional views. To customize it, follow these steps:

1. Click Arrange By at the top of the Task list (see Figure 9.10).

2. Select a new arrangement from the context menu: Categories, Start Date, Due Date, Folder, Type, or Importance.

3. Select Show in Groups to toggle grouping off and on. When grouping is enabled, the Task list is grouped by the Arrange By field.

4. Customize or reset the view by selecting View Settings.

5. Right-click Type a New Task to view a second context menu containing the same view options.

FIGURE 9.10

Click Arrange By: and select a different arrangement for the Task Peek.

 NOTE The Tasks Peek also contains email messages that are flagged for follow up.

Configuring Task Options

You can configure limited options for Tasks. Following are the steps.

1. Click the File tab, then click Options.

2. Select Tasks to open the Task Options dialog box (see Figure 9.11).

3. Configure the task options, and when you are finished, click OK to return to Outlook.

The task options that users can configure include the following:

- **Set Reminders on Tasks with Due Dates**—With this enabled, every task with a due date will have a reminder set, using the default reminder time.

- **Default Reminder Time**—Choose the time of day you want to use for default reminders on tasks and to-do's that are due "tomorrow" or later in the week. Tasks and to-do's created and due today have a reminder time 1 hour before the end of the workday, as set in Calendar Options.

- **Keep My Task Updated with Copies of Tasks I Assign to Other People**— With this enabled, you'll receive updates for tasks you assign to others.

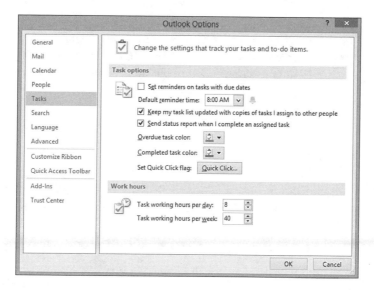

FIGURE 9.11

Use the Task Options dialog box to choose an automatic formatting color of overdue and completed tasks, whether to use reminders on tasks with due dates, and how you want to handle assigned tasks.

- **Send Status Report When I Complete an Assigned Task**—When someone else assigns a task to you, a status update is sent to the originator.

- **Overdue Task Color**—This sets the color of the subject in list views. The default color is red, and you can choose another color from the menu, if desired.

- **Completed Task Color**—This option sets the color of completed tasks used in list views. The default color is gray.

- **Set Quick Click Flag**—Set the default due date when you click in the flag column for email or create a task using the Type a New Task row. The default is Today.

Work house is the final setting in Task options. You'll use this to set the length of your working day. This setting is used to calculate how many working days you work on a task. This should be set to the average length of your workday and workweek.

In addition to setting a default reminder time in File, Options, you can choose a specific date and time for your reminder on the task form. These fields accept natural language entries.

NOTE   When you create a new task by typing in the Type a New Task field in a view, the task is automatically flagged using the Quick Click flag. If the Quick Click flag is Today, the reminder is automatically set for 1 hour before the end of your working day. When the Quick Click flag is tomorrow or later, the task uses the default reminder time set in options.

Creating To-Dos

A To-Do is a flagged message or contact. It acts like a task, supports reminders, and displays with your tasks in the To-do List, but the item you flagged remains in its own folder.

Setting a flag on a message is easy: move your mouse over the message in the message list then click on the Quick Flag icon when it comes into view to use the default flag or right click on the Quick Flag icon to choose a different flag (Figure 9.12).

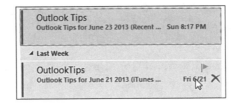

FIGURE 9.12

Move your mouse over a message to display the Quick Flag icon. Click or right-click on it to set a flag.

You can use the Follow Up button on the ribbon, which is located above the reading pane and also in opened messages and contacts. You can click on the Follow Up button and choose one of the preset flags (see Figure 9.13). You'll flag a contact in the same manner—either by selecting the contact and clicking the Follow Up button on the toolbar, or by right clicking on the contact and choosing the Follow Up menu.

The Flag to Follow Up choices are:

- **Today**—Due at the end of the day. When the default reminder is used, the reminder is set for 1 hour before the end of the workday, as set in Calendar Options (click File, then Options, and select Calendar).

- **Tomorrow**—Due tomorrow, uses the default Task reminder time.

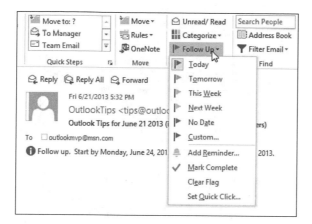

FIGURE 9.13

Select a Follow Up flag to create a To-Do for a message or contact. The start and due date as well as the Flag to phrase are added to the Infobar under message header.

- **This Week**—Due at the end of the work week; uses the Work week setting in Calendar Options and the default Task reminder time.

- **Next Week**—Due at the end of the next work week.

- **No Date**—Sets a flag but without a due date or reminder.

- **Custom**—Choose your own due date and change the Flag to phrase. Uses the default Task reminder time.

- **Add Reminder**—Use to Add or edit a reminder to items currently flagged.

In addition, you'll have these options available on most of the Follow Up menus:

- **Mark Complete**—Mark To-do complete after you finish the task if you want to keep it in the To-do List.

- **Clear**—Clears the flag and removes the item from the To-Do List.

- Add a flag to messages and contacts to create To-Do's. Flagged items are shown in the To-Do List with your tasks.

 CAUTION Outlook.com and IMAP accounts do not support all of the Follow up options. You are limited to setting a flag and clearing it. You can't customize the flags or choose a due date.

You can change the phrase "Follow Up" which displays in the Infobar under the To field in a received message or above the contact's name in a contact. Either choose from one of the predefined Flag to phrases or type over Follow Up to add your own text. You can type up to 255 characters in the Flag to field. (See Figure 9.14)

FIGURE 9.14

Type your own Flag to phrase in the Custom Flag dialog box.

When you no longer need the flag, you can either clear the flag or mark it complete using the same steps: click on the Follow Up button and choose Mark Complete or Clear. Choosing Mark Complete keeps the item in the To-Do List for future reference, while Clear removes the flag and removes the item from the To-Do List.

 NOTE Do not delete the item from the To-do List or you'll delete it from Outlook.

Sending tasks to and linking with OneNote

Office 2013 owners can send email, tasks, and appointments to OneNote and create Outlook tasks in OneNote. When Outlook Tasks are linked to OneNote pages, you can mark the task complete in either Outlook or OneNote and it will be marked complete in the other application. Notes added in OneNote won't sync to the Outlook Task but you can open the task from OneNote and the OneNote page from the task.

Why would you want to use OneNote for task notes instead of adding notes to the task body? The most obvious reason is because you already use OneNote for note taking and want to keep all of your notes together. If you aren't using OneNote, you need to try it: you can store your notebooks in SkyDrive and access them on your smartphone, tablet, or another computer.

To link a task to a OneNote page, follow these steps:

1. Open or select the Task.

2. Click the OneNote button on the ribbon. In an open task, it's on the Task tab (Figure 9.15); when you select a task, it's on the Home tab.

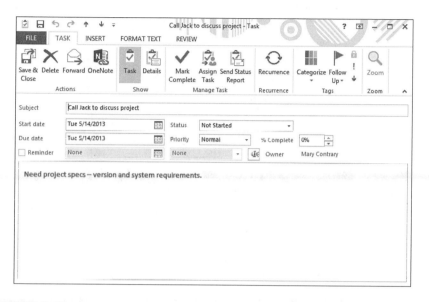

FIGURE 9.15

Click the OneNote button to copy the task's subject to a OneNote page.

3. If this is the first time you've linked an Outlook item to OneNote, the Select Location in OneNote dialog box opens for you to select the location where you want the task (see Figure 9.16).

4. You can set the selected location as your default location by checking Always send task notes to the selected location. If you change your mind later, you can change it in OneNote's Options.

5. The Task's subject is used as the OneNote page title and flagged with the due date.

After the OneNote page is created, clicking the OneNote button in Outlook will open the page in OneNote. You can open the Outlook task from OneNote by right-clicking on the flag and choosing Open Task in Outlook from the menu. You can also change the due date, mark the task complete, remove the tag, or delete the task from Outlook. Changing the due date or marking it complete will update the Task in Outlook. Of course, if you choose Delete Outlook Task, it will be deleted from Outlook (Figure 9.17).

FIGURE 9.16

Select the OneNote location where you want the task to go.

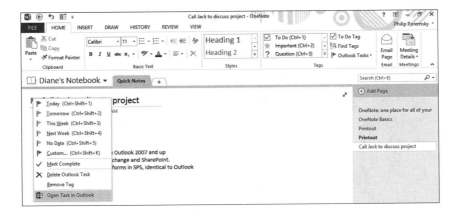

FIGURE 9.17

Use the right-click menu to change the due date, mark it complete, delete the task, or open the task in Outlook.

NOTE If you remove the tag, you won't be able to open the Outlook task from OneNote but the Outlook task will open the OneNote page.

The steps to create an Outlook Task from OneNote are just as easy:

1. Click in front of the line you want to use as the task subject

2. Click Outlook Tasks button and select a Flag.

3. A task is created in Outlook, with the line as the subject. The line is added to the task body as text and a copy of the OneNote page is attached (Figure 9.18).

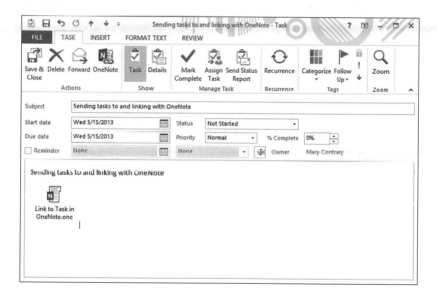

FIGURE 9.18

A task created in OneNote includes a copy of the OneNote page.

THE ABSOLUTE MINIMUM

Here are the key points to remember from this chapter.

- You can create a task by typing in the new item row at the top of the view, by dragging email messages to the Task button, or you can create a to-do by flagging a message.

- Add a flag to messages and contacts to create To-Do's. Flagged items are shown in the To-Do List with your tasks.

- View your tasks in the Tasks Peek, in the task list at the bottom of the calendar, or in the Task or To-Do List folder.

- Assign tasks to co-workers and receive status updates.

- When you link Outlook Tasks to OneNote and store the notebook in SkyDrive, you'll be able to read and edit the task from your smartphone, tablet, or another computer. If you don't have OneNote installed you can use the OneNote application in SkyDrive.

10

SOCIAL CONNECTOR

Outlook's Social Connector does a little of everything. It displays a person's recent activities, including email, appointments, and attachments, in a pane at the bottom of an email message or contact. If you have a Facebook or LinkedIn account and have Outlook signed into the accounts, you'll also see updates the person posts to these social networks.

Meet the Social Connector

When you first open Outlook, the Social Connector is empty, displaying only email to or from the sender or recipients of the selected email messages. If you look at a contact, the Social Connector shows messages sent or received by the contact or meetings with the contact. Activity feeds and profile photos from networking sites, such as Facebook, LinkedIn, or SharePoint Server, are displayed in the Social Connector's pane after you configure Outlook to connect to the social networking service.

Configuring the Social Connector

Out of the box, the Social Connector's People pane acts like a search folder—messages and meetings between you and the sender are displayed in the People pane (see Figure 10.1). Selecting a message in the list opens the message.

When a message is sent to more than one person, each person is listed in the People pane, and selecting any of the pictures or the icon representing the person displays your activities with that person: messages to or from that person, their social networking feeds (based on their social network security settings), appointments, or attachments to or from them.

If you don't want to see the People pane, you can turn it off or minimize it. See Showing or Hiding the Social Connector Pane, later in this chapter.

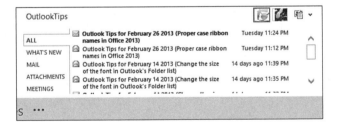

FIGURE 10.1

The People pane displays at the bottom of the Reading pane and contacts. Click the contact photos to view email and other activities between you and that person.

TIP You can use the People pane without connecting to social networks. The People pane displays Outlook items—email, meetings, and email attachments—and the sender or recipient's photo when a photo is added to that contact.

To view updates from social networks in the pane, you need to configure the social providers in Outlook. Outlook 2013 includes Facebook, LinkedIn, and SharePoint providers with the default installation, and you can go online to download additional connectors (when available).

 NOTE To see a person's Facebook profile picture or activity feed, the person needs to have a public profile picture and have an email address configured in his or her Facebook account.

Setting Up Social Networking Accounts

Before you can view profile photos and status updates for people who send you email, you need to connect Outlook to the social network. Follow these steps:

1. Switch to the View tab.

2. Expand the People pane button.

3. Select Account Settings from the menu.

4. Click to select a social network you want to use.

5. Enter your name and password (see Figure 10.2).

FIGURE 10.2

Sign in to the social networks. Outlook 2013 includes Social Connector providers for Facebook, LinkedIn, and SharePoint server.

6. Click Connect to link the social network to Outlook.

7. If you want the social network to be the default source for contact photos, select By Default, Show Photos and Information from This Network When Available.

Select the next social network and repeat the process.

 TIP If you are unable to connect Outlook to Facebook and you receive an "invalid username or password" message, check your security settings at Facebook. You need to give Outlook permission to access Facebook.

If you want to remove a social network, select the network and click the X on the right to delete your username and password for the social network (see Figure 10.3).

FIGURE 10.3

To sign out of the social network, click the X. To change your account, click the white Paper icon.

If you change your username or password on the social network, you'll need to change it in the Social Connector. Click the Paper icon to change your username and password. Click the Options button to view or change the settings Office applies to data shared between Office and the social network, which is contacts, profile photos, and status updates (see Figure 10.4)

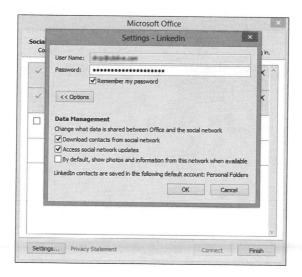

FIGURE 10.4

Click the white Paper icon to change social network settings, including which network is the default for contact photos.

- **Download Contacts from Social Network**—This setting creates a contact folder in Outlook and syncs your social network connections to Outlook, if the social network allows it. Only LinkedIn allows contacts to sync, whereas Facebook does not.

- **Access Social Network Update**—This syncs your Facebook and LinkedIn status updates to Outlook and displays them in the People pane when you view email to or from your friend, or view their contact.

- **By Default, Show Photos and Information from This Network When Available**—This sets the default network for contact photos. If a contact is a Facebook friend and a LinkedIn connection, this setting controls which photo you see in Outlook.

If you use Outlook 2013 at work, the Social Connector can sync updates from Active Directory and update your local contacts with the contact's job title, address, and phone number from the Active Directory. The Settings button is used to set the Contact update option. Users can choose to be prompted before the contacts are updated, to update without prompting, or to never update (see Figure 10.5). If your Active Directory is kept up-to-date, you'll always have the correct job title, address, and phone numbers for your contact when automatic updates are enabled. If the Active Directory is not updated often but you keep your contacts updated, you'll want to use Never update.

FIGURE 10.5

Control the contact update feature in the Social Connector's Settings.

When a contact is updated from the Active Directory, a change log is added to the Contact's Notes field. The log lists the fields that were updated and the date they were updated.

Turning Off Contact Photos

Although the Social Connector displays contact photos, the option to display photos throughout Outlook and other Office applications is a People option. If you don't want to see the photos, you can disable this feature.

To turn contact photos off, click File, click Options, click People, and then deselect the Show User Photographs When Available option (see Figure 10.6). You must restart Outlook for this to take effect.

Showing or Hiding the Social Connector Pane

As useful as the People pane may be, you probably won't want it open all the time. You can minimize and open the pane by clicking the caret icon on the right edge of the pane (see Figure 10.7).

If you want to turn the People pane off, you need to use the People Pane button on the View tab.

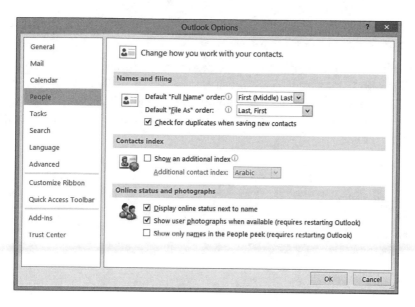

FIGURE 10.6

Turning off Contact photos in People Options.

FIGURE 10.7

Open and minimize the People pane using the caret on the right.

When the pane is open, you can drag the upper edge to make the panel larger or smaller. This can be helpful when you are reviewing a list of messages in the People pane.

Social Connector Security

Most questions about Social Connector security are about Facebook. This is because Facebook contains more personal information, whereas LinkedIn targets businesspeople. In either case, if you don't want people you correspond with to see your profile photo or status updates, you need to make your profile private.

Facebook

When the Facebook provider is installed, the profile photos and status updates of people who send you email or are in your contacts will be shown in the People pane if the person has the profile publicly searchable and has associated the email address with his or her Facebook account.

Just being Facebook friends with someone is not enough to ensure that their status updates or profile picture will be visible when they send you email. The email address you have for the person must be linked to the person's Facebook account, and the correct Facebook profile privacy settings must be set (see Figure 10.8).

	Privacy Settings and Tools		
General			
Security			
Privacy	**Who can see my stuff?**	Who can see your future posts?	Friends of Friends	Edit
Timeline and Tagging		Review all your posts and things you're tagged in		Use Activity Log
Blocking		Limit the audience for posts you've shared with friends of friends or Public?		Limit Past Posts
Notifications	**Who can look me up?**	Who can look you up using the email address or phone number you provided?	Friends	Edit
Mobile				
Followers		Do you want other search engines to link to your timeline?	Off	Edit
Apps				
Ads				

FIGURE 10.8

Adjust your Facebook security settings to prevent people you send email to from seeing your Facebook status in the People pane.

Following is an explanation of various privacy settings:

- **Publicly Searchable**—You will be able to see the person's status in the social connector even if you are not friends.

- **Not Searchable**—No status information is returned from Facebook.

- **Searchable to Friends Only but the person's email address is not visible to friends**—No status information is returned from Facebook even if you are a friend.

- **Searchable to Friends Only AND their email address is visible to friends**—That person's status information is returned from Facebook if you are a friend.

The address associated with Facebook must be the same email address used for email (or on the contact record in Outlook), or registered as a secondary address in the Facebook Profile.

 NOTE If the email address used to send messages or listed on the contact is not registered with the social network, the user's activities will not appear in the People pane.

If you want your activities to appear for your colleagues at work, add your work email address as an additional email address under account settings for the social network. Or, to ensure business colleagues can't see your Facebook posts, don't link your business address to your Facebook account.

 NOTE Even people who do not use Outlook or the Social Connector need to check their Facebook and LinkedIn settings; otherwise, people they send email to may be able to see their profile picture or feeds.

Who Sees Your Photo and Your People Pane Content?

Following are two frequent questions:

- Are the messages in the People pane sent with replies?

- Is my picture sent with my messages?

A surprising number of people see the search results in the People pane and are concerned that their replies will include all these messages.

No one except you sees this list of messages. The messages do not leave your computer. Other Outlook users you send email to will see a similar list, but it contains only the email in their mailbox. You'll only see what is in your mailbox or what they have allowed on social networking sites. Others will see only what is in their mailbox or what you allow on social networking sites. You can't "see" messages in their mailbox, even if you use Exchange server.

The Contact photo that displays on messages and in the People pane also generates a lot of questions from people worried it's going to be sent with their email. You aren't sending your photo with your messages; the photo you see on messages is also not sent with the message. If recipients have a contact for you and have added a photo to it, they will see that. They could also see your Facebook or LinkedIn photo, if your security settings on either site allow it.

 NOTE Occasionally, you might see a photo that does not belong to the sender. This happens when someone mistypes an address in their social network profile. Create a contact for the people and use a logo or correct photo for the person.

THE ABSOLUTE MINIMUM

Here are the key points to remember from this chapter:

- You don't have to use the People pane and Social Connector if you don't want to. You can minimize the People pane or set it to Off.

- You can use the People pane to view recent messages sent to or from a message's sender or recipients. You don't need to sign into a social network to view messages, appointments, or attachments associated with a contact.

- Even if you decide not to use the People pane or log into a social network, anyone with Outlook may be able to see your profile photo and status updates if your profile is set to public and your email address is in your social network profile.

11

NOTES AND JOURNAL

Outlook is loaded with features, some of which are complicated and confusing, but one of the most basic features is Outlook's Notes. It doesn't do much, but it's handy if you need to securely store bits of text and notes.

Notes resemble sticky notes, and you can use them to replace the paper version, but they lack a lot of functionality you would expect to find in onscreen sticky notes. That's not to say they aren't useful—they just don't have the features many people expect from electronic sticky notes.

If you used a previous version of Outlook and are familiar with either Notes or Journal, you'll notice a number of changes. Microsoft has removed some functionality from Notes to make them simpler, and Microsoft removed all automatic Journal features.

Using Outlook's "Sticky Notes"

Outlook's Notes are useful for storing small pieces of text. You can add contacts or categories to your notes and locate the note quickly using Find. Because URLs in notes are clickable, you can paste a URL in a note and include comments about the site. You never have to remember to save notes; Outlook automatically saves them as soon as you move focus away from the note.

To simplify things and make Outlook's options less overwhelming, Microsoft removed all the note options. A medium yellow note is your only choice, although you can drag the edges of a note to make the note larger (or smaller) and Outlook will remember the note size. If you want notes in different colors, assign Color Categories and the note will pick up the category color.

Notes uses a simple text editor that doesn't support rich text formatting. As a result, you can't highlight words or phrases with different colors or fonts or include images in a note. This doesn't mean Notes aren't useful—as an electronic version of Post-it style notes, simple is better. Notes are great for small snippets of text—usernames and passwords, email settings, and other short blocks of text are well suited for Notes.

The Notes feature is not listed on the Folder bar by default. Click the three dots on the bar and select Notes to open the Notes folder. Choose Navigation Options and create the maximum number of visible items or change the order of the folders on the Folder bar (see Figure 11.1). This allows you to see Notes on the Folder bar.

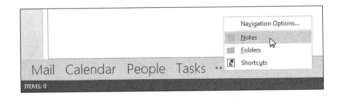

FIGURE 11.1

Select Notes from the Folder bar to view your notes.

Creating Notes

As with all Outlook items, you can create new notes in several ways (see Figure 11.2).

- From the Notes module, use the mouse to select New Note from the ribbon. Type or paste text into the note form.

Click icon for options

FIGURE 11.2

Outlook's note has a simple interface and no toolbar. Click the small icon in the upper-left corner to access the options available for individual notes.

- From anywhere in Outlook folders, use the keyboard shortcut Ctrl+Shift+N to create new notes. If you prefer using menus, you'll go to New Items, More Items, Choose Form, and select Note from the list of forms.

- Double-click between notes in the Notes list to open a new note. If you use an Icon view, double-click between the icons or double-click after the last note in List view. The note is now ready for you to enter text.

- Drag and drop a message to a note folder to save the entire message as a note.

- Select part of a message and drag the selection to a note folder. You aren't limited to dragging selections from Outlook items; this works for any OLE document, such as Word documents, Excel spreadsheets, and Internet Explorer pages.

The status bar displays the time and date the note was last modified. The Modified Time field is updated to the current time when you edit a note.

 NOTE If it's important for you to know the date a note was created, type the date into the note body—don't rely on the Created and Modified Date fields in Outlook.

When you drag Outlook items to create notes, drop the text or message on the Note link at the bottom of Outlook's window, on a Note folder, or anywhere in the Note list area.

When you're done creating your note, you can use the Esc key or Alt+F4 to close it.

Outlook uses the first line of the note for the name of the note. The maximum length for the name is 256 characters, unless you begin a new paragraph. If you want a shorter name, press Enter to begin a new line.

Assigning Categories to Notes

Although you can't see a Category field on a note form, you can assign categories to notes. When you use categories, you can create a group by category view, display the Category field in the Notes List view, or use Instant Search to find your notes.

You can add a category to notes in three ways:

- Click the Note icon in the upper-left corner and select Categories from the menu to display the Categorize menu.

- Right-click a note in the folder and choose Categorize.

- Use the List view and click to assign the Quick Click category or right-click in the Category field to choose a category (see Figure 11.3).

FIGURE 11.3

Assign categories to notes.

You can assign a category to several notes at once. After selecting the notes, right-click the selection and choose Categorize. You can also create a group by Category view and drag notes between category groups.

Saving Notes

Outlook automatically saves your notes to the default Notes folder when you close the note or when focus is no longer on the note.

When you use the File menu or keyboard shortcut to create a note, it's saved in the default Notes folder. If you want to save a note in another note folder, you must open that folder, create the note, or move it from the default Notes folder after it's created.

You can use the mouse to move or copy notes to another note folder. Drag and drop with the left mouse button to move the note, or use a right-click drag and drop to select between Move or Copy.

When you select two or more notes and right-click, one of the menu options is Move to Folder. Selecting this option opens the Move Items dialog; select the folder to move the notes to.

Instead of copying the content of a large note and pasting it into a document, you can save the note as an RTF file type and open it in a word processor.

You can save contents of a note to the Windows file system as notes, RTF documents, Outlook templates, or text files.

Outlook provides two print styles you can use—Table Style and Memo Style—for printing copies of your notes (see Figure 11.4). Use Table Style to print a list of your notes or Memo Style to print individual notes. For most views, you'll choose your print style; however, Icon view supports Memo Style only.

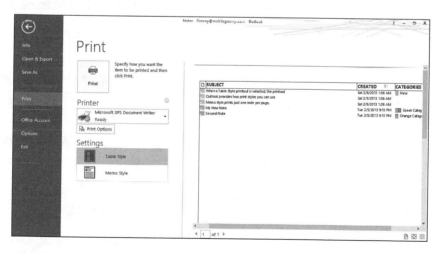

FIGURE 11.4

Print a list of notes or individual notes.

Memo Style prints just one note per page. When the notes are short, use the Table Style to print your notes on one page. This style offers limited configuration settings beyond the type of paper used.

When a Table Style printout is selected, the printout contains all the fields exactly as they're seen on the screen, including Message Preview lines, if enabled. Notes that contain fewer than 256 characters of text might print in their entirety when Message Preview is enabled.

Emailing Notes

It's easy to send your notes to other people; just drag and drop the note on the Inbox or any mail folder. A new message form opens with the text of the note in the body of the message. The first line of the note is used for the subject, and the note's last modified date is added to the message.

When you select multiple notes and drop them on the Inbox, one message is created with the contents of the notes in the message body. The subject field is left blank.

You can send notes as attachments, too. If you've already started an email message, choose the Insert File, Item toolbar selection when using Word as your editor or Insert, Item menu with the Outlook editor, and then browse to the Notes folder and select the note. When you select the note first, you can use Ctrl+F, or right-click and choose Forward Note.

Organizing Your Notes

When you have a lot of notes, you'll want to organize them, either using folders or views. In some cases, creating additional note folders makes sense, but you can create custom views to show certain notes. Switch to the View tab and you'll see the predefined views that are included with Outlook 2013:

- **Icon**—Choose from Small Icons, Large Icons, or List (see Figure 11.5).
- **Notes List**—Similar to the view used in the Inbox. Arrange by category or created date.
- **Last Seven Days**—A filtered view that shows only new notes.

You can customize these views or create new custom views. Select the View Settings button to customize a view.

This view uses the Notes List view with the notes grouped by date. Shared Notes is available for Exchange server users only.

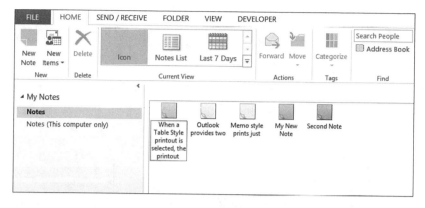

FIGURE 11.5

The Large icon view of the Notes folder.

Keyboard Shortcuts

Notes uses a very basic text editor that doesn't have a ribbon or toolbars. Some of the commands, like New Note and Print are available on the ribbon when you select a Note, but not all commands are in the ribbon. Many users, myself included, use the mouse for everything, but with no toolbars, the mouse is useless. Keyboard shortcuts work in Notes and can be used for simple tasks, such as center text or align it to the right.

Many of these shortcuts work with the other Outlook items too.

TABLE 11.1 Keyboard Shortcuts to Use with Outlook Notes

Shortcut	Action
Shift+Ctrl+N	New note
Ctrl+N	New note when Outlook is opened to the Notes folder
Escape	Close the note you are reading
Ctrl+D	Delete the open or selected note
Ctrl+D or Delete key	Delete selected note from List view
Ctrl+E	Center text
Ctrl+R	Block text right
Ctrl+L	Return to left block
Ctrl+F	Forward selected note using email

Shortcut	Action
Ctrl+P	Print
Ctrl+S	Save
Shift+Ctrl+V	Move selected note to new folder
Shift+Ctrl+F	Advanced Find

Outlook's Hidden Journal

Outlook includes a hidden module called Journal. This can be used as a diary to create a record of your activities. However, Microsoft removed as much of the Journal as possible from Outlook 2013. If you used it in a previous version of Outlook, you can access your old journal entries and create new ones, but the best features of the Journal were removed.

 NOTE If you need to keep a journal or diary, I recommend creating a new calendar to record your activities in or use Microsoft OneNote, which is included with all Office suites.

Creating Journal Entries

To open the Journal folder, you can use the keyboard shortcut Ctrl+8 from anywhere in Outlook 2013 or by selecting the Journal folder in the Folder pane (Ctrl+6).

The keyboard shortcut for new journal entries was removed from Outlook. You can open a new journal by clicking New Item, then More Items, and selecting the Choose Form menu to open the Journal form; or you can switch to the Journal folder by using the Ctrl+8 shortcut and clicking the Journal Entry button to create new entries.

Yes, Microsoft is trying to discourage people from using the Journal, and they may eventually remove it from future versions of Outlook.

 TIP If you are going to use the Journal, I have a macro that creates new journal entries and one that switches to the Journal folder. When you add the macro to the ribbon, creating new journal entries is much easier. See http://slipstick.me/journal for the code.

Although Microsoft is discouraging its use, you may find it useful to keep a record of phone calls, meeting notes, and other activities such as the following:

- Letters, documents, and faxes you send or receive

- Telephone calls or conversations

- Meetings you plan or are invited to

- Remote sessions you participate in

 NOTE The list of Journal Entry types is hard-coded, and although you can't type a new entry type into the field, you can edit the Registry to add new entry types. The instructions needed to edit the Registry are at http://slipstick.me/je.

The journal form (see Figure 11.6) contains a few basic fields:

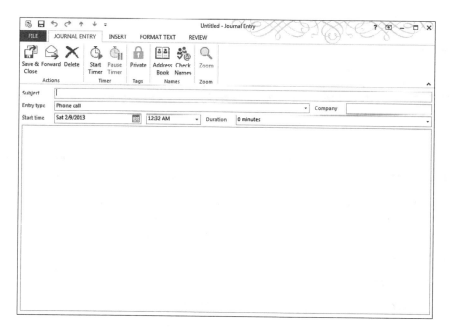

FIGURE 11.6

The journal form contains just a few fields that must be filled in.

- Subject
- Entry Type
- Company

- Start Time

- Duration

- Notes

After you've entered the information in the fields, click the Save button and your journal item is finished. You can create your own entries for anything you want to keep in your journal, including home and car repairs or visits to the doctor. Because Outlook doesn't have entry types for all the types of items you might need, you'll have to make do with one of the existing entry types or create new entry types that meet your unique needs.

Create Journal Items

1. Switch to the Journal folder and select Journal Entry to open a new journal form.

2. Enter a subject and select an Entry Type for your new journal entry.

3. Enter the Start date and time.

4. Click the Start Timer button if you need to record the duration. If the activity has already ended, select the duration from the Duration menu.

5. Enter notes in the Notes field, insert links to attachments, and add color categories to the journal item, if desired.

When you've finished entering notes, click the Save and Close button. The timer stops and the duration field updates to the elapsed time.

If you're inserting documents or files, use the Attach File button on the ribbon; use the Outlook Item button to insert Outlook items. When you insert file attachments, you can select how to insert the files on the expanded Insert button (see Figure 11.7):

- **Insert**—Insert the file as an attachment.

- **Insert as Text**—Available only for text files.

- **Insert as Hyperlink**

FIGURE 11.7

You can insert files as text, attachments, or hyperlinks.

Using the Insert as Hyperlink option keeps the size of your mailbox smaller and is recommended.

You can also insert any item from Outlook's data file as text only, as an attachment, or as a shortcut to the item. In most cases, you'll want to use the As Shortcut to the Item or As Text Only setting, rather than duplicating an existing item.

Choose As Attachment or As Text to ensure that you always have the original item saved with the journal entry. Hyperlinks fail if you move, rename, or delete documents or Outlook items that the journal's hyperlinks point to.

Journaling Appointments, Tasks, and Email

You can use several ways to create your own journal entries, often with very little typing. These methods create a new journal entry with the fields already filled in.

1. Use the Move, Copy to Folder command and select the Journal folder as the Copy To folder. This creates a journal entry with the item attached.

2. Drag the Outlook item to the Journal folder.

3. Right click and drag an Outlook item to the Navigation bar button. When you release the right button, you can choose between copying the entry as a shortcut to the original item, copy as an attachment, or move as an attachment.

When you are using one of the preceding methods to journal calendar or task items, the new journal entries have the same subject as the appointment or task. The start time, duration, contacts, and categories are also the same as on the appointment. A shortcut to the appointment is added to the notes field of the journal entry. After adding notes about the meeting, you need only to save and close the journal entry.

When you drag an email to the Journal folder, the message subject is used for the journal subject, and the date and time the message was received are the start date and time. The Contact field contains the sender's name if a contact exists or the email address if you don't have a contact record for the sender, and a shortcut to the message is added to the journal body.

You can also create new journal entries and insert calendar or task items using the Insert, Item menu selection. However, you'll need to complete the journal fields yourself.

Journal Views

The journal comes with four predefined views, using Timeline or Table layouts. You can customize these views or create your own custom views. You aren't limited to using Timeline or Table views with the journal: Day/Week/Month views also work well, but Icon and Card views do not.

The timeline view defaults to showing the journaled items for the current week. You can change this to Day, which is segmented by the hour, or one month by clicking the Day or Month toolbar button. You can return to a seven-day view by clicking the Week button. You can jump to any date by selecting the date in the Go to Date dialog. Open it using the Ctrl+G shortcut, right-clicking in an open area, and selecting Go To Date, or by clicking the expand arrow in the lower-right corner of the Arrangement section of the Journal ribbon (see Figure 11.8).

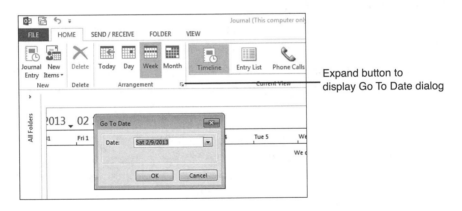

Expand button to display Go To Date dialog

FIGURE 11.8

Click the Expand button in the Arrangement section of the ribbon, and then select a date from the Go to Date command to jump to a date.

The predefined Table views have filters controlling what you see:

- **Entry List**—No filter used
- **Last 7 Days**—Filtered to display entries created within the past seven days
- **Phone Calls**—Filtered to display only phone calls.

You can customize any of these views and create new views using your own criteria. Switch to the View ribbon and choose View Settings to open the Advanced View Settings dialog and customize the current view to your liking. If you want to restore the default settings for the view, click the Reset button in the View ribbon.

THE ABSOLUTE MINIMUM

The key points to remember from this chapter include the following:

- Outlook Notes are a safe and secure place to store short snippets of text, such as usernames and passwords.

- Because Notes don't have a toolbar to use with a mouse, you need to use keyboard shortcuts when you have a note open.

- Although the Journal is useful for record keeping, it is being discontinued.

12

SYNC AND SHARE OUTLOOK DATA

When you use more than one computer, or if you have a smartphone or a tablet, you'll probably want to sync your Outlook data with the other computer or smartphone. You might want to share your calendar and contacts with another user or use the data in another program. If you have an Exchange Server mailbox, syncing your mailbox to other computers is as easy as configuring your account in Outlook. Sharing your calendar and contacts with other users is also easy, as long as the other users also have mailboxes on your Exchange Server. If you aren't using Exchange Server, it's not so easy.

Sharing Calendar and Contacts

Most people who use Outlook on more than one computer want to use their calendar and contacts on their other computers or share them with other people. Sharing works best if you use an Exchange Server mailbox or an Outlook.com email account, because your email, calendar, and contacts will be stored on the mail server and synced to any computer or device.

If you use a POP3 (Post Office Protocol 3) email account, your choices are to leave the mail on the server and download it on each computer or use a utility to sync your email, calendar, and contacts. IMAP (Internet Message Access Protocol) accounts sync email only; you need to use a utility or another method to move your calendar and contacts between computers and devices.

You can share your calendar and contacts by exporting your contact to a personal folder file (*.PST) or exporting to a CSV file and importing on the other computer. I recommend using a PST file to move Outlook items to another computer whenever possible. When you use a CSV file, attachments and contact photos are not included when the file is imported.

Syncing with Smartphones and Tablets

The easiest way to sync your mailbox with smartphones or tablets, or even other computers, is with an Outlook.com or Exchange Server mailbox, such as Office365. Apple, Android, Windows Phone, and Blackberry 10 smartphones and tablets sync directly with Outlook.com and Exchange Server mailboxes.

If you're using an IMAP account, email syncs to all your devices, and changes you make on one device, such as reading a message or replying, are seen on your other devices.

If your email account supports only POP3 accounts, you'll need to configure Outlook to leave mail on the server so it will be available to download on all devices.

 NOTE   If you want the best experience using email, calendaring, and contacts on multiple computers and portable devices, you need to use an Exchange Server mailbox, such as offered by Office365 for business users. The accounts are targeted to businesses, but can be used by individuals as well.

Apple iPhone and iPad users who do not use Outlook.com or Exchange mailboxes can share Outlook Calendar, Contacts, and Tasks using the iCloud add-in. The iCloud moves appointments, contacts, and tasks to an iCloud data file in Outlook, which then syncs to the iCloud and all Apple devices linked to your Apple ID account.

The iCloud works well, but many users don't like that all appointments, contacts, and tasks are removed from Outlook's folders, even though they are still visible in Outlook.

Android and Windows Phone users will need to use a third-party utility to sync with Outlook if they don't have Outlook.com or Exchange server mailboxes. A list of third party utilities can be found here: http://www.slipstick.com/smartphones.

Sharing with a Second Computer

If you're sharing with a second Outlook on another computer, one of the easiest ways to do it is to copy the PST file to the other computer and open it in the profile. Go to the File tab, click Open & Export, click Outlook Data File, and then select your PST file. This is recommended over Import and Export because views and other customizations are not exported. If you need to export, use the native Outlook Data File format to export to a .pst file.

Moving the Data File

Before you can move the data file, you need to find it on your hard drive. The easiest way to do this is by using the Account Settings dialog.

1. Click the File tab and select Account Settings.
2. Select the Data Files tab.
3. Select the .pst file.
4. Click the Open File Location button to open Windows Explorer to the location of the .pst file (see Figure 12.1).
5. Close the Account Settings dialog box.
6. Close Outlook, and then copy the .pst file.

Copy the data file to the second computer. You can put it anywhere on the hard drive, but I recommend using Outlook 2013's default location for .pst files and place it in the My Documents\Outlook Files folder. This makes it easier to make a backup copy of your Outlook data (which you should do on a regular basis).

Open the data file in your profile by going to Outlook's File tab, selecting Open & Export, then Open Outlook Data File to select your .pst file.

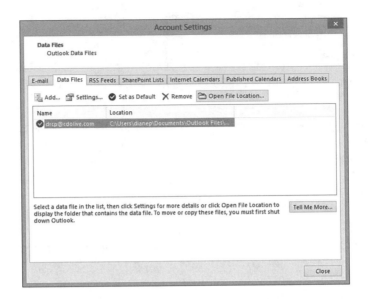

FIGURE 12.1

Click the File tab, click Account Settings, and then click Data Files tab to go the location of the .pst file.

 NOTE Only .pst files can be used in other profiles. IMAP, Outlook.com, and Exchange offline files can't be opened in other profiles.

Using Export and Import

Although I generally recommend moving the entire .pst to a new computer to preserve views and other hidden data, as well as the modified dates, it is easier to export if you need to move your calendar and/or contacts to another computer also using Outlook. When you use the data in another copy of Outlook, export in Outlook Data File (.pst) format. Use CSV format when the data will be used in other programs.

To Export Outlook data, open the Import/Export wizard by clicking the Open & Export menu, and choosing Import/Export. Choose Export to a File and click Next. If you are using the data in Outlook, choose Outlook Data File (.pst).

Sharing Calendar

You can use one of several methods when you need to share a calendar in Outlook 2013. In addition to exporting the calendar or copying the .pst file, you can share the calendar by email or publish it to a WebDAV server.

To access these options, right-click the Calendar folder and choose Share.

Sharing by email creates an iCalendar (.ics) file of your calendar and inserts it in an email message; it also creates a planner-style calendar in the message body. For more information on these options, see Chapter 7, "Using the Calendar."

Using Outlook.com to Share Calendar and Contacts

Outlook 2013 syncs with Outlook.com calendar and contacts using the Outlook.com (EAS) account type. When you use a POP3 or IMAP email account, you can use an Outlook.com account to sync your appointments and contacts with other computers and smartphones.

All you need is a Microsoft account. Although you could use an Outlook.com or Hotmail address, you can create a Microsoft account using any valid email address because you'll use this account only for appointments and contacts, not email.

If you don't have a Microsoft account for your email address, go to https://signup.live.com/signup.aspx and complete the form to create a Microsoft account, entering your email address in the Microsoft account name field.

After the Microsoft account is

created and verified, log in to http://outlook.com to begin using the account. You'll receive a couple of welcome emails in the account online.

Next, you'll need to add your email account and the Microsoft account to Outlook 2013.

1. Go to File tab and click on Account Settings then select Account Settings.

2. Click New to open the Add Account dialog.

3. If you need to add a POP3 or IMAP account, you can use Auto Account Setup. If you aren't using Auto Account Setup and need instructions to configure POP3 and IMAP accounts, see Chapter 3, "Setting Up Accounts and Personalizing Outlook."

You'll need to manually configure the Microsoft account, selecting the Outlook.com account type.

From the Account Settings dialog box, follow these steps:

1. Click New to open the Add Account dialog box.

2. Select Manual setup or additional server types from the lower left.

3. Click Next.

4. Choose Outlook.com or Exchange ActiveSync compatible service (see Figure 12.2).

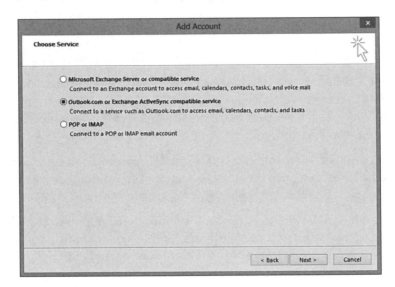

FIGURE 12.2

Choose the Outlook.com or Exchange ActiveSync account type when using a Microsoft account to share calendar and contacts.

5. Type in your name and email address.

6. Enter m.hotmail.com as the server address, then enter your email address again and your Microsoft account password (see Figure 12.3).

7. Click Next to test the settings and exit the dialog.

The Microsoft account is added to your profile.

Before closing the Account Settings dialog box, switch to the Data Files tab. Select the new account's data file and click Set as Default so appointments display on the Calendar Peek, and new appointments and contacts will be added to the Outlook.com folders and sync to the server. Now you can close the dialog box.

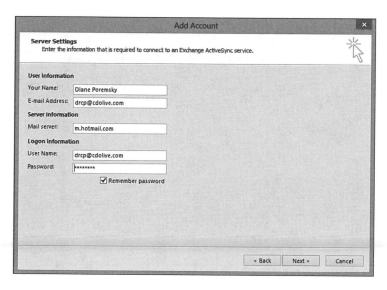

FIGURE 12.3

Enter your account information on the Server Settings screen, using m.hotmail.com for the server address.

 NOTE Your email account should be set as default on the Account Settings, E-mail tab.

When you return to Outlook, you'll have two accounts in the folder list: your ISP or "real" email address for email and the Outlook.com account for calendar and contact sync. Both accounts will have the same email address.

It's confusing to have two accounts with the same address in your profile, but you can rename the Microsoft account. To do this, open the Send/Receive Groups dialog using Ctrl+Alt+S, and then click Edit. Select your Microsoft account and click the Account Properties button in the upper-right corner. You'll enter a friendly name for the account on the General tab in the dialog (see Figure 12.4). Click OK to change the name.

You'll need to close and restart Outlook to finalize the changes.

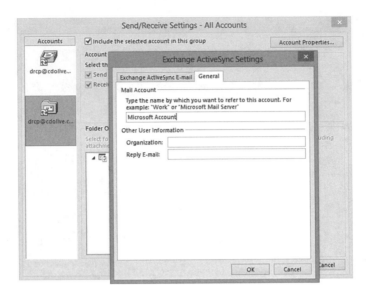

FIGURE 12.4

Change the account's display name to a friendlier name.

You'll need to move or copy existing appointments and contacts to the Microsoft account data file. This is easier if you use a List view and then select all and drag to the folders.

1. Switch to the Calendar folder.

2. Select the View tab.

3. Click the Change View button and select List.

4. Select an appointment and press Ctrl+A to select all.

5. Use the Move to command on the Home ribbon or drag the appointments with your mouse to move them to the new calendar folder.

6. Switch to the Contacts folder, select all contacts, and move to the new contacts folder.

If you want Outlook to open to your Inbox, go to File, Options, Advanced, and select your Inbox to be the default start up folder.

Out of the box, Outlook 2013 uses the email account that belongs to the folders you are viewing. This means if you compose a new message while viewing the Microsoft account calendar, the message will be sent using the Microsoft account by default. This is not the desired behavior when you are using an Outlook.com account only for syncing calendar and contacts, because the From address is a long Hotmail address.

To fix this, you need to add Registry value to force Outlook to always use the default account for new email messages.

To force all new messages to use the default email account, regardless of which data file you are viewing, follow these steps:

1. In the Windows Search dialog, type **regedit** to open the Registry Editor.

2. Browse to HKEY_CURRENT_USER\Software\Microsoft\Office\15.0\ Outlook\ Options\Mail.

3. Right-click on Mail and choose New, DWORD (32-bit) Value.

4. Type **NewItemsUseDefaultSendingAccount** as the value name (see Figure 12.5).

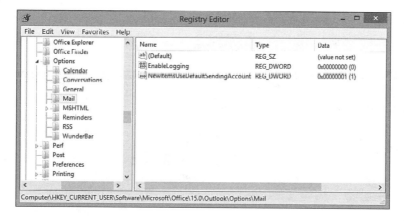

FIGURE 12.5

Edit the Registry to make the default email account the default for all new messages.

5. Right-click the name and choose Modify. Enter a value of 1.

6. Restart Outlook.

If you prefer not to edit the Registry yourself, I have a Registry file that will update the Registry for you. Download it from http://www.slipstick.com/outlook-com.

Using Contacts in Other Programs

You can use contacts in other programs by exporting to a CSV file. You can even use a List view, then select all the contacts, and copy and paste into any application that accepts paste.

Most applications can import (and export) CSV files.

To copy and paste a List view, create a custom view containing only the fields you need. (See Chapter 17, "Working with Views.") Select the contacts you need using Select All (Ctrl+A) or hold Ctrl as you click specific contacts. Use Ctrl+C to copy the selected contacts and paste into any application that accepts paste. If you paste Outlook data into Word, you'll need to paste as text.

Using Contacts in Word

There are two ways to use Outlook Contacts in Word: you can use Outlook's address book in Word to address letters and envelopes or you can use mail merge. These features are discussed in Chapter 20, "Using Mail Merge."

THE ABSOLUTE MINIMUM

Here are the key points to remember from this chapter:

- You can use Outlook's calendar and contacts on other computers.

- It's possible to sync calendar and contacts to any smartphone. If you use Outlook.com or Exchange Server, you can sync over-the-air and do not need to use an add-in.

IN THIS CHAPTER

- Sharing folders with other users
- Using Delegates
- Using Public Folders and Shared Mailboxes
- Connecting SharePoint and Outlook

13

USING EXCHANGE SERVER AND SHAREPOINT

This chapter covers features specific to Outlook users with Exchange Server mailboxes or users who can access SharePoint servers. Everything in this chapter applies to Office365 business accounts or corporate Exchange Server accounts. Users with Exchange mailboxes will have a few more features and additional buttons on the ribbon. For example, Exchange server mailboxes were designed to allow users to share calendar and contacts with co-workers.

If you don't use Exchange and SharePoint, you may want to skip this chapter. Or you can read it to see what you are missing. Many individuals and families have Office365 Business accounts because it is the best way to share a calendar and contacts among family members and to sync calendar and contacts with smartphones.

Sharing Folders with Other Users

Sharing can be as simple as letting others see your calendar to know if you are busy, or you can share folders in your mailbox with co-workers. For example, an administrative assistant can be delegated to manage a mailbox, which may include the capability to send messages for the mailbox owner.

At many organizations, an administrator configures permissions so everyone can see the Free/Busy status of their co-workers in the Scheduling Assistant screen of a Meeting Request. Depending on the permissions given to your account, you may be able to see if the person has an appointment, but you won't be able to see the appointment details.

To check the permissions on your calendar, follow these steps:

1. Click File, click Options, and then select Calendar.

2. Click the Free/Busy Options button to open the Calendar Properties dialog box shown in Figure 13.1.

    Individuals and groups who have permission to view your Free/Busy are listed at the top of the Calendar Properties dialog box, along with their permission level.

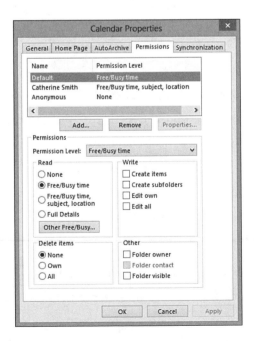

FIGURE 13.1

Check your calendar's Free/Busy permissions.

3. To change the permissions for any person or group, select the name and choose a new Permission Level from the drop-down list. When you select different permission levels, the settings for Read, Write, Delete Items, and Other will change so you can see what rights each permission level has.

4. Click Apply to apply changes, and then click OK to close the dialog box.

 NOTE If you change the permissions, other people may be blocked from viewing your Free/Busy or will see more information about your appointments than you want to share.

Located under the Free/Busy settings is the Other Free/Busy button with a couple of additional options (see Figure 13.2). The button opens the Internet Free/Busy Options dialog box which is not usually used when you have an Exchange Server mailbox, and you should not change these settings unless told to do so by your administrator.

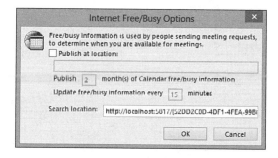

FIGURE 13.2

Additional Free/Busy Options are available in Other Free/Busy settings.

Users with Outlook.com, POP3, or IMAP email accounts will use the Internet Free/Busy Options dialog box to configure Free/Busy publishing, using a file server or web server. If your Free/Busy is published to a server accessible by other Outlook users, they can check your availability before sending you a meeting request, or to see if you are free at a certain time. Outlook will publish your Free/Busy at the Publish at location and look for your co-workers Free/Busy information for at the Search location.

You need to enter a file path or web address in the Publish at location field, using one of the following formats and replacing "alias" with your email alias (the part before the @ sign).

http://webserver/directory/FreeBusy/alias.vfb

file://\\server\directory\FreeBusy\alias.vfb

The Search location uses the same web address or file path as the publishing address, except it uses %NAME% instead of alias, as in this example:

file://\\server\FreeBusy\%NAME%.vfb

When Outlook looks for Free/Busy information, it replaces %NAME% with the other person's alias.

 NOTE When everyone at work or at home uses Outlook, you can publish Free/Busy to a folder on a shared computer and only people who can access the network folder will see your Free/Busy.

You can tell Outlook how much Free/Busy data to publish. The default is 2 months, this month, or next month. This setting is in calendar months, not the next 60 days, so at the end of each month, you'll have only 30 or 31 days available in Free/Busy. The Search location is a file path or URL, usually the same path used for publishing, where Outlook checks for the attendees' Free/Busy when you create a meeting request.

Sharing Mailbox Folders

You aren't limited to sharing just your calendar. Any folder in your Exchange mailbox can be shared with co-workers. Sharing default folders—your Inbox, Calendar, Contacts, or Tasks—is the easiest, but it is also possible to share folders you create.

To share a folder with another user, you'll need to give the user permission to see your mailbox (view the name only) and to view the contents of the folder you want to share. To do this, follow these steps:

1. Click the top level of your mailbox, bringing Outlook Today into view.

2. On the ribbon, switch to the Folder tab and click Folder Permissions to open the Properties dialog box.

3. Click Add and double click on a person's name or group in the Global Address List (GAL), and then click OK to return to the Properties dialog.

4. Set the Permission Level to None.

5. Enable Folder Visible, and then click OK and return to Outlook.

6. Select the default folder you want to share and repeat the previous steps. In this example, we use Contacts.

7. With the Contacts folder selected, switch to the Folder tab, then click Folder Permissions tab.

8. Click Add and select the person you want to share the folder with. Click Add again, and then click OK.

9. Select the name you just added and change the permissions. Because we want the person to be able to view contacts but not make changes to them, we select Reviewer from the Permission Level drop-down list. When you are finished, your screen will look like Figure 13.3.

10. Click OK and return to Outlook.

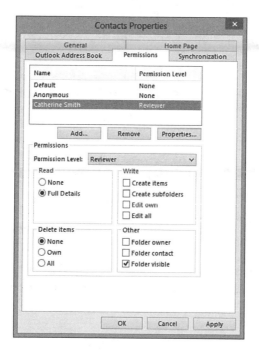

FIGURE 13.3

Use the Properties dialog to give other people permission to access your folders.

The following permissions are available for each folder type:

- **Owner**—Has full permission to the folder. Can read, create, edit, and delete items.

- **Publishing Editor**—Can read, create new items, edit or delete all items, and create subfolders.

- **Editor**—Can read, create new items, edit, or delete all items.

- **Publishing Author**—Can read, create, and edit or delete items they created and can create new subfolders.

- **Author**—Can read items, create new items, and edit or delete items they created.

- **Nonediting Author**—Can read items, create new items, or delete items they created.

- **Reviewer**—Can read items in the folder but can't create new items or delete items.

- **Contributor**—Can create new items in the folder but cannot see items already in the folder.

- **None**—No permissions. Cannot see items in the folder or create new items.

 NOTE   There are two options for the None permission: absolutely no permission and Folder Visible permission. Folder Visible permission allows the person to see the name of the folder only, not the contents, and is required in order to view subfolders.

Opening Shared Mailbox Folders

The person we shared contacts with will use the Open Shared Contacts command on the Folder tab to open the contacts. Any shared folder can be opened by clicking the File tab, clicking the Open & Export group, and clicking the Open User's Folder.

Click Name to browse for the person whose folder you want to open, or type a name into the field. Select the folder you want to open and click OK (see Figure 13.4).

FIGURE 13.4

Click Name to browse the address list, or type a name to open a shared default folder.

Sharing Nondefault Folders and Subfolders

Sharing folders you created requires the same steps you used to share the default folders: the person you are sharing with needs Folder Visible permission on the top level of your mailbox, plus permission to the folder you want to share.

When the folder is a subfolder, the other person needs at least Folder Visible permission on each folder in the path. For example, if you want to share a subfolder under your Inbox but not share your Inbox, you need to give the other person Folder Visible permission on the Inbox.

The persons you share with will not use the Open Shared Folder command to open nondefault folders. They need to add your mailbox to their profile.

To add a shared mailbox to a profile, follow these steps:

1. Click the File tab, then Account Settings and select Account Settings to open the Account Settings dialog box.

2. Double-click your Exchange server email account. Click the More Settings button. Click the Advanced tab.

3. Click Add and type the user's name or alias in the Add mailbox field. Click OK (see Figure 13.5).

4. Click OK, then Next and then click Finish to return to Outlook.

FIGURE 13.5

Add another user's mailbox to your profile to view shared folders.

The shared mailbox is added to the folder list. The names of the folders that have Folder Visible permission can be seen in the list (see Figure 13.6), but you will see only the contents of the folders that have read permission, which is Editor or higher.

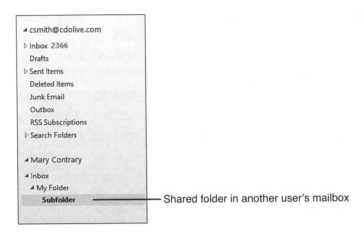

Shared folder in another user's mailbox

FIGURE 13.6

Add another user's mailbox to your profile to view the folder the user created in the mailbox.

Using Delegates

The final method for sharing mailbox folders is with delegation. This is used to give people (such as assistants) permission to manage your mailbox. The delegate can view your mailbox folders, send email on your behalf, schedule meetings for you, and accept meeting requests. You can have multiple delegates, if needed.

To make an assistant your delegate, follow these steps:

1. Click the File tab, and then click Account Settings.

2. Select Delegate Access from the menu.

3. Click Add and select your assistant from the GAL.

4. Change the default Delegate Permissions if desired (see Figure 13.7). I recommend selecting Automatically Send a Message to Delegate Summarizing These Permissions to let the delegate know that he or she is your delegate.

5. Click OK when you are finished to return to the Delegates dialog box.

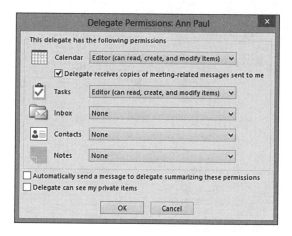

FIGURE 13.7

Select the permissions you want to give to your delegate.

After adding the delegate and returning to the Delegates dialog box, you need to choose how you want to handle meeting requests: send requests to your delegates and a copy to you; send meeting requests to your delegates only; or send meeting requests to both you and your delegates. It is recommended that you use the default option of delivering meeting requests to the delegate and sending a copy to you. Avoid the last option of delivering the meeting request to both you and the delegate. It can result in deleted or duplicated meetings.

If you need to change the delegate permissions, open the Delegates dialog box (see Figure 13.8), select the delegate name and click Permissions. Select a delegate and click Remove to delete a delegate.

 NOTE   Delegates should be reserved for people who are acting on your behalf. It should not be used to give permission to people who just need to see a folder.

Delegates can open your mailbox in their profile, as explained in the previous section. They can open specific folders by clicking the File tab, clicking Open & Export, and then clicking Open User's Folder. Your calendar will be added to the delegates' Other Calendars group on the calendar navigation pane automatically.

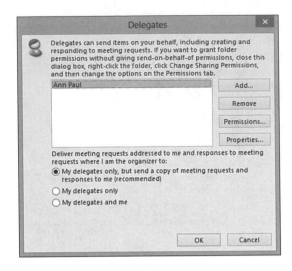

FIGURE 13.8

View your delegates and the meeting request options on the Delegates dialog.

Using Public Folders and Shared Mailboxes

In addition to user mailboxes, Exchange Servers can be configured to use Public Folders or shared mailboxes. The Exchange administrator needs to set them up for you and give you permission to access the public folders or shared mailboxes.

A shared mailbox, also called a Managed Mailbox, is often used for general addresses, such as info@domain.com or sales@domain.com, where multiple people need to access the mailbox. The users can be given Send As permission by the administrator so users can reply using the shared address. It's a full mailbox and has all the default folders.

With Full Access permission, the shared mailbox is added to your navigation pane so you don't have to use the Open User's Folder command.

When the Exchange Server has Public Folders enabled, you'll have an extra set of folders on the folder navigation pane named Public Folders (see Figure 13.9).

The folders work like your mailbox folders but are usually shared with groups, departments, or companywide. If you have permission, you can create new items in the folders. Public Folders can be mail enabled, and people can send email to the folder.

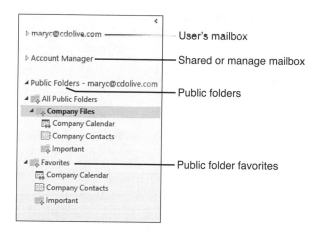

FIGURE 13.9

Public Folders and managed mailbox are added to the folder list.

To make the public folders easier to access, you can add the folders to the Favorites section of the Mail navigation pane. Right-click a frequently used public folder and choose Add to Favorites to add it to the Public Folder Favorites.

Public calendar, contacts, and task folders that are added to the Favorites list are automatically added to your Calendar, People, and Tasks navigation pane. Mail folders are not automatically added to the Mail Favorites. If you want the public folder added to the Favorites list on the Mail navigation pane, right-click the folder in the Favorites list and choose Show in Favorites.

Connecting SharePoint and Outlook

If you are lucky enough to have a SharePoint server, you can link SharePoint folders to Outlook. This is handy if your organization keeps a company calendar or contacts in SharePoint. When the lists are added to Outlook, they can be used just like any other folder in Outlook: contacts folders can be enabled as address books, and calendar folders can overlay your other calendars. You can create new items or edit existing items in the folder in Outlook, and as long as you have write permission on the server, the new items and changes sync up to the server.

To open a SharePoint list or library in Outlook, open the SharePoint website and click the Connect to Outlook button on the List tab (see Figure 13.10).

FIGURE 13.10

Click the Connect to Outlook button to add the list to your Outlook profile.

Although you cannot add SharePoint lists to your profile using the SharePoint List tab of the Account Settings dialog, you'll use this dialog to change whether the list roams with you or to enter a friendly name for the list. You can also deselect the Update Limit to turn off automatic syncing.

To change the SharePoint List settings, follow these steps:

1. Click File tab, click Account Settings, and then select Account Settings from the menu.

2. Select the SharePoint lists tab.

3. Double-click the list you want to change to open the list Options dialog (see Figure 13.11).

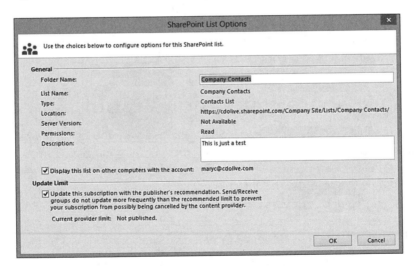

FIGURE 13.11

Change the display name and disable roaming in the Options dialog.

4. You can enter a friendly display name for the list, change the default setting to roam the list with your profiles, or change the Update Limit.

SharePoint lists that are connected to Outlook are stored in a .pst file used only by SharePoint. If you use multiple SharePoint sites, all sites will share one .pst file.

FIGURE 13.12

Link SharePoint lists to Outlook. You aren't restricted to calendar, contacts, and tasks. Documents libraries can also be opened in Outlook.

THE ABSOLUTE MINIMUM

Here are the key points to remember from this chapter:

- There are two ways you can share your Exchange Server mailbox with co-workers: by giving them permissions or making them a delegate.

- Don't make everyone delegates; change the folder properties if you want to share with people who shouldn't be your delegate.

- If you need to share your calendar, you don't need to share your entire calendar, share just your Free/Busy status.

- SharePoint lists can be synced with Outlook; changes made in Outlook sync back to the server.

14

USING COLOR CATEGORIES

We could all be organized, right? Outlook has a great feature that helps you get organized, makes it easier to use your contacts, see the important appointments when you view your calendar: color categories. You can use color categories to create contact groups, use Group by Category views to view related items together. Or use Instant Search or Search folders to find your categorized items.

Color categories take categories to a new level by highlighting the item with color when you assign a category. This allows you to color code Outlook items so it's easier to visually identify them, or use Instant search to find the items within a specific category.

You can "group" categories that have similar purposes by assigning them the same color or color family. For example, you are working on several projects for a client and created categories for each project, calling them Project1, Project2, and Project3. You are using the blue category colors for this client. Project1 is active and uses the dark blue category color. Project2 and Project3 are still in the planning stage, and the category color is light blue. All email, appointments, and tasks that are associated with these projects are assigned the appropriate category. When you glance over your calendar, you know which client and project the appointment is for, just by seeing the category color.

You can assign more than one category to an item. For example, John's contact belongs in the Friends category and also in the Softball team category. Instead of creating folders for each group of contacts (and creating duplicate contacts), you use categories to mark contacts belonging to the softball team and your friends.

You can use categories to create dynamic Contact Groups, instead of adding contacts to a Contact Group. By using categories to create groups, you don't need to update the Contact Group to add or remove members or after updating a contact's email addresses. When you send email to the category, you'll always have the updated addresses.

Assigning Color Categories to Outlook Items

Assigning a color category to an email message, appointment, task, or contact is simple. First, select what you want to categorize. Like all things in Windows, there are several ways you can assign a category:

- Right-click a message in the message list and choose Categorize, and then select a category from your list of categories

- Choose a color category by clicking the Categorize button on the ribbon and choosing a category from the menu.

- Click in the category column to apply the Quick Click category or right-click to choose from your list of categories.

- When an Outlook item is open and has a category assigned, double-click or right-click the category in the message header to access the Category menu.

To assign color categories to an email message follow these steps:

1. Select the message.

2. Right-click on the message and choose Categorize from the menu.

3. Select a category from the list (see Figure 14.1).

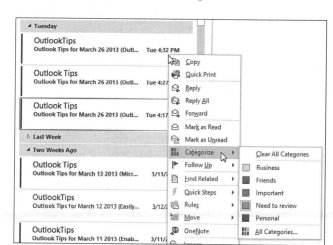

FIGURE 14.1

Right-click a message and choose Categorize; then select a category from the menu to add it to the email message.

4. Repeat to add more categories.

After you assign a category to a selected item, the category is highlighted with a pale blue border on the Categorize menu or has a checkmark beside the category name in the Color Category dialog box.

The 15 most recently used categories are shown on the Categorize menu in alphabetical order. Select All Categories from the bottom of the Categorize menu to open the Color Category dialog box, and then select a category from your entire list of categories, including those not listed in the menu. The Clear All Categories command removes all categories assigned to the currently selected item.

You can clear one or all categories assigned to an item:

1. Select the categorized item.

2. Click the Categorize button to expand the menu.

3. To remove one category, select it from the menu.

4. To remove all categories, select Clear All Categories (see Figure 14.2).

NOTE   The first time you select each one of the default color categories, Outlook brings up the Add New Category dialog box so you can give the category a more descriptive name.

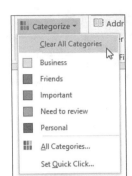

FIGURE 14.2

Use Clear All Categories to remove all categories from an item.

Using the Quick Click Category

Outlook has a handy little feature to help you out, called the Quick Click Category. You set your most frequently used category to use the default color category. Then when the category field is shown in a view, you can click in the color category column to add the color category to the item, saving time and a lot of mouse clicks.

To select other color categories, you right-click the category field and choose a category.

Set a Quick Click Category

You'll want to set one of your most frequently used categories to the Quick Click.

1. On the ribbon, click the Categorize button to expand the category menu.

2. Select Set Quick Click (see Figure 14.3).

FIGURE 14.3

Select a Quick Click color category.

3. Choose the color category you want to use as your default category and click OK.

4. Click the color category column. Outlook adds this color category, allowing you to categorize an item as the default color. If you click again, the category is removed from the color category column.

The Quick Click Category field is supported only in single line List views; it is not available in the Compact view, which is the default view in all Mail folders. Turning the Reading pane off will switch the Inbox to a single line view.

 NOTE   The Quick Click category is not available in the Compact message list view in Outlook 2013.

Clicking in the category field toggles on and off the category assigned to the Quick Click. Right-click the Category field to select from the list of most recently used categories. Selecting a category from the Category menu toggles the category on and off, allowing you to add more than one category to the selected item (see Figure 14.4).

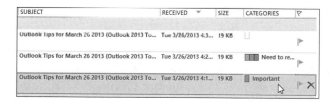

FIGURE 14.4

When the view shows the Category field, you can click in it to apply the Quick Click category.

 NOTE   The Color Category Picker is not available in Internet Message Access Protocol (IMAP) accounts. You can assign keyboard shortcuts to color categories, and then use the shortcuts to add categories. You can also add categories to an open appointment by clicking File, then clicking Properties to open the Properties dialog box.

Assigning or Removing Color Categories

To assign a color category to an email message, follow these steps:

1. Select a message in your Inbox.

2. Right-click anywhere on the message and choose Categorize.

3. Select a category from the list.

4. Right-click again and choose another category. Notice the color block for the category selected in step 3 is highlighted.

5. On the ribbon, expand the Categorize button and choose Clear All Categories to remove the categories from the message.

 NOTE In the Calendar view, the Category color takes precedence over colors applied using views. This means that you can't use Conditional Formatting to highlight appointments in color if they are assigned a category. If you use a List view, you can use both Conditional Formatting and Color Categories to highlight appointments. See Chapter 17, "Working with Views," to learn more about Conditional Formatting.

Creating Color Categories

Outlook comes with six predefined color categories. You can add as many additional categories as you need and assign keyboard shortcuts on up to 11 categories. You are limited to 25 colors, but each color can be assigned to multiple categories.

The first time you choose one of the default color categories, a dialog box opens so you can assign the category a more descriptive name (see Figure 14.5). If later you decide that you want to rename a category, you can rename it and all items assigned to the category will be renamed.

FIGURE 14.5

Use the Rename Category dialog box to change the default category names to something more meaningful.

You use the Add New Category dialog box to create as many new categories as you want or need (see Figure 14.6).

FIGURE 14.6

Use the Color Categories dialog box to create new color categories or edit existing categories.

Follow these steps to create new Color Categories.

1. Click the Categorize button to expand the Category Picker.

2. Select All Categories to open the Color Categories dialog box.

3. Click New.

4. Type a name for your new category.

5. Select a color.

6. Select a shortcut from the list of available Shortcut Keys, if desired.

7. Click OK to create the category.

If you decide you want to delete the category, change the category name, use a different color, or assign (or change) the shortcut key, select the category name and use the buttons on the right. When you choose Rename, you'll edit the name in place (see Figure 14.7).

 TIP Assign keyboard shortcuts to your frequently used color categories, and you'll be able to assign categories without using the mouse.

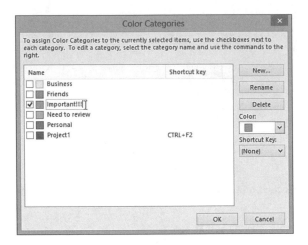

FIGURE 14.7

Rename color categories using the Color Categories dialog box.

Upgrading to Color Categories

When you import an Outlook Personal Folders file (.pst) that has categories assigned to items, you need to use Outlook's Upgrade to Color Categories command to add these categories to your Master Category list. Outlook assigns random colors to the categories.

How to Upgrade to Color Categories

When some of your categories are not listed on the Master Category list, or are not assigned a color, you'll need to follow these steps to add the Categories to the Master Category list. If you aren't sure, go ahead and run Upgrade to Color Categories; it is completely safe to use.

1. Right-click the top-level folder in your mailbox. This is the folder that displays your email address; if it's your default data file, clicking on this folder opens the Outlook Today screen.

2. In the menu, click Data File Properties.

3. Click the Upgrade to Color Categories button (see Figure 14.8).

If you don't use the Upgrade to Color Category option, categories not in the master list are colored white and marked "not in Master Category list" (see Figure 14.9) These one-off categories cannot be used on other Outlook items until they are added to the Master List.

FIGURE 14.8

If you previously used Outlook, upgrade your categories to color categories before creating new color categories.

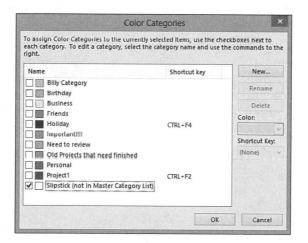

FIGURE 14.9

Categories not in the master list are white and marked "not in Master Category list."

You can add categories to the master list without using Upgrade to Color Categories.

1. Open or select the Outlook item containing one-off categories.

2. Click Categorize then click the All Categories box.

3. Select the category, and then click the New button.

4. The Name field contains the category name, and a color is assigned. Select a different color and choose a shortcut, if desired, before clicking OK to add the category to the master list.

Using Color Categories to Create Contact Groups

Color categories might be one of the most underutilized features available for Contacts. Many people choose to use multiple folders to categorize their contacts, with one for personal contacts and another for business contacts. Other people go so far as to create one contact folder per company or organization.

Using multiple folders is often the worst way to manage your contacts. One of the biggest problems you encounter when you use multiple folders is maintaining multiple copies of contacts when they are filed in more than one folder, such as someone who is both a personal and business contact.

Another problem concerns how the automatic resolution feature of the address book works. When Outlook is trying to resolve a name, it searches all the address books in order and stops at the end of the first address list in which it finds a match. For example, if you have Wayne Johnson in your business contacts folder and John Archer in personal contacts, and you type **John** in the To field, Outlook stops looking for matches to John after finding Wayne Johnson in the business contacts folder. When both men are in one contacts folder, Outlook finds both and enables you to choose the correct person.

Instead of using multiple folders to group similar contacts, you can use categories. Each contact can belong to multiple categories.

Figure 14.10 shows a contact list grouped by color category. Although it might seem that there are duplicates of the contact, it's really just one contact. If you need to remove a contact from one category, open the contact and remove the category using the category picker. Don't delete the contact from the category in the List view.

▲ ■ Categories: Friends: 2 item(s)			
Billy241 Smith241	Smith241, Billy241	Billy241@Smith241.com	■ Friends
Alice Arbuckle	Arbuckle, Alice	alice@domain.com	■ Friends
▲ ■ Categories: Personal: 1 item(s)			
Billy241 Smith241	Smith241, Billy241	Billy241@Smith241.com	■ Personal
▲ ■ Categories: Project1: 1 item(s)			
Mary Contrary	Contrary, Mary	mary@gmail.com	■ Project1

FIGURE 14.10

Use Color Categories to group contacts together.

Sharing Color Categories

Color categories are stored in the mailbox and are available only to the current mailbox. If you have multiple accounts in your Outlook profile, each account will have its own set of color categories. If you want the same categories available in each account, you need to create the categories in each account.

This same limitation applies to shared mailboxes and folders; when you share folders in an Exchange mailbox with co-workers, they won't be able to see the colors assigned to categories or create and edit exiting categories unless they have Owner permission to your mailbox.

 TIP   Outlook doesn't provide a built-in method to share categories with other people. It is possible to create a list of your categories and add the list to the Master Category list using a macro or a third-party utility. We have provided a macro that does this at http://slipstick.com/categoriesmacro and a list of utilities at http://slipstick.com/categories.

Discovering tips for using categories

How would you use Color Categories? The obvious and most frequently used method is just to mark items so they are more easily found or to signify importance: Important is the red category, yellow is used for Needs Attention, and green is Complete. But there are other ways to use color categories.

As previously mentioned, and one of my favorite uses, is using categories to create a dynamic Contact Group. When the group membership changes, you need to edit and update the Contact Group. It's easier to add and remove a category from the contacts. If a contact is in several Contact Groups and has a new email address, you need to update every group his contact is in. Plus, you can't easily use Contact Groups in Mail Merges, but you can create a mail merge using just the contacts in a specific category.

I also like to use the same shade of color on related categories. Suppose you want your contacts organized in folders, with each country in a different folder. You should use categories instead of folders. Create a category for each country and assign colors by continent or region. For example, categories assigned to contacts in the Northern European countries have the dark blue color, North America is green. This solves the problem of "too many categories, not enough colors" while making it easier to glance over the list and know who is in Europe and who is in America.

Although not a favorite of mine, a number of users use a black category to cross "yesterday" off or mark appointments completed. Simply create a category named Completed and assign black or another dark color. When the appointments are finished, assign the completed category to the appointment. The appointment picks up the color of the most recently assigned category. To cross off dates in the monthly calendar, create an All Day Event and assign the Completed category to it.

THE ABSOLUTE MINIMUM

Here are the key points to remember from this chapter:

- You can organize your Outlook items by creating new categories and editing existing categories.

- Assigning color to categories, creating color contact groups, and sharing contact colors can help you organize your appointments, email, and contacts.

IN THIS CHAPTER

- Creating new folders
- Managing data using folders
- Using Conversation view
- Adding more data files

15

USING FOLDERS

Many users like to file their mail into folders, if only to keep the Inbox empty. Although I don't recommend using a lot of folders because it makes managing Outlook items more difficult (especially contacts), filing mail into a few folders and then using Instant Search to find the messages can be useful.

The most common reason many people use more folders in Outlook is to file their email and get it out of the Inbox. Some people like to create a folder for each person they receive email from, but this makes it harder to work with long email exchanges when several people are replying, because each message is stored in a different folder.

If you want to move messages out of the Inbox to keep it clean, move the messages to a folder named Completed, or use separate folders for personal and business messages, plus one for receipts for online purchases.

In this chapter, I'll show you how to manage your Outlook data using folders and data files.

Creating New Folders

You can create as many folders as you need at either the Inbox level or as a sub-folder to any other folder. The default folder type is the same type as the parent folder or parent module. You can create subfolders of any type under any folder. For example, you can create contacts and calendar folders under the Inbox.

 NOTE Is there a limit to the number of folders you can create in Outlook 2013? No! The data file format Outlook 2013 uses supports unlimited subfolders and Outlook messages or other items per folder. The default data file size is 50GB, so it can hold a lot of email, appointments, and contacts (somewhere around one million items, depending on size). If you need a larger data file, the file size can be increased by editing the registry. See http://support.microsoft.com/kb/832925 for instructions.

When you need to create a new mail folder, you can click the New Folder button on the Folder tab or right-click an existing folder, and then choose New Folder from the context menu. When you are creating Mail folders, type the name for your folder right in the folder list (see Figure 15.1).

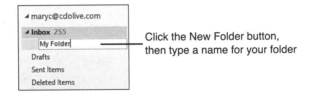

FIGURE 15.1

New Mail folders are added directly to the folder list in the Mail module.

When you are working in other modules and choose New Folder from the right-click menu or Folder tab, the Create New Folder dialog box opens (see Figure 15.2). Type a name for your folder, verify that the desired folder type is selected in the Folder contacts drop-down, and select the folder that the new folder will be placed in. If you want it at the same level as the Inbox, select the top level of the mailbox. Press OK to create the folder and exit the dialog box.

 NOTE You won't see the New Folder command on the context menu or ribbon in the Calendar module; look for the New Calendar command instead.

FIGURE 15.2

Choose any folder type in the Create New Folder dialog box.

After you've created the folders, you can move them to another position in the folder list by dragging the folder with your mouse.

 NOTE   If you have a habit of accidentally picking up folders and dropping them inside other folders, try enabling the mouse's ClickLock feature in Control Panel, Mouse. With ClickLock enabled, you need to click once to pick up a folder and click again to drop the folder.

Managing Folders

In addition to creating new folders, you can move, copy, rename, and delete your folders. These commands are available on the Folder tab and on the context menu when you right-click a folder, or you can use your mouse.

When you delete a folder, it's moved to the Deleted Items folder. The Calendar, Contact, or Tasks folders won't be visible in the Deleted items folder when you use the Mail pane. You'll need to switch to the folder list to see the nonmail folders.

 NOTE   If you need to delete a lot of folders, drag the folders into one folder, and then delete that folder, or drag the folders into the Deleted Items folder. This will avoid the annoying "Move [folder name] to the Deleted items folder?" dialog box that comes up when you use the Delete command.

If you need to move a folder a short distance on the folder list, you can drag it with your mouse. Use Outlook's Move Folder and Copy Folder commands when you need to move the folders a longer distance, because it uses the Folder picker, which is usually easier than dragging a folder up or down the folder list (see Figure 15.3).

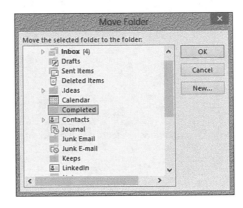

FIGURE 15.3

Use Move Folder when you need to move folders into other data files.

The Folder tab on the ribbon contains these commands (see Figure 15.4):

FIGURE 15.4

The Folder tab contains the commands you need to manage your Outlook folders. This screenshot shows the commands for an IMAP account.

- **New Folder**—Opens the Create New Folder dialog box.

- **New Search Folder**—Opens the New Search Folder dialog box.

- **Rename Folder**—Click to rename the selected folder. Instead of using the button, you can click twice on the folder name to initiate a rename.

- **Copy Folder**—Opens the Copy Folder dialog box. Select the folder and then click the Copy Folder button to choose the folder you want to copy the selected folder into. Instead of using the button, you can hold Ctrl as you drag the folder with your mouse. The cursor will include a + sign, indicating it is being copied.

- **Move Folder**—Opens the Move Folder dialog, where you'll select the folder you want to move the folder into, or you can drag the folder using the mouse.

- **Delete Folder**—Select the folder you want to delete and press the Delete button. If you prefer using the keyboard, select the folder and press the Del key.

- **Mark All as Read**—Select a folder and then click the button to mark all messages in the folder as read.

- **Run Rules Now**—Use to open the Rules and Alerts dialog box to run rules. Note that this button is not shown on the ribbon with all account types.

- **Show All Folders A to Z**—Previous versions of Outlook sorted folders in alphabetical order, but Outlook 2013 lets you arrange the folders in any order you desire. If you decide alphabetical order is better for you, click Show All Folders A to Z to sort the folders. When the button is highlighted, the sort order is locked alphabetically. Click it again to unlock.

- **Clean Up Folder**—Use this button to remove redundant messages from threads.

- **Delete All**—Move the contents of the folder (but not the folder) to the Deleted Items folder.

- **Purge (IMAP accounts only)**—Permanently deletes messages marked for deletion.

- **Recover Deleted Items**—Used with Exchange Server mailboxes to recover recently deleted messages after the Deleted Items folder is emptied.

- **Show in Favorites**—Adds the selected folder to the Favorites list. You can also drag folders to the Favorites list and drag to reorder the folders.

- **View on Server (Exchange server only)**—Includes the messages that are on the server when using Sync Slider to limit the amount of messages stored in Outlook.

- **Policy (Exchange Server only)**—Policy settings used for archiving older messages.

- **IMAP Folders (IMAP accounts only)**—Opens the IMAP folders dialog box.

- **Update Folder List (IMAP accounts only)**—Updates the IMAP folder list.

- **AutoArchive Settings**—Opens the autoarchive settings dialog box.

- **Folder Permissions (Exchange Server only)**—Opens the Folder Properties dialog box to give other users permission to view your folders.

- **Folder Properties**—Opens the Folder Properties dialog box.

Managing Data Using Folders

Common usage of folders is to sort Contacts into groups. Some people sort their contacts into folders by state or country, others use 26 folders and sort the contacts alphabetically. Some Outlook users sort by company or social group.

Although it makes sense to keep the contacts for members of the civic club or baseball team in a separate folder, if the members are also friends you'll have a copy of the contact in your Friends folder. If you need to update their address, you'll need to remember to update both contacts. For this reason, it's usually better to use fewer folders, and then group contacts or appointments using color categories.

My recommendation for calendar and contacts folders: one folder each. If you want or need more, use two: one for business and one for private or personal contacts or appointments. Use categories to group contacts together instead of separating them into different folders.

Most users, myself included, use folders to sort email. Some of the messages are moved using rules as the messages arrive in Outlook's Inbox. Other messages are moved to other folders after reading them.

As with contacts, fewer folders is better, but most people will have more than two folders for email. At the very least, have a folder for messages that you are finished with but don't want to delete, one for messages you need to keep forever, and folders for messages from email lists. Most people have at least a dozen folders, and it's not uncommon for some users to have several hundred folders. I don't recommend several hundred folders; it's too hard to manage that many folders, and it's harder to navigate the folder list.

More than one person has created deeply nested folders and then forgot where a folder was. In some cases, they forgot where the folder was and what it was called; other times, they accidently picked up the folder with their mouse and then dropped it. Because Outlook can't search for folder names, finding the folder involves a lot of browsing unless you know the tricks.

If you can find a message in the folder, you can use these steps to find where the folder is.

1. Use Instant Search to find an email message in the folder you are looking for. You may want to add the In Folder field to the view so you can see if a message is in the "missing" folder.

2. Double-click the email to open it.

3. Click the opened email to make sure that is your active window.

4. Press Ctrl+Shift+F (Advanced Find). If the folder name you are looking for is not shown in the In field, the message was not the active window or the message is not in that folder.

5. Click the Browse button to reveal the full path to the email (see Figure 15.5).

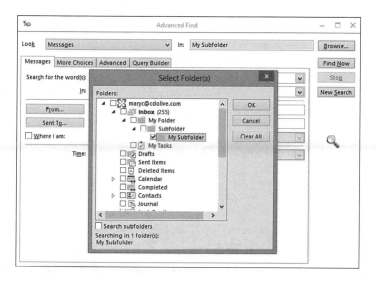

FIGURE 15.5

Use the Select Folder(s) dialog box in Advanced Find to find where folders are in your folder list.

 NOTE You can use a macro to find folders. See http://www. slipstick.com/find-folder for the code.

Conversation View

Although I don't recommend either using a large number of folders to sort your email or filing mail in folders by sender, you can use the conversation feature in Outlook 2013 to show all mail in a conversation. With the Conversation Settings option enabled to Show Messages from Other Folders, all messages in a conversation, including sent messages and messages stored in other folders, are shown in the conversation.

To enable conversations, switch to the View tab and add a check mark to Show as Conversations; then expand conversation Settings and select Show Messages from Other Folders (see Figure 15.6).

FIGURE 15.6

Use Show as Conversations and Show Messages from Other Folders to view all messages in a conversation together.

If you have multiple Personal Folders files in your profile and are not delivering mail to the Personal Folders, you'll need to enable it for Search if you want to include the results in the Conversation view. You can also enable an option for reminders.

To include the data file in searches, open the Search tab by clicking in the Search field, and then expand Search Tools, Locations to Search. Select the data files you want to include in the searches.

If you want to display reminders for items in Personal Folders files (.pst), you'll need to right-click the top-level folder, Choose Data File Properties from the bottom of the context menu to open the Properties dialog box. Add a check to Display Reminders and Tasks from This Folder in the To-Do Bar (see Figure 15.7). With this option set, reminders on items in the data file are displayed.

Adding More Data Files

Outlook can open as many Personal Folders files as you want, within reason. However, after you get above 50 .pst files open in your profile, Outlook may start to slow down. Multiple .pst files are used for different email accounts or to archive older messages.

You can open existing Personal Folder files (.pst) in Outlook or create new .pst files.

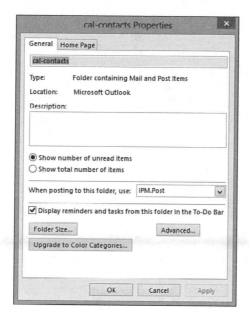

FIGURE 15.7

Enable Display Reminders and Tasks from This Folder if you want to include the contents of the folder in the Conversation view.

To open an existing .pst or create a new one, switch to the File tab.

1. Click Account Settings. Switch to the Data Files tab.

2. Click Add.

3. From the Save As Type list, select Outlook Data File.

4. Browse to find the .pst file you want to open, or type a name for the new .pst in the Name field (see Figure 15.8).

5. Click OK and return to the Account Settings dialog box in Outlook.

 NOTE When you create new Personal Folders (.pst) files, you can put them anywhere on your hard drive.

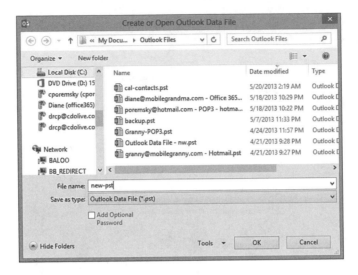

FIGURE 15.8

Use the Create or Open Outlook data File dialog box to create a new .pst file or select an existing .pst file to open in your profile.

THE ABSOLUTE MINIMUM

Here are the key points to remember from this chapter:

- You can create as many folders as you want or need; however, sorting mail and contacts using folders can make it harder to manage your data. Using fewer folders is better.

- Outlook's data files can hold well over one million messages, appointments, and contacts. If you need more storage space, you can edit the registry to allow larger data files or create more Personal Folders (.pst) files.

- If you file your mail in folders, Outlook 2013's Conversation View can display all messages in the conversation, including messages in other folders and in other data files.

USING SEARCH

Finding your messages in a large mailbox isn't difficult when you use Instant Search. If you use the same search over and over, you can create a search folder, which contains always-up-to-date search results.

Outlook offers several ways to find things in your mailbox: Instant Search, Search folders, Find Related, Advanced Find, filters in custom views, and the People pane. Each method uses essentially the same search criteria, and each method has benefits.

Instant Search

Instant Search is a quick and easy way to find your messages, contacts, or appointments. Type a keyword into the search field or refine the search query using field names and wait a few seconds for Outlook to find items matching the keyword. If you don't refine the search to specific fields, all common fields will be searched.

The Search context tab displays when you click in the Search field or press Ctrl+E on your keyboard, so you can select the fields to refine the search (see Figure 16.1). After you learn the common field names, it's usually faster to type the query into the search field.

FIGURE 16.1

Click in the Search field to display the Search tab.

Choose the folders you want to search in the Scope group on the left of the Search ribbon, choosing from All Mailboxes, Current Mailbox, Current Folder, Subfolders, and All Outlook Items.

To set a specific scope as your default search scope, open the Search Options dialog box (see Figure 16.2). From the Search tab, choose Search Tools, and then click Search Options.

Other options you can enable or disable are as follows:

- Include messages from the Deleted Items folder in each data file when searching in All Items.

- When possible, display results as the query is typed.

- Improve search speed by limiting the number of results shown.

- Highlight search terms in the results and choose the highlight color.

- Notify me when the search results might be limited because indexing is not complete.

You can include or remove a data file from the index using the Search tab's Search Tools menu. Expand the Locations to Search menu and select a data file to toggle the setting. Data files with check marks beside their name are indexed. In most cases, you'll want all data files selected.

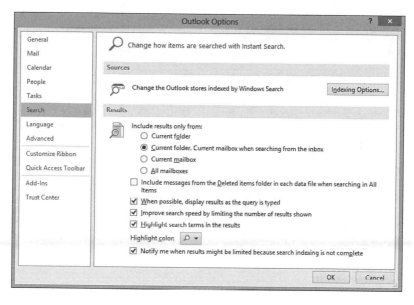

FIGURE 16.2

Configure the search options, including the default scope, the search term highlight color, and whether to include the Deleted Items folder in the results.

NOTE Searching for mail, calendar, or contacts in Windows Start Search field or Windows Explorer's Search field will not include items in Outlook 2013. You can search for Outlook email, appointments, and contacts only by using Outlook 2013's Instant Search or Advanced Find.

Instant Search Queries

Instant search includes a number of commands you can use to refine a search. These commands can be inserted by clicking buttons on the Search tab, or you can type the query into the search field directly. Typing the query can be a faster and more efficient way to do a search when you know the commands to use.

To search by a field name, type the Outlook field name into the search field. Don't use a space in multiple-word field names. Following are examples:

from:john

firstname:mary

To search between (but not including) two dates, use the following format with any date field. The following example finds messages received 1/2/2013 through 4/14/2013:

received:(>1/1/2013 AND <4/15/2013)

To include the two dates in the results, add an equal sign or use two periods between the dates. These two queries will find messages received 1/1/2013 through 4/15/2013:

received:(>=1/1/2013 AND <=4/15/2013)

received: (1/1/13..6/15/13)

To find messages of a certain size or within a size range, use the greater than, less than, and equal signs or two periods, as shown in these examples:

size:10kb

size:=50kb<60kb

size:3mb..12mb

In addition to greater than (>), less than (<), and equal symbols (=), you can use commas, AND, or OR operators between search terms.

from:(mary NOT smith)

cc:(mary AND sue)

to:(mary OR billy)

You can use some natural language words with Instant Search. Search recognizes days of the week (Sunday, Monday, Tuesday), the months (March, April, May), as well as today, tomorrow, yesterday, week, next month, last week, past month, and coming year. The space between multiple word phrases is optional: thisweek, nextmonth, lastweek, pastmonth, comingyear are valid in Instant Search.

received:(last week)

start:(nextmonth)

Partial Word Searches

Instant Search can't do the type of partial word search most people want, with the search term found anywhere in the word. Instant Search looks for the search term at the beginning of each word. This means searching for **ann** would include Anniversary in the results but not MaryAnne. The search engine sees most punctuation as the end of a word, so it would find **ann** in Mary-Anne.

Finding Mail Sent to or from Specific People

There are several ways to find mail sent to or from a specific person. You can use the Find Related, the People pane, or Search Folders.

Find Related

Find Related is a predefined Instant Search query found on the right-click context menu (see Figure 16.3) or on the Message tab in an open message. To use it, right-click a message and move the mouse over Find Related, selecting Messages in This Conversation, Messages from Sender, or if a category is assigned to the message, Messages in [category name].

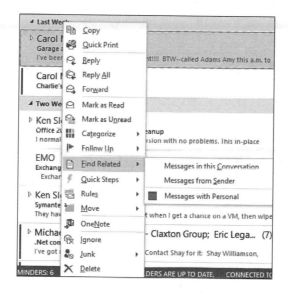

FIGURE 16.3

Right-click a message and choose Find Related from the context menu.

The Find Related commands create an instant search using one of the following queries:

Messages in this Conversation: **[Conversation]:="message subject"**

Messages from Sender: **from:(sender display name)**

Messages in Category: **category:="category name"**

People Pane

If you need to find recent messages, attachments, or appointments from a person, the message will be listed in the People pane at the bottom of the Reading pane, in an open message, or on the person's Contact information.

The sender and each person the message was sent to will be listed in the People pane, represented by the contact's photo, if available, or a generic people icon. Click on the photo or icon to view messages from that person and click any message to open it.

Minimize and maximize the People pane by clicking the top of the bar (or use the arrow on the right side as shown in Figure 16.4). You can adjust the height of the maximized window by dragging the top edge. To turn the People pane off completely, switch to the View tab and select People Pane, Off.

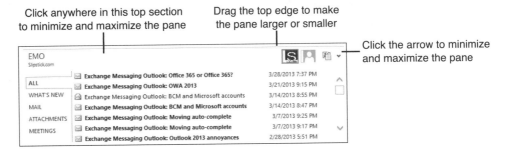

FIGURE 16.4

The People pane displays recent messages from the sender or any recipient of the current message.

The People pane works best when you need to find recent messages, because it is limited to the 100 most recent items, including Facebook or LinkedIn status updates.

Search Folders

If there is an instant search you use a lot, you can create a search folder for it. Search folders are virtual folders that can display messages from any folder in the data file (unlike Instant Search, which can search all data files in the profile). If a search folder is used at least once every 8 days, the folder watches for messages meeting the condition of the search and adds them to the search results.

To create a search folder, follow these steps:

1. Right-click Search Folders in the folder list.

2. Choose New Search Folder.

3. Select from one of the predefined searches or create a custom search folder (see Figure 16.5).

4. Choose the criteria.

5. Click OK to close the dialog box.

6. Right-click the new search folder and choose Show in Favorites.

FIGURE 16.5

Create search folders for frequently used searches.

 NOTE Search folders are limited to email only. They cannot be used with other Outlook item types.

Search folders display the results of a search; messages are not moved to search folders.

Advanced Find

Although Instant Search is powerful and can handle most searches, there are times when Advanced Find is useful. Like Search Folders, Advanced Find is limited to searching one data file at a time. But unlike Instant Search, the results are listed in a separate window (see Figure 16.6). This enables you to keep the search results open onscreen as you work in other Outlook folders.

FIGURE 16.6

When you use Advanced Find, the search results are displayed in a separate window.

The context menu is available when you right-click items in the Advanced Find results, allowing you to flag messages, add categories, reply or forward messages, and more. You can also customize the view in the Advanced Find results pane; to do this, right-click the row of field names to select from the various options.

AND and OR operators are supported in the Advanced Find filters (see Figure 16.7). When the criteria uses the same field, the conditions use the OR operator. You can put the conditions together on one line or use separate lines for each criteria.

From contains Mary OR John

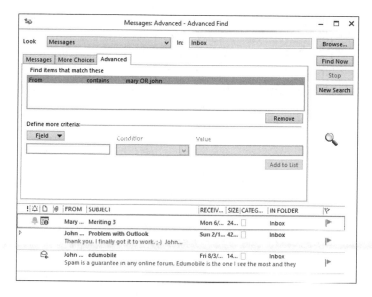

FIGURE 16.7

Use the Advanced tab on the Advanced Find dialog to create advanced searches.

When the criteria uses different fields, the criteria uses the AND operator. This filter would search for messages from Mary and sent to John (see Figure 16.8).

From contains Mary

To contains John

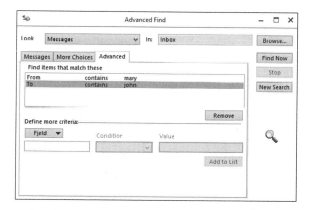

FIGURE 16.8

When you use two different criteria, the search uses the AND operator.

To use the AND and OR operators together with different fields, you need to use a hidden feature called Query Builder, which allows users to create complicated queries using AND and OR operators (see Figure 16.9). When it is enabled, it works with all uses of the Filter dialog box, including custom views, search folders, and Advanced Find, and you will be able to use queries such as this:

From contains Mary

OR

To contains John

FIGURE 16.9

Use the Query Builder to create complex filters using the AND and OR operators.

To enable Query Builder, perform these steps:

1. Press Windows key+R to open the Run command.

2. Type **regedit** in the Open field and click OK.

3. Browse to HKEY_CURRENT_USER\Software\Microsoft\Office\15.0\Outlook.

4. Right-click Outlook and click New, and then Key.

5. Type **QueryBuilder** as the new key name, and then press Enter.

6. Close the Registry editor and return to Outlook.

7. Press Ctrl+Shift+F to open the Advanced Find dialog box. A new tab called Query Builder is added after the Advanced tab.

NOTE   Enable Query Builder using a ready-to-use .reg file available at http://www.slipstick.com/query.

Search Troubleshooting

If the Instant Search results don't include content from all data files in your profile, verify that the data file is enabled for search. To check, click in the Search field, expand the Search Tools button, and then click Locations to Search and verify the data file is selected.

On the rare occasion when Instant Search doesn't seem to be working correctly, you may need to rebuild the Search Index.

To rebuild the index, go to File, Options, Search, and click Indexing Options. Click the Advanced button, and then click Rebuild. This rebuilds the instant search index and should fix most search problems.

Although it's generally better to use the Rebuild button when you need to rebuild the index, you can delete the search index files from the hard drive to force Windows to rebuild the index.

To do this, delete all files and folders in C:\ProgramData\Microsoft\Search\Data.

ProgramData is a hidden folder, and you'll need to type the entire path in the address bar of Windows Explorer to see it. You need to reboot before Windows starts to index your Outlook files over again.

THE ABSOLUTE MINIMUM

Here are the key points to remember from this chapter:

- Outlook offers several methods you can use to find email, appointments, and contacts.

- Use the People Pane to find recent messages and attachments from your contacts.

- Instant Search is faster and powerful enough for many search needs.

- For persistent search results, use Search Folders or Advanced Find.

- When you need to search using complex criteria, you'll need to enable Query Builder.

IN THIS CHAPTER

- Changing views
- Creating new views
- Conditional formatting
- Creating custom views

17

WORKING WITH VIEWS

Outlook contains a lot of data, including all your email, contacts, appointments, and tasks—often several years' worth of data. If you send and receive a lot of email, you could have thousands of messages in your inbox to sort through. Views can help you manage your email, calendar, and contacts, making it easier to find the information you need. You can use Outlook's default views or create your own custom views, with conditional formatting to color code items or filters to show only the item you want to see.

Views are a powerful way to manage your email, but because they were buried in menus in previous versions of Outlook, few people used the views included with Outlook and even fewer people created their own customized views. The View tab in Outlook 2013 (see Figure 17.1) makes it easy to use the supplied views and to create your own customized views.

FIGURE 17.1

The View tab has the commands you need to change the view and arrangement of your email messages.

You change the view on the folder using the Change View command. You edit the view using View Settings and change how the items are grouped by selecting one of the commands in the Arrangement section. Use the Reverse Sort command to change the sort order. Finally, to undo all changes and return the view to the default settings, click the Reset View button.

Changing Views

Changing the view in Outlook is simple:

1. Select the Views tab.

2. Click Change View to expand the menu and select a new view (see Figure 17.2).

FIGURE 17.2

Click Change View to select a new view.

Outlook includes several predefined views for each folder type. Each folder type has different views that work best for each specific folder type, such as the monthly calendar view for the calendar folders and the business card view for the contacts folders. One or more list views are available for each folder type.

Items in a list view can be grouped together by the category, date, subject, or several other fields. Outlook 2013 refers to this as Arrangement. The fields you can arrange by vary with the folder type, but you'll have category and date arrangements available in each folder type (see Figure 17.3) .

FIGURE 17.3

Use Arrangement to change how you group Outlook items.

 NOTE You don't need to use the Views ribbon to change the Arrangement or sort order. In the message list, click By [field name], and then choose a different arrangement from the menu. To change the sort order, click the field name you want to sort by, and then click again to reverse the sort order.

Email Views

The predefined views for folders containing email are all list views and include the following:

- **Compact**—Default two-line view containing the subject, sender, and date
- **Single**—The subject, sender, date, and other fields on one line
- **Preview**—A single-line view with the Reading pane turned off

Some folders have views that were designed specifically for the type of messages stored in the folder, such as a Sent To view in the Sent Items folder which shows the name or address the message was sent to. There is also an RSS view for the RSS feeds, and Documents and Site Mailbox views for Search Folders.

IMAP accounts have their own views:

- **IMAP Messages**—A Compact view, the default for IMAP accounts.
- **Hide Messages Marked for Deletion**— When you delete messages from an IMAP account, they get marked for deletion (crossed out) and deleted later. This view hides these messages.

- **Group Messages Marked for Deletion**—This view groups messages that are marked for deletion.
- **Preview**—A two-line view with the reading pane turned off.

You can use a 1-, 2-, or 3-line message preview with each of these views to display up to the first 256 characters in a message (see Figure 17.4).

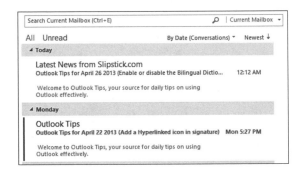

FIGURE 17.4

The email message list with three-line preview enabled.

 NOTE To view only unread messages, click Unread at the top of the message list. Click All to show all messages.

The Compact view was designed to provide more information about each message when the Reading pane is on the right, whereas the Single-line view works better with the Reading pane off or on the bottom.

 NOTE Message Preview previews all messages if enabled. There is not an option to preview only unread messages.

Calendar Views

The calendar comes with the standard calendar views and list views with filters, which include the following:

- **Calendar**—This is the familiar Day, Week, and Month view of the calendar.
- **Preview**—Day, Week, and Month views that include the contents of the notes field, as space allows. This is most useful with longer appointments.

- **List**—A list of all appointments in table format. The appointments can be sorted or arranged in groups.
- **Active**—This view shows the upcoming appointments in a table format.

To view multiple calendars at once, add a check beside the calendar's name in the Navigation pane. Click the arrows in the calendar tabs to switch between overlay and side-by-side view.

In addition to the typical day, week, and month layouts, the calendar includes a Schedule View (Figure 17.5). The Schedule View was designed to display multiple calendars, with the calendar names listed top to bottom and the hours going left to right.

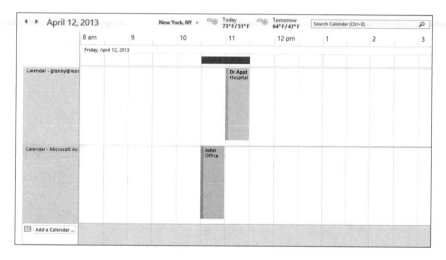

FIGURE 17.5

Use the Schedule view with multiple calendars.

Each calendar can be displayed using a different color. You can let Outlook pick the color automatically or permanently assign a color to a calendar. To change the calendar color, select a calendar and on the View tab, click the Color button or right-click the calendar and choose Color.

People Views

Outlook's People module, formerly known as Contacts, contains all of your contacts and the traditional address card and list views as well as a new People view.

- **People Hub**—An aggregate view of your contacts. When you have more than one contact for a person, the details from each contact are combined on the Contact Card in the People Hub, with links to each contact. (Figure 17.6)

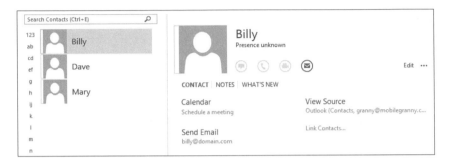

FIGURE 17.6

The People Hub displays contacts in an easy-to-use format.

- **Business Card**—A business card-like view. The cards can be customized with company logos and photos.

- **Card**—A simple card view, displaying the contact's information in a list.

- **Phone**—A list view containing name, company, and the phone number fields.

- **List**—A list in table format containing the company-related fields as well as address and phone fields.

The People Hub displays "contact cards" and links to the person's contact(s), with all data on each contact displayed as one contact on the contact card. If you use the LinkedIn or Facebook social connector in Outlook, contacts in the People Hub will include links to their LinkedIn or Facebook profiles.

The People Hub may seem confusing at first. When you have more than one contact for a person, the People Hub displays the information from all of the contacts, including Facebook and LinkedIn, on one card. To open the person's contact, click the link under View Source.

Task Views

All task views are simple table or List views, using predefined filters. You can sort and arrange tasks in groups using any of these views.

- **Detailed**—Includes most task fields.

- **Simple List**—Includes only the basic task fields: Subject, Due Date, and Categories field.

- **To-Do List**—Task list with the Preview pane turned on. This view is useful in the To-Do List with flagged email messages.

- **Prioritized**—Groups tasks and flagged messages by the Importance field (High, Normal, Low).

- **Active**—Completed tasks are hidden.

- **Completed**—Only completed tasks are shown, using a normal font, not the strikeout text normally used for completed tasks.

- **Today**—Shows only tasks due today or overdue.

- **Next 7 Days**—Tasks due in the next 7 days or those that are overdue.

- **Overdue**—Shows only overdue tasks.

- **Assigned**—Shows only the tasks assigned to others.

- **Server Tasks**—This view includes custom Priority and Status fields used only with SharePoint Tasks.

Notes Views

Outlook 2013's "sticky notes" use two types of views, list and icon, and come with these default views:

- **Icon**—Displays the notes as Small or Large icons or in an icon list arrangement

- **Notes List**—A list view, with the note subject (the first sentence or 256 characters), the created date, and categories shown

- **Last 7 Days**—A list view that shows only the notes created within the last 7 days

Journal Views

The journal is well hidden and will eventually be removed from Outlook, so I don't recommend using it; however, if you do, you'll have Timeline or List views to choose from; these are as follows:

- **Timeline**—The dates scroll across the top of the view.

- **Entry List**—A list view.

- **Phone Calls**—Shows journal items marked "phone calls."

- **Last 7 Days**—Shows journal items created within the last 7 days.

Applying Views to Folders

After you change a view on one folder, you can apply the view to many other folders at once. You need to view the folder whose view you want to apply to other folders. You can apply views to any or all folders of the same folder type. Follow these steps:

1. Open the folder whose view you want to apply to other folders.

2. Switch to the View tab.

3. Expand the Change View button.

4. Select Apply View to Other Folders.

5. In the Apply View dialog box, select the folders you want to apply the view to.

6. Select the top-level folders and add a check to Apply View to Subfolders to apply the view to all folders of that type within your mailbox or data file.

7. Click OK when you are finished selecting folders. This applies the current view to all the selected folders (see Figure 17.7).

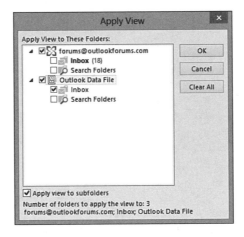

FIGURE 17.7

Select the folders to apply the view to, and then press OK.

 TIP   When you use a list view, if you press and hold Shift as you click field names, you can sort by multiple fields.

Creating Custom Views

Customized views can be used to show or hide Outlook items meeting certain conditions. You can use custom views to filter contacts before doing a mail merge. If you use the same search queries over and over, a custom view can be used as a more permanent instant search.

Views offer seven areas you can customize:

- **Columns**—Add the fields you want to see in your view.

- **Group By**—The default setting is to Automatically Group According to Arrangement.

- **Sort**—Change the sort order of your Outlook items.

- **Filter**—Create filters to show or hide Outlook items. Choose from preselected options or use the Advanced tab (and SQL tab, when available) to create your own filters using any available field.

- **Other Settings**—The options available in Other Settings depend on which folder you view. Use this dialog box to change fonts and customize your layout.

- **Conditional Formatting**—Conditional formatting changes the color or font of an item in List view when the item meets the conditions in the conditional formatting rule. Not all views support conditional formatting.

- **Format Columns**—Use this to change the format used in columns containing dates or numbers or to change Yes/No fields to check boxes or words.

To create a custom view, you need to switch to the View tab. Click View Settings to customize the current view or click Change View, Manage Views to create a new custom view.

To create a new custom view, follow these steps:

1. On the View tab, click the Change View button.

2. Select Manage Views.

3. Click New.

4. Enter a name for your view.

5. Select the type of view.

6. Select who can see the view.

7. Click OK.

8. In the Advanced View Settings, select the Columns (fields) that will be used in the view (see Figure 17.8).

FIGURE 17.8

Create a custom view in Outlook 2013.

9. Configure the other options, including filters and conditional formatting.

Close the dialog box when you are finished to apply the view to your folder.

Resetting Views

Although a rare occurrence, occasionally one or more views become corrupt and prevent Outlook from displaying the folder contents. To fix it, press the Reset View button on the View tab, as shown in Figure 17.9.

FIGURE 17.9

Click Reset View to restore the view to its default settings.

You can also reset views using the Manage Views dialog box. Select the view you want to reset and click Reset View. You can reset only the default views; custom views are deleted instead.

If Outlook won't open and you suspect the view is corrupt, or resetting the view on the folder does not fix the problem, you'll need to close Outlook and restart using the cleanviews switch.

To use the cleanviews switch, close Outlook, and then press the Windows key+R to open the Run command and type the following:

outlook.exe /cleanviews

Press Enter or click OK to start Outlook and then reset all the views in Outlook.

All custom views are deleted, and the default views will be reset to their original settings.

Copying Views

Imagine this scenario: you spent an hour creating a number of conditional formatting rules in one of Outlook's default views. Because Outlook does not offer an easy way to lock a view, you accidently reset the view and lost all of your hard work.

Although you can't lock views to prevent changes, you can make copies of custom views to use as backups if the original is lost or changed.

Create a copy of the current view from the View tab by selecting Change Views, Save Current View as a New View.

If you want to copy other views, choose Manage Views, then select the view and click Copy and enter a new name for your view.

Using Conditional Formatting

Conditional formatting is used to format messages or other Outlook items that meet specific conditions. For example, messages from your boss can be shown in the message list with a larger red font, and messages from friends can use a smaller purple font (see Figure 17.10).

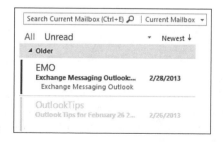

FIGURE 17.10

Use colors to highlight messages for better visibility.

Conditional formatting rules are part of a view; if you change the view, you'll lose the conditional formatting rules.

 NOTE Outlook includes default conditional formatting rules for read, unread, expired, and overdue messages. The formatting can be changed, but the conditions cannot be changed.

To create a conditional formatting view, follow these steps:

1. Switch to the View tab.

2. Click the View Settings button.

3. Click the Conditional Formatting button.

4. Click Add to create a new Conditional Formatting rule.

5. Enter a name for the rule (see Figure 17.11).

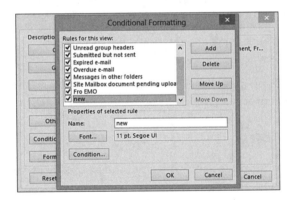

FIGURE 17.11

Create a conditional formatting rule.

6. Click Font to select a color. You can also change the font and font size.

7. Click Condition to open the Filter dialog box to create your filter.

 NOTE To create a filter for an email address or part of an address, use the From field on the Messages tab. To use the display name, use the Advanced tab and select the From field from the list of fields.

THE ABSOLUTE MINIMUM

Here are the key points to remember from this chapter:

- Use Views to sort and filter Outlook items instead of using multiple folders.

- Don't be afraid to customize the views. If you mess up a view, reset the view and start over.

- Use conditional formatting to highlight messages in color so they are easier to find.

18

PRINTING

Although Outlook is primarily an electronic personal information manager, at times you'll need to print out messages, appointments, or tasks.

Outlook supports the calendar and contact formats used by popular planners, including Day-Timer, Day Runner, and Franklin Planner, using a wide range of paper sizes and layouts.

Printing Basics

Outlook doesn't offer a lot of print options; in fact, many people consider Outlook's printing capabilities primitive and limited. There are two basic print styles for all Outlook items: Table Style and Memo Style, with additional print layouts available for Calendar and Contacts.

The Table Style printout creates a list of the contents of the selected folder, exactly as shown on your screen. This style is good if you need a checklist of tasks or a list containing the sender, email subject, and received dates.

The Memo Style prints an individual item, one per page. When you open a message, appointment, or contact before printing, Memo is the only style available.

You can open the Print dialog box from the File tab by clicking Print or using the keyboard shortcut Ctrl+P to select the layout and printer configurations. The available styles are listed under Settings, and on the right is a print preview of the selected style (see Figure 18.1).

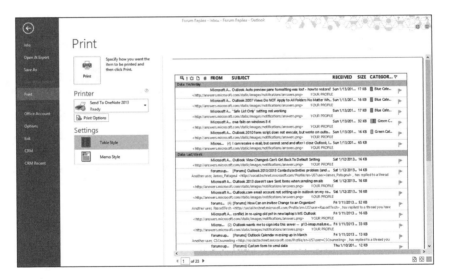

FIGURE 18.1

Available print styles are shown on the Print page, along with Print Preview.

The basic elements of the Print dialog box include the following:

- **Print button**—When you are ready to print, select this button.

- **Printer**—Select the printer you want to print to here. Most people will have an electronic format, such as OneNote, in addition to a standard printer.

- **Print Options**—Use this to include attachments in the printout, change Page Setup, save custom print settings, or select the number of pages to print.

- **Settings**—Choose Table Style or Memo Style here.

- **Preview**—Previews the pages before printing. When you select one item to print Memo Style, print preview is automatically enabled. If you select more than one item to print in Memo Style, or have a large number of items in the folder and are using Table Style, they are not automatically previewed.

 NOTE   Messages with Rights Management (IRM) enabled will have the Print menus disabled and are not printable.

Printing Email

When you print most Outlook items from a table view, including email messages, tasks, and lists of calendars or contacts, the default print settings are often acceptable. You can print one or more items in their entirety using the memo format, or you can print a list of the selected items or a list of all items in the folder. When you print a list of Outlook items, the fields visible in the folder are included in the printout.

Table Style includes all the fields used in the current view, on one line; if Message Preview is enabled, the preview is included in the printout (see figure 18.2). Additionally, all formatting shown in the view is printed when you use Table Style. This includes icons, dates, flags, and category fields. Unread messages are printed using bold formatting.

Group headings are included in the printouts. If you are using a view that groups items, such as Arrange by Date or by category, the group titles are included in the printout. Conversation groups are not expanded when printed; however, the message count is included in the printout.

If you want to include specific fields in Table Style printouts, create a custom view and select it before printing.

You'll use the Memo Style when you want to print messages or items in full, with one Outlook item per page. When you open an item and choose File, Print, the only style available is Memo Style.

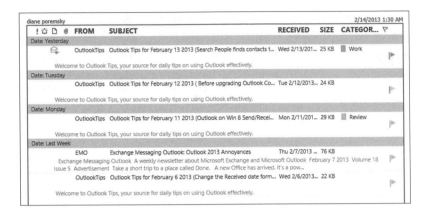

FIGURE 18.2

Printing a list of messages in Table Style includes all the fields in the view.

The Memo Style doesn't give you control over the fields that are included. The header fields will print, including all the recipients listed in the To and CC fields. Attachments included on the message can be printed along with the message. All fields in appointments or contacts are printed.

 TIP If you need to print a message but don't want to include the list of recipients, click the Forward button, delete the names and email addresses from the message body, and then print. After the message is printed, close the Forward without sending it.

Print Styles

A print style is a combination of page settings and paper sizes that let you control the way items print. Outlook includes a number of built-in styles that can be customized to create additional styles. Additionally, you can choose the font and other formatting options and can create custom styles to use again and again.

You can use custom styles to use a specific paper size, fonts, or header and footers. For example, if you use a Day Planner, you can create a custom print style that uses the correct paper size for the planner.

The two basic print styles give you the choice of printing individual items or printing a list of all items in the folder. For example, you can print a single appointment on one sheet of paper or print a list of appointments in the Calendar folder (see Figure 18.3).

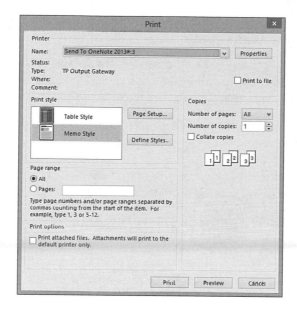

FIGURE 18.3

Choose Memo Style to print the Outlook item or table view to print a list of all items in the current folder.

All Outlook items types support these two basic print styles:

- Table Style prints Outlook items in a table format similar to the List Style view used in Outlook folders.

- Memo Style is used to print out an Outlook item on a single sheet of paper.

In addition to Memo Style and Table Style, the Calendar and Contacts folders have additional print styles, which are similar to layouts used in day planners. These Calendar print styles can be selected when you use the Day, Week, Month, or Schedule view:

- Daily Style prints appointments in a daily appointment-style list by the hour, similar to the 1-day view available in Outlook and used in day planners.

- Weekly Agenda Style creates a printout with the week displayed in two columns and three rows.

- Weekly Calendar Style prints the calendar using the daily format, but with all seven days included.

- Monthly Style prints your calendar in a traditional monthly style, similar to the monthly style used onscreen.

- Tri-fold Style creates a trifold calendar. By default, it contains appointments for a specific date, along with your tasks or a blank area for handwritten notes and a weekly calendar. The content of each section is configurable.

- Calendar Details Style prints a simple list of appointments, grouped by date. The printout includes the appointment details.

When you are viewing Contacts in People, Business Card, or Card views, the following styles are available for printing:

- Card Style prints your contacts using the same fields that are visible in the Card view.

- Booklet Style offers small or medium booklets. Use this style to create an address book you can take with you. This style can be printed on both sides of a sheet of paper that folds into a booklet.

- Phone Directory Style prints your contacts in an alphabetical list, similar to the format used in commercial phone books.

The print styles that are available to use depend on the folder view. When you use a List view, only the Memo and Table Styles are available. When you use an Icon or Timeline view, only Memo Style printing is an option.

The additional print styles for calendar and contacts are present only when you use Day, Week, Month, or Schedule views or the People, Business Card, or Card views. If you don't see these print styles listed when you choose File, Print, you need to change the view on the folder before opening the print dialog.

 NOTE You can change the fonts and paper sizes, but you cannot customize the templates.

When you customize a print style, the customization is stored in a file called OutlPrnt, located in C:\Users\username\AppData\Roaming\Microsoft\Outlook. If you have multiple Outlook profiles, they will share the OutlPrnt file and custom styles will be available in all Outlook profiles.

Some printing errors, including Outlook crashing when you try to print something, can be fixed by deleting or renaming the OutlPrnt file. It's safe to delete this file; Outlook will create a new OutlPrnt the next time you print, but you will lose any custom settings or styles.

Configuring Printing Options

Outlook comes with preconfigured print styles, and many people never change the defaults. However, you can change them if you want to, or you can create your own print styles using Page Setup or Define Styles. If you use several different paper sizes, you can create a style for each paper size.

You can manage the Printing Options using these two dialog boxes:

- **Page Setup**—Change the fonts, paper size, margins, headers, and footers.
- **Define Styles**—Save custom settings to use again.

If you want to use the print style again, follow these steps:

1. Open the Print dialog by clicking the File tab, then Print.
2. Click the Print Options button.
3. Choose Define Styles, and then click Copy.
4. Enter a name for your style and then click OK in the Define Styles dialog to save it.

To open the Page Setup dialog box (see Figure 18.4) choose Define Print Styles, and Edit or Copy. The Format tab will get the most use, with different options available for each Outlook item type.

Although the available options vary with the print format, the Fonts settings and Column Shading settings are available in all print styles and enable you to customize the style's properties.

Use the Paper tab, as shown in Figure 18.5, to choose the paper type, the size of the printed page, and the page orientation. Many paper types are included in the list, but you also can create a custom type. The page size reflects the size of the finished page, with many sizes defined, including pages for popular planners. As you select different page sizes, a preview of the page is shown in the orientation preview section.

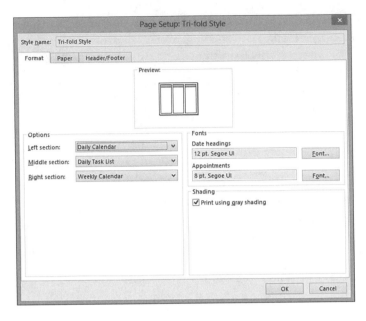

FIGURE 18.4

Use the Page Setup dialog to customize your printout, add a basic header or footer, and select from an assortment of paper sizes.

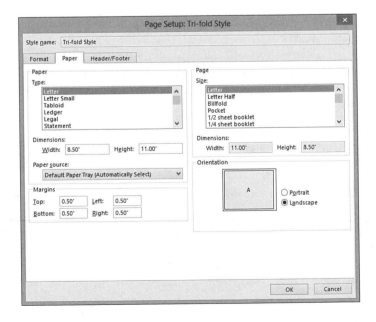

FIGURE 18.5

Choose your paper size and orientation in Page Setup.

The Header/Footer tab has your options for headers and footers (see Figure 18.6). Click your mouse in any of the sections and click the icons at the bottom of the footer area to insert the page number, date and time, and username. Text entered into the left block is blocked left, text in the center section is aligned center, and text on the right is blocked right.

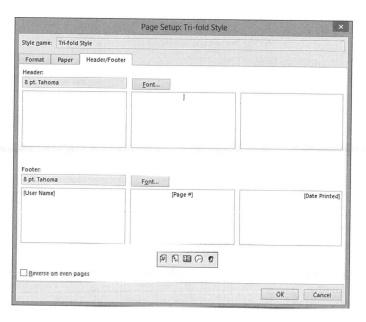

FIGURE 18.6

Customize the header and footer.

You can type anything into the header and footer blocks, such as your name, company name, and other information. Add page numbers, number of pages, printed date, printed time, and username to the headers and footers. Font changes apply to the entire header or footer.

 NOTE A frequent question is how to remove the user's name from the top of the page. Although you can't remove the line under the name, you can use a font that has a blank character set, such as WP MultinationalB Courier font. If this font is not installed on your computer, search for a copy online.

You can edit the style from the Print dialog box by clicking the Page Setup button, but if you want to create a new print style, choose Define Print Styles. This opens the Define Print Styles dialog box, which enables you to select the default style that you want to work in creating your new style (see Figure 18.7). Select the style that's closest to your needs and click Copy.

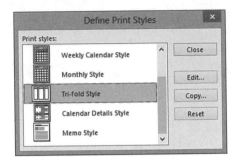

FIGURE 18.7

Copy, edit, or reset a style in Define Styles.

When you choose Edit or Copy, the Page Setup dialog box opens, as shown in Figures 18.4 and 18.5. Use it to create the style you need. For example, if you often print out copies to carry in your planner, you'll want to create a style with the paper options set for your planner.

When you Copy a style you are creating a new style, whereas Edit changes the configuration of the selected style. Reset will reset the default styles to the original state. You should use Copy when you want to save custom styles, rather than editing the default styles.

Removing Your Name from the Printout

People don't always like to see their names at the top of the menu style printouts. Although you can't edit the template to remove the name or the bold line, you can make your name invisible by changing the font used for the page title. If you choose a font that does not contain the alphabet, the name will be blank (see Figure 18.8).

1. Click File, and then click Print.

2. Click Print Options.

3. Click Page Setup.

4. On the Format tab, click Title Fonts.

5. Select a font that does not include the characters in the western alphabet, such as WP MultinationalB Courier or Adobe Blank font, and then select OK.

6. Click Print.

From:	OutlookTips <tips@outlook-tips.net>
Sent:	Wednesday, February 13, 2013 5:32 PM
To:	dianep@outlook-marketplace.com
Subject:	Outlook Tips for February 13 2013 (Search People finds contacts that don't exist)

FIGURE 18.8

Change the title font to hide your name in the header.

If you don't have a font installed that has blank squares for the alphabet, you can download Adobe Blank from SourceForge. You can find that download at http://slipstick.com/adobeblank.

Printing Calendars

The layout options you'll have to choose from when you print your calendar vary with the print style you choose. Among the options you can select is the number of pages to use per selected time period, which is usually one or two pages per day, week, or month. You'll also use this dialog box to include a task list or a blank area for handwritten notes.

You can change the Page options to include only your workdays, not weekends, in a printed calendar, leaving more room for your important appointments.

 NOTE   When you have the option to include a notes area, it's for handwritten notes, not Outlook notes.

Calendars have additional print styles available when you use the Day, Week, Month, or Schedule views on the folder. When you use a Table view, you'll have Memo and Table styles only.

Although the options you'll have available depend on the print style you choose, some of the options include the following:

- The time range to include for daily calendars; the default is 7 a.m. to 7 p.m.
- Exclude weekends on monthly calendars.
- Force a full month per page when you select a date range that spans months.
- Arrangement used for days in a weekly calendar (left to right or top to bottom).

The paper type and size selections and header/footer options are the same used for Table and Memo styles.

You can print your calendar using a wide range of styles, options, and paper sizes. The Print dialog used for the calendar has some options not found in the Print dialog for Table and Memo views. In addition to several styles to choose from, if you have multiple calendars, you'll be able to choose which calendar to print when you display multiple calendars.

1. Open your Calendar folder and apply a Calendar view if you're currently using a List view. The configuration of your calendar might affect the printout. For example, if you show end times, they may be included in the printout of your calendar.

2. Open the File menu and select Print.

3. Select the calendar you'd like to print from the Print This Calendar drop-down list. The list will contain multiple calendars when you have more than one displayed side-by-side in Outlook.

4. Select the date range to print.

5. Add a check to Hide Details of Private Appointments if you want to hide the details of appointments marked private.

6. Select the print style you want to use. You can choose from

   - **Daily Style**—A daily calendar divided into hours.

   - **Weekly Agenda Style**—A planner-style format, two columns by three rows; dates can go left to right or top to bottom.

   - **Weekly Calendar Style**—Similar to the daily calendar, it can be configured with the dates across the top of the page and hours down the side or dates down and hours across the top.

   - **Monthly Style**—Traditional monthly calendar. Print all dates or weekdays only.

   - **Tri-fold Style**—A three-column printout, your choice of calendar or tasks in each column.

   - **Calendar Details Style**—A simple list of appointments.

7. After selecting a style, choose Page Setup to set additional options (see Figure 18.9).

8. After selecting all your options, choose Print from the Page Setup dialog or click OK in the Print dialog.

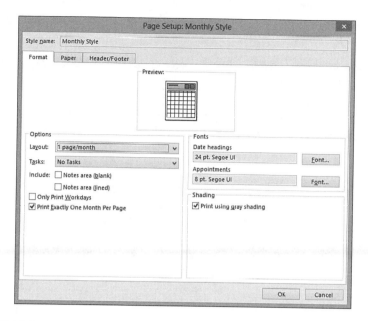

FIGURE 18.9

Use the Page Setup dialog box to control the layout of your printed calendar.

That's all there is to printing out your calendar. When you save the styles, you can print out your calendars in just three steps: Choose the File, Print command; select your style from the Print Styles list; click OK to print it.

 TIP You can double-click the style when you select it to open the Page Setup dialog.

Printing Contacts

As with the calendar, there are print styles specifically for contacts. You must view your Contacts folder using an Address Card view to access the special print styles. The special print styles available for contacts are the following:

- **Card Style**—Large booklet style, contacts are displayed in 2 columns. All fields in the view are included in the printout.

- **Small Booklet Style**—A small version of the Card style, containing 8 small columns of contacts. Suitable for folding into a booklet for your purse or pocket.

- **Medium Booklet Style**—Similar to the Card style, but with 4 columns. Suitable for folding.

- **Memo Style**—Prints one contact per page, with all fields included in the printout.

- **Phone Directory Style**—Formatted similar to a phone book, with only the contact name and phone number listed.

The Card and Booklet Styles are similar and have the same Page Setup options (see Figure 18.10). Phone Directory Style prints a phone-book–style list of your contacts.

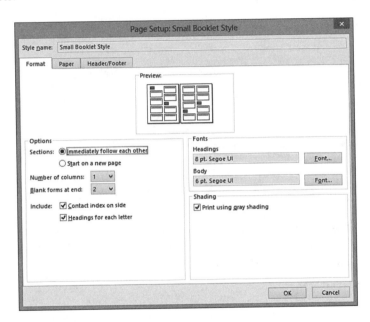

FIGURE 18.10

Configure the options for the Card and Booklet Style listing.

 NOTE Contact photos and business cards are not included in the printouts. If you want to print the photos, you'll need to use screenshots or a utility to print.

When you print a Card or Booklet Style listing, a section is created using the first letter or number of the File As name. If you want the sections on separate pages, choose Start on a New Page; otherwise, leave it set to Immediately Follow Each Other.

Choose the number of columns you want to use. Unless you're using landscape format, you'll want to limit this to three or fewer.

Blank Forms at the End prints blank forms so you can add new contacts to your booklet. Naturally, you'll have to write the contact information into the fields by hand. Later, you can enter the information into Outlook.

You can include the contact index on your printout. This is a vertical list of letters down the right edge of the printout, similar to the index many address books have. Unless you are printing a large number of contacts, it's probably better to use the default setting of Headings for Each Letter, which adds a letter between each contact section.

Use the Paper tab to select the paper types, sizes, and layouts for your printout. Customize the header and footer using the Header/Footer tab.

Choose OK to return to the Print Options dialog. If you want to use the style you created again, save it using a new name. To do this, click Define Styles, select the style you customized, then choose Copy. Enter a new name for your style and save it.

To preview your printout, choose Preview, and when you are ready to print your address book, click Print to send it to your printer.

Phone Directory

The Phone Directory Style prints a list of your contacts in a format similar to traditional phone book listings. The Page Setup options available for Phone Directory Style are limited to the number of columns and whether to use headings for each letter or the contact index (see Figure 18.11).

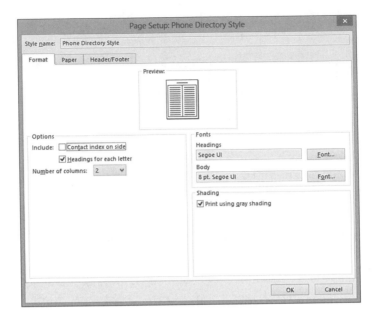

FIGURE 18.11

The Phone Directory Style has a few available options.

THE ABSOLUTE MINIMUM

Here are the key points to remember from this chapter:

- The view you are using in Outlook will affect the styles you'll have available in the Print dialog box.

- Printouts will include all fields in the current view. If you don't want something printed, remove the field from the view first.

- Create custom styles, and then save them to use the next time you print.

DATA FILE MANAGEMENT

Outlook uses two types of data files to store your email, calendar, contacts, and tasks on your computer: Personal Folders and Offline Folders. All your Outlook data—email, calendar, contacts, tasks, and notes—are stored in one or more data files.

Understanding Outlook Data File Types

Personal Folders have the file extension .pst and are often referred to as simply "pst." Personal Folders files are used with POP3 (Post Office Protocol 3) email accounts or "No mail" profiles and can be moved from computer to computer. Archiving is always to a .pst file.

Offline files have the extension .ost. These are used with Exchange server accounts in cached mode, IMAP accounts in Outlook 2013, and Outlook.com Exchange Active Sync accounts. The offline files contain a replica of your online mailbox and do not need to be backed up.

While the Personal Folders files (.pst) can be moved to other computers or used in other profiles, the offline data files (.ost) can be used only by the account that created it.

Moving Data Files

Outlook 2013 stores the .pst files in a folder under your My Documents, typically at C:\Users\username\Documents\Outlook Files. They are backed up when you back up your other documents.

You can move .pst files to any location on your hard drive. However, it's not recommended that you store .pst files you are actively using on a network drive because you risk corrupting the data file. You can keep backup copies on a network drive.

Offline files are difficult to move to a new location. Because the offline files are copies of your mailbox, .ost files don't need to be backed up. Third-party .ost recovery software is needed to recover data from orphaned files.

To find out where a .pst (or .ost) that is used by your profile is stored, open File, Account Settings, and then click the Data Files tab. Select the data file and click Open Data File Location. This opens Windows Explorer to the folder where the data file is stored.

Follow these steps to move a .pst file to a new location:

1. Open the folder where the .pst file is located.

2. Close Outlook. If you use Lync, you'll need to exit it as well.

3. Move the .pst file by dragging it to a new folder, or use cut and paste and paste it in the desired location.

4. Open Control Panel, search for the Mail applet, and open it.

5. Click the Show Profiles button.

6. Select your profile and click Properties, and then click Data Files.

7. Select the .pst file from the list and then click the Settings button (see Figure 19.1).

8. Because the file was moved, you'll receive a warning message saying that the file can't be found.

9. Click OK. The Create or Open Outlook Data File dialog box opens for you to find the .pst file.

10. Browse to the location where you moved the .pst file to, select it, and click Open.

11. Click OK to return to the Account Settings dialog box. Close the dialog box.

When you restart Outlook, it will use the .pst file that you put in the new location.

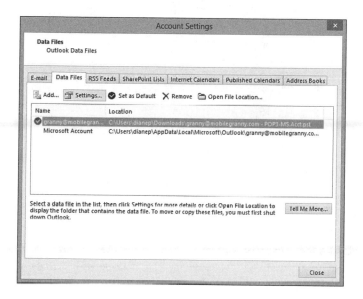

FIGURE 19.1

Select the .pst file and then click the Settings button.

Importing and Exporting Data Files

Outlook can import or export your calendar, contacts, appointments, and tasks in Comma Separated Values (CSV) or Outlook Data File (pst) format. In addition, you can also import vCards, iCalendars, and vCalendars.

Which format should you use? When you need to import data stored in another application, you need to export it in a format Outlook can import. In most cases, your only choice is to export it to the CSV format. If vCard (.vcf) or iCalendar (.ics) is an option, you can choose either format, but CSV is generally easier to import. If you need to edit the CSV file before importing it, you can open the CSV in Excel or Notepad for editing.

To use the Import and Export Wizard to import a CSV exported from another application, follow these steps:

1. Open the File tab, and then click Open & Export.

2. In the Open list, select Import/Export.

3. Select Import from Another Program or File, and then click Next (see Figure 19.2).

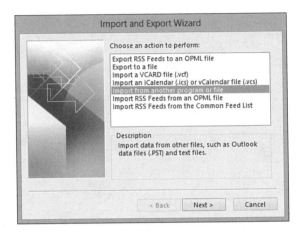

FIGURE 19.2

Select your desired import or export action from the list. Import from Another Program or File is chosen here.

4. Select Comma Separated Values and click Next.

5. Select the file to Import.

6. Choose how you want Outlook to handle duplicates, and then click Next.

7. Select the folder you want to import the file into, and then click Next.

8. Click the Map Custom Fields button.

9. Verify that the fields are mapped correctly. If you need to change any field mappings, drag the field from the left side of the dialog box to the field name on the right. When the field name is highlighted, drop the field to set the mapping (see Figure 19.3).

10. Click OK to exit the Map Custom Fields dialog, and then click Finish to complete the import.

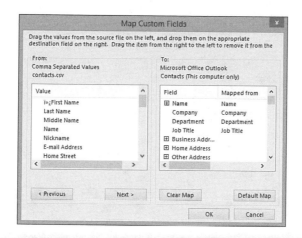

FIGURE 19.3

Check the field mappings and drag fields from the left to the right column to correct incorrect mappings.

NOTE Outlook can't import Apple's multiple contact vCards; it imports only individual vCards, one vCard at a time. There are third-party utilities that can import multiple vcards, and you can use a VBA macro to import vCards in bulk. More information is available at http://www.slipstick.com/vcards.

The process is the same when you export your Outlook data. You have two choices for the file types to export to: Comma Separated Values or Outlook Data File (.pst) format. Choose the CSV format if you need to use the data in another program, and choose Outlook .pst if you need to use it in Outlook.

To use the Import and Export Wizard to export your Outlook data, follow these steps:

1. Go to the File tab, and then click Open & Export.

2. In the Open list, select Import/Export.

3. Select Export to a File, and then click Next (see Figure 19.4).

4. Select Comma Separated Values (CSV) if you are going to use the data in another program or Outlook Data File (.pst) if you will be using it in Outlook. Click Next.

5. Select the folder you want to export. You can export only one folder at a time when you export to CSV.

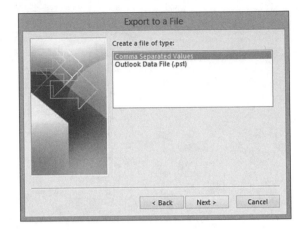

FIGURE 19.4

You'll have two choices for exporting Outlook data: CSV or Outlook .pst file.

6. Click Browse. Select the file you want to export to, or type a name to export to a new file. If you are exporting to a .pst file, you'll need to choose how you want Outlook to handle duplicates.

7. Click Next to export the data.

NOTE If you are going to use the data in Outlook, you should export to the Outlook Data File (.pst) format. If you are moving your Outlook data to a new computer with Outlook, don't use export. Instead, copy your existing .pst file to the new computer and add it to your profile.

NOTE When you export to a CSV file, you need to export each folder separately. When you export to a pst file, you can include subfolders.

Backing Up Your Data

When you use a POP3 account or have Outlook data stored in a .pst file, it's important that you make frequent backups because the items in your .pst file may be the only copy you have. If you use IMAP, Outlook.com, or Exchange Server accounts, you don't need to back up the data file your email is delivered to because a copy of your mail is stored on the server. You need to back up your calendar, contacts, tasks, and notes if you use IMAP, or your notes if you use

Outlook.com, because these item types are not synced to the server. Everything in your mailbox is synced with the server when you use an Exchange server mailbox.

Making a backup is as simple as locating your data file. By default, it is in your My Documents folder, in a folder named Outlook Files. Close Outlook and copy the data file to back up media or cloud storage, such as SkyDrive or Dropbox. It can be as complicated as configuring a backup program to back up your entire hard drive. The important thing is that you make frequent backups. You should also test the backup occasionally to ensure that your Outlook data file is not corrupt.

 NOTE If you use an online backup such as Mozy or Carbonite, you need to check the backups every now and again. Outlook puts a lock on the .pst file when the .pst file is open, and if the backup tries to run while the lock is on, the Outlook data file is not backed up.

Archiving Email

As email ages and the data file grows, many people archive their email to remove it from their mailbox, while saving it in case they need it years from now. However, many people never access the archived mail; being a pack rat with computer files only means you need more storage space.

 NOTE Always follow company policy for archiving. If the administrator wants business email deleted, don't move it to a data file to save it.

You can use either AutoArchive to move or delete email, appointments, or tasks to the same folder in an archive .pst or use manual archiving to move or delete messages in a specific folder and its subfolders at any time. Contacts are not archived.

Each folder can be configured to have unique AutoArchive settings, or you can apply the same setting to all folders.

 NOTE When you use an Exchange server mailbox with an online Archive mailbox, Archiving in Outlook is disabled.

To enable AutoArchive, open the AutoArchive dialog and click File, then click Options, click Advanced, and then click AutoArchive Settings. These enable you do to the following:

- Check Run AutoArchive Every 14 days, and change the number of days if desired. To disable or turn off AutoArchive, deselect this option. Maximum value is 60 days.

- If you want to be notified before AutoArchive runs, enable Prompt Before AutoArchive Runs. With this enabled, you will be able to cancel archiving if you think it will interrupt your work.

- If you use expiration dates on email, select Delete Expired Items (email folders only). This removes messages marked as expired.

- To remove old email, appointments, and tasks, enable Archive or Delete Old Items. If this is not selected, only expired messages will be deleted.

- Select Show Archive Folder in Folder List if you want the archive .pst file added to your Outlook profile. If this is not checked, the .pst is added to your profile temporarily during the archive process and removed when the archive is finished.

- Select the default age for archiving old messages. This applies to all folders that do not have folder-specific settings (see Figure 19.5). The maximum time period is 60 days, 60 weeks, or 60 months. Choose the time period that is appropriate for most folders. By default, the age is based on the last modified date, not the received date.

FIGURE 19.5

Configure the global AutoArchive settings.

- Choose between moving old items to an archive folder or permanently deleting the old items. If you are moving old items, you can use the default archive .pst or choose a new one. You can return to this dialog and change the data file at any time. If you permanently delete old items, you will not be able to recover them.

- Click Apply These Settings to All Folders Now to apply the default settings to all folders; then close the dialog.

If you want any folders to use a different AutoArchive setting, you'll need to change the folder settings before AutoArchive runs. For example, you can configure the Deleted Items and Junk E-mail folders so that items older than three days are permanently deleted. Every time AutoArchive runs, these folders will be cleaned out.

To check for folder-specific settings, right-click the folder and choose Properties; then click the AutoArchive tab. You can also access this dialog from the Folder tab by clicking the AutoArchive Settings button (see Figure 19.6).

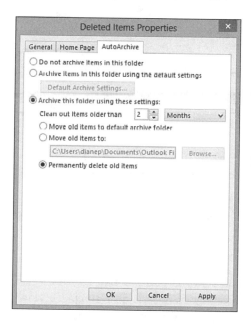

FIGURE 19.6

Configure folder-specific AutoArchive settings, such as to permanently delete older deleted items or junk mail.

These settings are specific to each folder and are not applied to subfolders. You'll need to change each folder individually.

You can run AutoArchive at any time using the AutoArchive option on the File tab. Click Cleanup Tools, and then click Mailbox Cleanup, then AutoArchive.

Mailbox Cleanup

Outlook has several built-in tools that make it easier for you to discover how large your data file is and to reduce the size. These tools are grouped on the Mailbox Cleanup dialog, click the File tab, and then Cleanup Tools (see Figure 19.7).

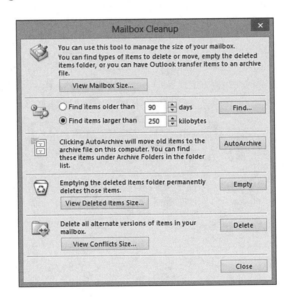

FIGURE 19.7

Mailbox Cleanup can help you reduce the size of your data file.

Following are options in the Mailbox Cleanup dialog:

- View Mailbox Size shows you the size of your mailbox and each folder within the mailbox. This information is also available when you right-click a folder, choose Properties, and then click Folder Size.

- Find Items Older Than and Find Items Larger Than. Select the age or file size and click Find to open the Advanced Find dialog using the selected criteria. You could use Instant Search with the criteria "size: > 250KB" or "received:(<12/1/2012)" right from your Inbox.

- As mentioned previously, the AutoArchive button runs AutoArchive.

- View the size of the items in the Deleted Items folder and empty it. You can empty the Deleted items folder by right-clicking the folder and choosing Empty Folder.

- View Conflicts Size shows you the size of the conflicts in your mailbox. Conflicts are created when Outlook creates a copy of an existing item, usually when the original item is being edited. This is more common with Exchange Server mailboxes, but is possible with Outlook.com accounts and IMAP accounts.

Outlook also has a manual Archive option, in File, Cleanup Tools. Manual archiving lets you select just the folder and subfolder that need to be archived, and you can choose a specific date to use. You can archive to your archive .pst file or select a different .pst file (see Figure 19.8).

FIGURE 19.8

Use Manual Archive to clean out specific folders.

If you select the top-level folder (where your account name is), you can archive the entire data file using a specific date.

For example, after a project has ended, you could use this to archive a folder created for that specific project.

Storing Data Files in the Cloud

With the popularity of cloud storage services, such as Dropbox and SkyDrive's inclusion in Office 2013 subscription, I'm often asked if the .pst file can be stored in the cloud.

Storing an active .pst file in the cloud (or on a network drive) is not supported for two reasons:

1. Outlook keeps a lock on the .pst file when it's open, and it cannot be uploaded to the cloud while the lock is on.

2. The typical .pst is around 1GB in size, but many are much larger. Not only do larger files take longer to sync, they also use a lot more of the available cloud storage.

You can store your archive .pst files in the cloud, provided you don't keep them open in Outlook. However, if there are problems syncing, the data could be corrupted.

 NOTE Some cloud services, such as Sugar Sync, create and delete temporary files when they try to sync a .pst opened in Outlook. If the deleted items count toward your cloud quota, you may find your free space is limited because of hundreds of temp files.

Outlook puts a lock on the .pst file when the .pst file is open. SkyDrive continually syncs the local folder. It won't be able to sync correctly when Outlook is open because Outlook has a lock on the data file.

Although you could use cloud storage to store backup copies of your data files, it's not recommended because of the large size of many .pst files: uploading a large data file can take "forever." If you want your Outlook data in the cloud, use Office 365 or other hosted Exchange service, Hotmail/Outlook.com, or an IMAP account. Office 365/Exchange will store all Outlook data online, whereas Outlook.com/Hotmail is email, calendar, tasks, and contacts only; IMAP is email only.

There are online backup services that can back up .pst files when Outlook is open and incrementally back up the .pst so that only changes are saved. These are safe to use because they are designed to work with Outlook data files. However, unlike backing up a file to SkyDrive or DropBox, you can't download the .pst file to another computer when needed. You need to restore it using the backup application.

Repairing the .pst Using Scanpst

Sometimes the Personal Folders file is damaged and needs to be repaired using the Inbox Repair Tool, or Scanpst, as it's more commonly called.

Scanpst.exe is included in your Office installation, which by default is at C:\Program Files\Microsoft Office\Office15 or C:\Program Files (x86)\Microsoft Office\Office15 if you installed Office 2013 32-bit in 64-bit Windows.

Most people will have Office 2013 Home Premium or University, which is installed from the Internet, also known as Click to Run. Look for scanpst.exe under the root directory in the install path. If you used the default path, Scanpst.exe is at C:\ Program Files\Microsoft Office 15\root\Office15\scanpst.exe. If you installed 32-bit Office in 64-bit Windows, Scanpst.exe is at C:\Program Files (x86)\Microsoft Office 15\root\Office15\scanpst.exe.

If you have Office 2013 Pro Plus and did not need Internet access during the installation process, scanpst.exe for 64-bit Outlook is at C:\Program Files\Microsoft Office\Office15\Scanpst.exe or C:\Program Files (x86)\Microsoft Office\Office15\ scanpst.exe for the 32-bit version.

 NOTE The icon used for Scanpst.exe is a broken envelope. This is supposed to indicate that it works with broken messages. It does not mean the application is broken.

When you need to repair your .pst file, you'll follow these steps:

1. Close Outlook.

2. Open Scanpst.exe.

3. Click Browse and browse to the location of the .pst. The file browser will open to C:\Users\username\Documents\Outlook Files, which is the default location for .pst files in Outlook 2013.

4. Select your .pst from the list (most people will have just one).

5. Click Open, Start to begin testing your .pst file. It can take several minutes if your data file is large.

When Scanpst is finished running the tests, a dialog reports the errors it found and tells you if you need to repair the data file (see Figure 19.9). If you need to repair the .pst, always make a backup.

Scanpst will almost always find errors in the .pst file, especially if you use add-ins or applications that use Outlook data, such as sync utilities. Not all errors need to be fixed, though. Outlook will fix minor errors as part of the startup process.

FIGURE 19.9

Use Scanpst.exe to repair your Personal Folders files.

 NOTE I do not recommend running Scanpst on a regular basis. Use it only when Outlook tells you to run it or when you suspect the data file might be damaged. Don't use it as part of your normal computer maintenance. Scanpst will almost always find errors but minor errors don't need to be fixed, and fixing the .pst file over and over can cause more corruption. Outlook checks the .pst file when it starts and will fix minor errors, and it will let you know when you need to use Scanpst.

Only POP3 accounts, archive files, and exported files use a .pst file. IMAP, Outlook.com, and Exchange server use offline files (.ost). If these files are corrupt, close Outlook, delete the file, and Outlook will create a new file when you restart it.

 NOTE In the rare event that Scanpst can't fix a corrupt .pst file, you'll need to use a commercial repair utility. You can find a list of programs that do this at http://www.slipstick.com/repair.

THE ABSOLUTE MINIMUM

Here are the key points to remember from this chapter:

- Protect your valuable data by making frequent backups of your Personal Folder files. IMAP, Outlook.com, and Exchange mail .ost files do not need to be backed up.

- Cloud storage or network drivers are fine for storing backups, but don't store the data files you are using in either location. You could corrupt the file and lose your email, contacts, and appointments.

- Use AutoArchive and Mailbox Cleanup to remove older messages and past appointments and tasks from your mailbox or data file to reduce the size of the file.

- If the data file is corrupt, you can use scanpst to repair it.

IN THIS CHAPTER

- Understanding the basics of mail merge
- Starting a mail merge in Outlook
- Using Word's Mail Merge Wizard

20

USING MAIL MERGE

Nothing says "impersonal" as well as a form letter. Fortunately, it's easy to use Outlook's Contacts to create customized letters or labels in Word for print or email.

Whether you are sending a traditional mailed letter or sending email, you can use Mail Merge to customize form letters to make them appear more personal and directed specifically at the recipient. Mail merge makes it easy to create address labels and address books too.

You can start mail merges from either Outlook or Word, and you can use a number of options for configuring the mail merge. Starting a mail merge in Outlook gives you much better filtering capabilities than you'll get by starting from Word.

Using Contacts for Mail Merge

One of the advantages to using Outlook for contacts is the capability to use your contacts for a mail merge. The benefits of mail merge include customizing and personalizing a form letter for each recipient. Mail merge can also be used for sending a group of people the same email message, enabling you to put the individuals' addresses in the To field without exposing all the email addresses to the other recipients.

How Mail Merge Works

Outlook and Word work together when you're doing a mail merge, and you can start the merge from either Outlook or Word. Where you begin the merge is important because it determines the fields you'll be able to use in the mail merge.

When you start the merge in Outlook, you'll be able to choose from all the Outlook contact fields, and you'll have better filtering. You can even select only the contacts you want to use in the mail merge.

Regardless of the method you use to begin the merge, the steps used to complete the merge are the same.

Start the merge by clicking Mail Merge on Outlook's Home tab. When you begin the merge from Outlook, you can filter the contacts using views and select the contacts you want to use for the merge. Although all contact form fields can be used in a mail merge when you start the merge from Outlook, only a limited set of fields are used when you start the merge using Word's Start Mail Merge command on the Mailings tab.

If you're more comfortable using the Mail Merge Wizard, show the Mail Merge task pane after the contacts are processed and Word opens. In Word, switch to the Mailings tab, then click on Start Mail Merge to select the type of merge you want to do.

Using Mail Merge

Using mail merge is as simple as selecting the contacts in Outlook and starting the merge.

1. Select all your contacts. On the Home tab, click the Mail Merge button (see Figure 20.1).

2. Click OK to create a form letter to the selected contacts.

3. Word opens and you type up your letter and insert Contact fields to use in the merge.

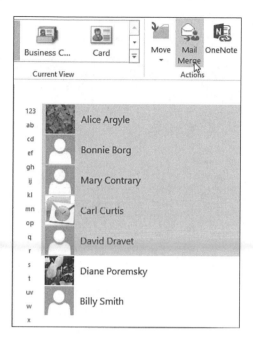

FIGURE 20.1

Select the contact you want to use in the merge and then click the Mail Merge button.

4. When you are finished composing the form letter, click the Finish and Merge button to print or email the letter.

That's a quick introduction to using mail merge. In the next section, you learn the finer points of doing a mail merge with your Outlook Contacts.

Starting the Merge from Outlook

When you start a mail merge in Outlook, the first thing you'll do is pick the contacts you want to include in the merge. I recommend selecting only the contacts you are going to use in the merge, either by choosing them while holding the Ctrl or Shift key as you select contacts or by using a filter to show the contacts you want to use.

If you want to use all contacts, you don't need to select them now; you can choose to merge all contacts in the Mail Merge Contacts dialog box.

 TIP   When you assign categories to your Contacts, you can group by category and then select the group of contacts to use in the mail merge.

After you've selected the contacts, on the Home tab, click the Mail Merge button to open the Mail Merge dialog box (see Figure 20.2).

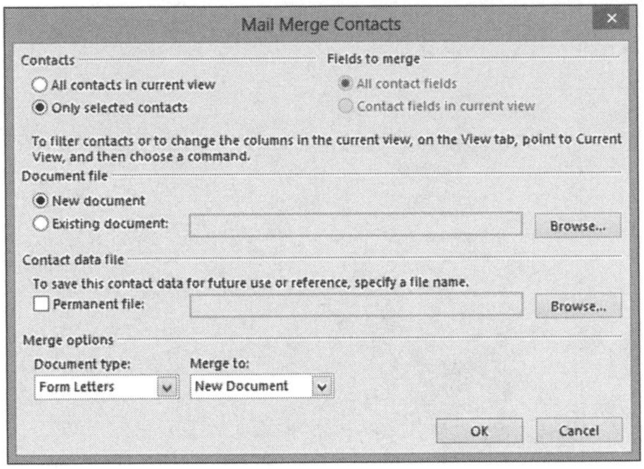

FIGURE 20.2

Use the Mail Merge Contacts dialog box to select the document type.

At the top of the dialog box, you have the choice of using All Contacts in Current View, or Only Selected Contacts. You can also choose to merge all fields or only those fields in the current view.

NOTE   Contact Fields in Current View means fields in the view, including any you need to scroll to see, not just the fields you can see onscreen.

Next, you can choose to merge to a new document or existing document. The default setting is New Document.

If you are going to use this merge data in the future or need to save a list of recipients, save a copy of the contact data to a permanent file.

Finally, you'll choose the type of document to merge to; the choices are Form Letter, Labels, Envelopes, and Catalog. Choose whether to merge to a document, printer, or email. If you change your mind, you can change the Document Type and Merge to type in Word.

After you make your selections and click OK, Outlook needs a few minutes to convert the contacts to a document, OMM0.doc, which it uses for the mail merge data source. When the conversion is completed, Word opens.

If you're new to mail merge, it's usually easier to use the Mail Merge Wizard to lead you through the final steps. After you're familiar with the merge options, you can skip the wizard and use the ribbon commands.

From the Mailing tab, click the Start Mail Merge button and then select the Step by Step Mail Merge Wizard (see Figure 20.3). Beginning the merge from Outlook puts you at step 3 in the Mail Merge Wizard. You can go back to step 1 if you need to select a different merge type. Move back to step 2 if you need to change the document type.

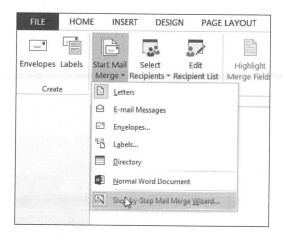

FIGURE 20.3

Use the Step by Step Mail Merge Wizard to guide you through the merge process.

Click the Next: Write Your Letter link at the bottom of the wizard. Compose your document and insert merge fields. When you're finished composing the message, at the bottom of the task pane wizard, choose Next: Preview Your Letters.

 NOTE You can't attach files to mail merges. Use a VBA macro or an add-in to include attachments in a merge to email. See http://slipstick.com/mailmerge for links to macros and add-ins.

When you're satisfied with the document, complete the merge. The Finish & Merge button on the ribbon can send the merged documents to a printer or to email.

After a couple of uses, you'll outgrow the Mail Merge Wizard, and you can use the command on the Mailings tab to insert fields, select the document to merge to, and use the Preview Results button to display your data in the merge fields (see Figure 20.4).

FIGURE 20.4

Use the Mailings tab instead of the Mail Merge Wizard.

 NOTE Mail merge to email is often better than sending BCC messages. Many anti-spam filters are configured to treat messages in which the user is blind carbon copied as spam. Mail merge puts the recipient's name in the To field, which allows it to pass through many anti-spam filters.

If you need to filter your list, open the Mail Merge Recipients dialog box. You can use the drop-down lists at the top of each column to set the criteria or remove the check marks from rows that you don't want included. However, it's usually faster and easier to filter your contacts in Outlook and then select the filtered records before beginning the merge.

Mail Merge Using Categories

One of the easiest ways to filter contacts to use in a mail merge is by grouping by categories. Select the contacts in the category and start the merge.

First, open Outlook's Contacts folder and switch to the View tab. If you are not using the List view, expand Change View and select the List view.

1. In the Arrangement group, select Categories.

2. In the category group, select the contacts.

3. Click the Home tab and click the Mail Merge button.

4. At the top of the Mail Merge Contacts dialog box, choose Only Selected Contacts.

5. At the bottom of the dialog box, select the document type. For this example, use Form Letter.

6. Select the type of document you want to create: a document, print, or email. Choose E-mail.

7. Enter a subject for the email message. This can be changed before sending it.

8. Click OK to complete Outlook's work and open Word.

Next, you'll complete the document in Word.

1. Type your letter and insert contact fields. You can use the Address block, Greeting Line, or insert the fields individually by selecting the fields from the Insert Merge Field menu. Choose Address block for this exercise.

2. Click Preview results to see what the finished messages will look like. Use the Go to Record command to check different contacts.

3. When you are satisfied, click the Finish & Merge button, and then select E-mail.

Starting the Merge in Word

When you start a merge using Word's Mail Merge menu, you lose the ability to use Outlook's filters or categories to restrict records included in the merge. All contacts in the selected Contacts folder are included in the recipient list; however, you can filter the contacts using Word's Sort and Filter dialog box. Outlook's filters are better than the filters available in the Mail Merge dialog and give you more control over the contacts that you include in the merge.

To start the mail merge from Word, start a new document and click the Mailings tab.

1. Expand Start Mail Merge and select the type of document you want to create.

2. Click Select Recipients button and then click Choose From Outlook Contacts.

3. Select the contacts you want to include in the merge (see Figure 20.5).

4. Compose your letter and insert the merge field.

5. Click the Preview Results button to review the letter; use the Previous and Next buttons to review the results for different contacts.

6. If you are satisfied with the results, click Finish & Merge, and choose Print Documents, Send Email Messages, or Edit Individual documents to complete the merge.

Create Envelopes and Labels

If you need to print an envelope or label for one person, or a small number of people, you can use Word's Envelopes and Labels feature to create envelopes or labels addressed to a contact in your Outlook address book. You can print the label directly from the dialog box or add it to the current document.

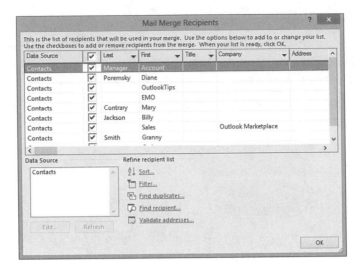

FIGURE 20.5

When you start the merge in Word, all contacts in the selected folder are included in the merge.

You open the Envelope and Labels dialog box by clicking the Envelopes or Labels button on the Mailing tab. These buttons open the Envelopes and Labels dialog box with either the Envelope or the Labels tab active.

Click the Address Book icon to open Outlook's address book and select a contact. You can select a previously used address by expanding the Address Book menu and selecting a name (see Figure 20.6).

If you frequently add addresses to your Word documents, you can add the Address Book button to the ribbon or Quick Access toolbar to make it easier to insert contact names and addresses in any Word document. Follow these steps:

1. In Word, click File, and then click Options to open the Options dialog and select Quick Access toolbar.

2. In the Choose Commands From drop-down, select All Commands.

3. Scroll down the list of commands to locate Address Book (see Figure 20.7).

4. Click Add, and then click OK to close the Options dialog box.

When you want to insert an address into a document, click the Address Book button, and then select an address.

You are limited to the name and mailing address fields only when you use either the Envelopes and Labels dialog box or the Address Book command.

FIGURE 20.6

Use Outlook's contacts to address envelopes or labels in Microsoft Word.

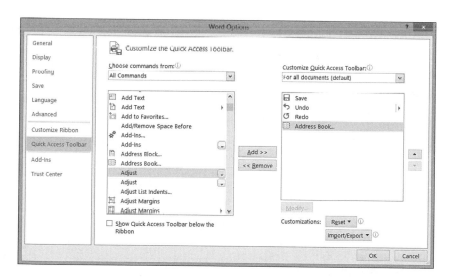

FIGURE 20.7

Add the Address Book command to the Quick Access toolbar.

THE ABSOLUTE MINIMUM

Here are the key points to remember from this chapter:

- Use mail merges to send email messages, printed letters, or to create labels for multiple contacts.

- Begin the merge by selecting Outlook Contacts; if you are working in Word, you can begin the merge from Word instead.

- Use a template or insert the merge fields into a new document.

Index

O

P

Q

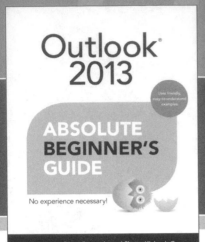

Outlook 2013
ABSOLUTE BEGINNER'S GUIDE
No experience necessary!

Diane Poremsky and Sherry Kinkoph Gunter

Safari
Books Online

FREE
Online Edition

Your purchase of **Outlook® 2013 Absolute Beginner's Guide** includes access to a free online edition for 45 days through the **Safari Books Online** subscription service. Nearly every Que book is available online through **Safari Books Online**, along with thousands of books and videos from publishers such as Addison-Wesley Professional, Cisco Press, Exam Cram, IBM Press, O'Reilly Media, Prentice Hall, Sams, and VMware Press.

Safari Books Online is a digital library providing searchable, on-demand access to thousands of technology, digital media, and professional development books and videos from leading publishers. With one monthly or yearly subscription price, you get unlimited access to learning tools and information on topics including mobile app and software development, tips and tricks on using your favorite gadgets, networking, project management, graphic design, and much more.

Activate your FREE Online Edition at
informit.com/safarifree

STEP 1:   Enter the coupon code: OSJMOGA.

STEP 2:   New Safari users, complete the brief registration form.
                Safari subscribers, just log in.

If you have difficulty registering on Safari or accessing the online edition,
please e-mail customer-service@safaribooksonline.com